Style and Rhetoric of Short Narrative Fiction

In many fictional narratives, the progression of the plot exists in tension with a very different and powerful dynamic that runs, at a hidden and deeper level, throughout the text. In this book, Dan Shen systematically investigates how stylistic analysis is indispensable for uncovering this covert progression through rhetorical narrative criticism. The book brings to light the covert progressions in works by the American writers Edgar Allan Poe, Stephen Crane, and Kate Chopin, and the British writer Katherine Mansfield. The analysis shows that to miss the covert progression is to get only a partial or false picture of the thematics, the characters, and the aesthetic values of the narrative.

"This important contribution to the stylistics of short fiction and poetics of narrative both enriches the theory of the short story and provides new interpretations of a range of major British and American stories. It is very relevant both for the teaching of short fiction and for the theory of narrative."

Jonathan Culler, Class of 1916 Professor,
Cornell University

"Dan Shen persuasively expands the scope of the rhetorical theory of narrative by showing that careful attention to easily overlooked patterns of meaning (what she calls "covert progressions") in fiction naturally lead to matters that previous rhetorical theorists have not done justice to, especially the interrelationships among style, ethics, and biography."

James Phelan, Distinguished University Professor,
Ohio State University

"A distinguished senior scholar makes a major contribution, combining in a rare way the perspectives of narrative theory, stylistics, and rhetoric to provide challenging new interpretations of major short fiction from nearly a century of English-language writing, ranging from Poe to Katherine Mansfield."

Jonathan Arac, Andrew W. Mellon Professor,
University of Pittsburgh

Dan Shen is Changjiang Professor of English Language and Literature at Peking University, China. She is on the advisory or editorial boards of the American journals *Style* and *Narrative,* the British *Language and Literature,* and the European *JLS: Journal of Literary Semantics,* as well as being a consultant editor of *Routledge Encyclopedia of Narrative Theory.*

Routledge Studies in Rhetoric and Stylistics

Edited by Michael Burke

1 **Literary Reading, Cognition and Emotion**
An Exploration of the Oceanic Mind
Michael Burke

2 **Language, Ideology and Identity in Serial Killer Narratives**
Christiana Gregoriou

3 **Beyond Cognitive Metaphor Theory**
Perspectives on Literary Metaphor
Monika Fludernik

4 **The Pragmatics of Literary Testimony**
Authenticity Effects in German Social Autobiographies
Chantelle Warner

5 **Analyzing Digital Fiction**
Edited by Alice Bell, Astrid Ensslin, and Hans Kristian Rustad

6 **Ulysses and the Poetics of Cognition**
Patrick Colm Hogan

7 **Style and Rhetoric of Short Narrative Fiction**
Covert Progressions Behind Overt Plots
Dan Shen

Style and Rhetoric of Short Narrative Fiction
Covert Progressions Behind Overt Plots

**Dan Shen
with a Foreword by J. Hillis Miller**

NEW YORK AND LONDON

First published 2014
by Routledge
711 Third Avenue, New York, NY 10017

and by Routledge
2 Park Square, Milton Park, Abingdon, Oxon OX14 4RN

Routledge is an imprint of the Taylor & Francis Group,
an informa business

© 2014 Taylor & Francis

The right of Dan Shen to be identified as author of this work has been
asserted by her in accordance with sections 77 and 78 of the Copyright,
Designs and Patents Act 1988.

All rights reserved. No part of this book may be reprinted or reproduced or
utilized in any form or by any electronic, mechanical, or other means, now
known or hereafter invented, including photocopying and recording, or in
any information storage or retrieval system, without permission in writing
from the publishers.

Trademark Notice: Product or corporate names may be trademarks or
registered trademarks, and are used only for identification and explanation
without intent to infringe.

Library of Congress Cataloging-in-Publication Data

Shen, Dan, 1958–
Style and rhetoric of short narrative fiction covert progressions behind
    overt plots / by Dan Shen ; with a foreword by J. Hillis Miller.
        pages cm. — (Routledge Studies in Rhetoric and Stylistics ; 7)
    Includes bibliographical references and index.
    1. Plots (Drama, novel, etc.)   2. Fiction—Technique.   3. Fiction—
Authorship.   4. Narration (Rhetoric)   I. Title.
    PN3378.S38 2014
    808.3—dc23
    2013025571

ISBN: 978-0-415-63548-6 (hbk)
ISBN: 978-0-203-09312-2 (ebk)

Typeset in Sabon
by Apex CoVantage, LLC

For my husband Xing, the star of my life

Contents

Foreword by J. Hillis Miller	ix
Acknowledgments	xiii
Introduction	1

PART I
Style and Covert Progressions in American Short Fiction

1 Style, Unreliability, and Hidden Dramatic Irony: Poe's "The Tell-Tale Heart"	29
2 Style and Unobtrusive Emasculating Satire: Crane's "An Episode of War"	50
3 Style, Surprise Ending, and Covert Mythologization: Chopin's "Désirée's Baby"	70

PART II
Style and Different Forms of Covert Progression in Mansfield's Fiction

4 Style, Changing Distance, and Doubling Irony: Mansfield's "Revelations"	95
5 Style and Concealed Social Protest: Mansfield's "The Singing Lesson"	111
6 Style and Secretly Unifying the Digressive: Mansfield's "The Fly"	125
Coda	145
Notes	151
Works Cited	161
Index	171

Foreword

It is a great pleasure and honor for me to write a Foreword for this distinguished book. Dan Shen is Director of the Center for European and American Literatures and Changjiang Professor of English Language and Literature at Peking University in Beijing. She has an international reputation as a narratologist and a stylistician. She serves on many Western editorial or advisory boards including those of the American journals *Style* and *Narrative*, the British *Language and Literature* and the European *JLS: Journal of Literary Semantics;* and she is also a consultant editor of *Routledge Encyclopedia of Narrative Theory.* Dan Shen has a distinctive, original, theoretical approach and a gift for perceptive close reading. Apart from her publication of numerous books and essays in China, she has published many essays in important journals in North America and Europe. She is in addition, as it happens, one of my oldest friends in China. I have watched with admiration the impressive development of her work and of her worldwide influence since I first met her in China some years ago.

Style and Rhetoric in Short Narrative Fiction: Covert Progressions Behind Overt Plots is the happy culmination so far of Dan Shen's scholarly work. It embodies the accumulated wisdom of years of thinking, teaching, and writing in the field of narratology, stylistics, and rhetorical studies. This book combines admirably two distinguished scholarly accomplishments. It develops with impressive rigor and exigency a powerful new theory of narrative progression. It then shows in detailed readings of six short fictions in English how this theory may be used to illuminate the way meaning is generated by the words on the pages of these stories. Her exemplary six stories include three by Americans: one by Edgar Allan Poe, one by Stephen Crane, and one by Kate Chopin. The second part of the book then reads three stories by the New Zealand-born British writer, Katherine Mansfield. Since these stories are often taught in undergraduate courses in literature, Dan Shen's book will be of great use to teachers of such courses.

This book is in the tradition of Neo-Aristotelian rhetorical narrative study, but significantly expands its scope by directing attention to the importance of stylistic analysis and the necessity for considering the context of creation, both having been consciously precluded by Neo-Aristotelian rhetorical critics in general. In the brilliant introductory essay to the book and in the

x *Foreword*

readings themselves, Dan Shen puts in question such exclusions. She sees no reason not to take into account in a rhetorical reading of a given story the author's life and social circumstances. An example is the brilliant and learned discussion of the "insanity debate" in American history in connection with her reading of Poe's "The Tell-Tale Heart." As regards her forceful argument for including in a rhetorical reading the stylistic analysis of verbal complexities, it is particularly well backed up by her admirable reading of Crane's "An Episode of War" and Mansfield's "The Fly," which convincingly demonstrates how stylistic analysis can make significant contributions to the interpretation of narrative texts. In addition, Dan Shen argues for the necessity in narrative criticism of making intertextual comparison between a given story and other related works, whether by the same author or by different authors. This point is especially well illustrated by her analysis of Mansfield's "Revelations" and Chopin's "Désirée's Baby."

Most brilliantly and of crucial importance in her theorizing and in her readings, however, is Dan Shen's recognition in various narratives of an often ironic discrepancy between the overt plot and what she calls a "covert progression" hidden behind the open one, as well illustrated by the six narratives analyzed in the book. The great Victorian poet and classicist Gerard Manley Hopkins, writing about the recurrent figures of speech in lyric sections of Greek tragedy, called a deeper level of meaning in a lyric passage an "underthought" hidden beneath the "overthought." What Hopkins says seems prophetically to anticipate Dan Shen's insights. "In any lyric passage of the tragic poets," Hopkins wrote in a letter of 1883, ". . . there are— usually; I will not say always, it is not likely—two strains of thought running together and like counterpointed; the overthought that which everybody, editors, see . . . and which might for instance be abridged or paraphrased . . . the other, the underthought, conveyed chiefly in the choice of metaphors etc used and often only half realized by the poet himself. . . . The underthought is commonly an echo or shadow of the overthought, something like canons and repetitions in music, treated in a different manner." The difference of course between Greek tragedies and Dan Shen's short fictions, as she observes, is that the "covert progression" in prose narratives is expressed not so much in metaphors as in many details of story-telling, and it is an undercurrent that runs throughout the text, rather than a local deeper meaning as the poetic "underthought." Hopkins, moreover, does not allow for the outright dissonance or contradiction that Dan Shen persuasively identifies in the relation between overt and covert progressions in some of her stories.

The "covert progression" in prose fiction is often ironic in nature. This type of irony, as Dan Shen convincingly argues and shows, differs from previously noticed types of irony in that it not only is pervasive, characterizing the text throughout, but also often constitutes an additional ironic layer behind the irony of the plot development, either complementing or subverting the latter.

Recognizing and demonstrating the presence of covert progressions in narrative fictions is the strikingly original and groundbreaking focus of *Style and*

Foreword xi

Rhetoric of Short Narrative Fiction. Starting from Aristotle, many narrative critics, for all their theoretical sophistication, tend to assume that a novel or short story has a single textual movement—the plot development (of course often with various forms of branching or narrative embedding). They have focused on the plot and have made diversified efforts to uncover its deeper levels of meaning. The "covert progression" is a different kind of deeper-level meaning, a hidden textual movement running parallel, or as an alternative, to the plot. But of course not every fictional narrative has a covert progression. Indeed, many do not, but in those narratives that have a covert progression, it is not to be missed since, as Dan Shen's analysis shows, our understanding of the ethical import and aesthetic value of the text or of the author's rhetorical purposes can be severely affected if we overlook the covert progression.

Dan Shen has a conspicuously sharp analytical mind. Her mind is much given to making distinctions and refinements in her theoretical formulations and in the details of her readings. She distinguishes, for example, between covert progressions that reinforce the overt action and those that contradict the apparent meaning of the story. An example of the latter is Kate Chopin's "Désirée's Baby." This story appears to be anti-racist, but it covertly reinforces racial stereotypes. A close reading not only of narratological complexities but also of subtle verbal complexities is necessary to uncover the covert progression. Shen Dan succeeds brilliantly in doing this.

A concern with the ethical implications of narrative fictions has been an important part of narrative studies ever since Wayne Booth's work and before. Dan Shen continues this tradition, but her recognition of covert progressions that work in sometimes dissonant counterpoint to overt progressions leads her to see and to show in detail that the ethical implications of a story like Poe's "The Tell-Tale Heart" or Mansfield's "The Fly" may be quite different from the evident one or from the one previous critics have identified.

Dan Shen's brilliant reading of Poe's story is characteristic of her interpretations of the six exemplary short stories she chooses. Her reading of "The Tell-Tale Heart" exhibits impressive mastery as well as sharp criticism of previous scholarship on the story. Dan Shen needs to clear the ground, so to speak, to make way for her strikingly original reading of "The Tell-Tale Heart." She also deploys thorough knowledge of relevant biographical and cultural contexts (such as the history of the "insanity debate" mentioned above). Bringing all these powerful tools of interpretation together, including an original analysis of the poetry/prose distinction in Poe's essays, Dan Shen shows in detail that "The Tell-Tale Heart" deploys "dramatic irony with a significant ethical dimension." While the plot development is marked by irony at the unreliability of the narrator, the "covert progression" of this story is one of the narrator's "unconscious self-condemnation" and "unconscious self-conviction." "Poe," says Dan Shen, "seems to make the protagonist's unconscious self-condemnation and unconscious self-conviction reinforce each other in order to convey the implicit moral in a highly dramatic and ironic manner."

xii *Foreword*

Another superb reading by Dan Shen is the chapter on Katherine Mansfield's "The Fly." After a succinct summary of the wide range of previous readings by other critics, Dan Shen turns to her own close rhetorical reading of textual detail in "The Fly." Her reading shows convincingly that the overt plot progression, the story of the protagonist's grief over his son's death in World War I and his wanton killing of the fly on his desk by dropping ink on it until it stops struggling to survive, is supplemented by a more covert textual movement ironically revealing the boss's vanity and self-importance. Dan Shen shows that in "The Fly" the covert progression supplements the overt plot progression and its meaning. Since none of the strikingly diverse previous published readings has noticed this covert progression, Dan Shen's brilliantly convincing new reading solves what has been a crux in the interpretation of a classic short fiction. As Dan Shen says in her concluding recapitulation, "Numerous existing interpretations of 'The Fly' have shed much light on the narrative from various angles and have greatly helped reveal the rich thematic significance and complicated dynamics of the plot development. But no matter how cogent, ingenious, thorough, and deep-going the analysis is, the picture that emerges is bound to be a partial one unless we perceive at the same time the ironic covert progression behind the symbolic plot development. The two progressions—the plot centering on war, death, grief, time, existence, victimization/being victimized etc. and the covert progression concentrating on the boss's vanity and self-importance—constitute two interacting dimensions of the whole textual dynamics. They complement each other in characterizing the boss and in generating thematic or ethical significance of the narrative." Dan Shen's chapter on Mansfield's "The Fly" is a spectacular confirmation of the heuristic power of her new theory of double textual dynamics in short fictions. Her theoretical presuppositions really do work admirably as a way of producing convincing and sharable readings.

I have singled out Dan Shen's readings of Poe's "The Tell-Tale Heart" and of Mansfield's "The Fly," somewhat arbitrarily, as exemplary of her procedures in all of her readings and of their uniform high quality. I leave it to the reader to find this out for herself or himself in the other readings. I have immensely enjoyed reading this superb book. I have learned much from it. It has led me, for example, to think about the way Dan Shen's assumptions and procedures work splendidly as a way of accounting for the narrative and ethical complexities of Ian McEwan's *Atonement*. Other readers will think of other texts that would be illuminated by Dan Shen's insights.

It is not often that a major breakthrough occurs in a well-established discipline like rhetorical narrative studies. *Style and Rhetoric of Short Narrative Fiction: Covert Progressions Behind Overt Plots* is definitely such a book. I commend it enthusiastically to all readers interested in narrative fiction.

—J. Hillis Miller
Deer Isle, Maine

Acknowledgments

I am grateful, first of all, to the late Emory Elliot, who, after reading some essays of mine in the summer of 2008, kindly suggested that I consider publishing a book in the West on narrative methods, aesthetics, and culture. At that time, I had published more than twenty essays in the West but had published my book-length projects only in my native China. Although this book takes up different issues from the ones Emory suggested, his encouragement and his confidence in me sustained me throughout the writing. I am also deeply grateful to Jonathan Culler for three things: suggesting that I write a book that uses stylistic analysis to offer new readings of short stories; commenting insightfully on the manuscript; and recommending the project to Michael Burke, the editor of this book series. To Michael I extend my gratitude for his keen interest in my project and for his valuable editorial support and advice.

Although I hope that this book breaks new ground in its attempt to explore *dual* narrative dynamics and *covert* progression, it is strongly influenced by the work of James Phelan, who has been leading the rhetorical investigation on narrative progression. Jim has read the drafts of almost all of my papers published in the West in narrative studies and has given me invaluable feedback. In the process of preparing this book, I have benefited immensely from his astute advice, trenchant questions, and incisive specific suggestions.

This project presents a challenge to the traditional critical focus on plot development and offers challenging new interpretations of some major short fiction. Although my basic stance is rhetorical (with an emphasis on shared reading) rather than deconstructive (with an emphasis on indeterminate reading), the project reflects the influence of my engagement with the work of J. Hillis Miller. He has given me unfailing support, advice, and encouragement since we first met in 1988. I am deeply grateful not only for his numerous helpful comments on the manuscript but also for his generously volunteering to write the Foreword.

I also owe debts of gratitude to numerous others: to Jonathan Arac for his thorough and perceptive reading of an earlier version of the Introduction and the first three chapters; to Meir Sternberg, the editor of *Poetics Today*,

xiv *Acknowledgments*

for his rigorous and insightful reviews of earlier versions of Chapter 3 and Chapter 6; to three anonymous Routledge reviewers for their helpful comments on an earlier version of the Introduction and Chapter 2.

Peter J. Rabinowitz, David Herman, Seymour Chatman, Porter Abbott, Monika Fludernik, Peter Messent, Paul Simpson, Michael Toolan, Ruth Page, Geoff Hall, Emma Kafalenos, Jakob Lothe, John Pier, Wolf Schmid, Donald Stone, Robyn Warhol, Brian Richardson, Susan Lanser, Alison Case, David H. Richter, and Alison Booth, among other Western colleagues and friends, have helped me clarify my thinking on various issues and have given me valuable support and encouragement.

I am also indebted to Felisa N. Salvago-Keyes, Margo Irvin, Katie Laurentiev, Renata Corbani, and the copy editor at Routledge for all their editorial support and help.

Many of my Chinese colleagues in Peking University and other universities have given me helpful comments and valuable support during the process of preparing this book. Let me mention in particular Yiqing Liu, Jie Tao, Jiaming Han, Xiaoyi Zhou, Jianhua Liu, Shusen Liu, Gengxin Su, Weixing Su, Feng Liu, Lu Liu, Fengfeng Gao, Liang Mao, Zhaoxiang Cheng, Ning Sheng, Xiangyu Liu, Yunte Huang, Shaobo Xie, Gang Zhu, Yiheng Zhao, Zhenzhao Nie, Yifan Zhao, Jianjun Liu, Wei Cheng, Zhongzai Zhang, Li Jin, Hong Jiang, Tie Li, Hailiang Ma, Xueyan Yang, Li Cao, Liya Wang, Yizhong Ning, and the late Bing Wu.

I am furthermore indebted to my undergraduate and research students at Peking University who have shared my interests in stylistics and narrative and whose stimulating discussions have helped advance my own thinking. In addition, my Ph.D. student Yanwei Hu has perused almost the entire manuscript with her sharp eyes and helped correct various slips. Thanks also go to Jing Chen, the secretary at the Center for European and American Literatures of Peking University, who has provided assistance in various ways during the process of preparing this book.

Finally, as a small recognition of my great fortune to live most happily in the many years of marriage, I dedicate this book to my husband, Xing Li.

Earlier versions of various segments of the book have previously appeared in print. Although I have significantly reworked most of them to fit the general argument of the book and my current understanding, especially in terms of the shift from the concern with subtext to a rhetorical concern with covert progression, I am grateful for permission from the publishers and editors to draw on the following essays:

"Neo-Aristotelian Rhetorical Narrative Study: Need for Integrating Style, Context and Intertext," *Style* 45 (2011): 576–97. Copyright 2011 by *Style*.

"Edgar Allan Poe's Aesthetic Theory, the Insanity Debate, and the Ethically Oriented Dynamics of 'The Tell-Tale Heart,'" *Nineteenth-Century*

Acknowledgments xv

Literature 63 (December 2008): 321–345. Copyright 2008 by the Regents of the University of California. Published by the University of California Press.

" 'Overall-Extended Close Reading' and Subtexts of Short Stories," *English Studies: A Journal of English Language and Literature* 91 (2010): 150–69. Copyright 2010 by Taylor & Francis Group.

"Implied Author, Overall Consideration, and Subtext of 'Desiree's Baby,' " *Poetics Today: International Journal for Theory and Analysis of Literature and Communication* 31 (2010): 285–312, used by permission of the publisher, Duke University Press.

"Subverting Surface and Doubling Irony: Subtexts of Mansfield's 'Revelations' and Others," *English Studies: A Journal of English Language and Literature* 87 (2006): 191–209. Copyright 2006 by Taylor & Francis Group.

"Covert Progression behind Plot Development: Katherine Mansfield's 'The Fly,' " *Poetics Today: International Journal for Theory and Analysis of Literature and Communication* 34 (2013): 147–75, reprinted by permission of the publisher, Duke University Press.

—Dan Shen

Introduction

In a letter of 1883 to his friend A. W. M. Ballie, Gerard Manley Hopkins draws a distinction between "overthought" and "underthought" when discussing lyric passages of Greek tragedy. The overthought is the surface meaning that the readers and editors see, and the underthought is another story carried on beneath the surface and expressed "chiefly in the choice of metaphors etc used and often only half realized by the poet himself" (Hopkins 1995: 174; see also Frye 1990: 57–58). A similar situation can be found in many fictional prose narratives, where our surface reading, or the way the overt plot moves, exists in tension with a very different and powerful dynamic that focuses, at a hidden and deeper level, on aesthetics and ethics, among other kinds of thematic import.[1] This hidden dynamic, which complicates the audience's response in various ways, is what I call "covert progression." But of course, the covert textual progression in prose fiction differs from the poetic underthought in more than one way. While the poetic underthought is a local deeper meaning "in any lyric passage" (Hopkins 1995: 174), the covert progression is an undercurrent running throughout the prose text; while the poetic underthought rests on the suggestive meaning of figurative language, the covert progression in prose narratives characteristically relies on non-metaphorical stylistic and structural techniques; while the underthought is often only half-consciously conveyed by the poet, the covert progression usually forms a purposeful rhetorical strategy of the prose writer. Moreover, while the underthought Hopkins had in mind is a positive undercurrent of the text, the covert progression this book investigates conveys an ethical import that can either be harmful (see Chapter 3) or beneficial (see all the other Chapters). Despite all these differences, the covert progression in prose fiction and the poetic underthought have essential similarities: both are a deeper-level textual movement that is aesthetically conveyed, and both form a significant counterpoint that supplements or contradicts the surface meaning, thus complicating the audience's response in various ways.

This book selects six short stories to illustrate how stylistic analysis is indispensable for uncovering the covert progression through rhetorical criticism. Short fiction is chosen as the object of investigation chiefly out of two

2 Style and Rhetoric of Short Narrative Fiction

considerations. First, using short stories as illustrations facilitates the revelation of a typology of different forms of covert progression. In *Understanding Fiction*, Cleanth Brooks and Robert Penn Warren only use short stories to illustrate the functioning of different elements of fiction, and, in like manner, this book uses short stories to show the different ways in which the covert progression relates to the thematic implications of the overt plot development. Second, we are hard put to carry out a comprehensive analysis of style in long fictional narratives. Stylistic analyses of novels usually only deal with certain passages, a tiny portion of the long text. Although we can assume that "any passage is a microcosm of the whole" in terms of the importance of style in a given text (Phelan 1981: 20), to uncover the covert progression we have to trace the stylistic patterning from the beginning to the end of the text. This can only be conveniently carried out in short texts. Not surprisingly, this book, as a pioneering attempt to show different forms of covert progressing, confines its analysis to short fiction.

COVERT TEXTUAL PROGRESSIONS: BRIEF SKETCHES

Since the late 1970's there has been an increasing study of narrative sequence, dynamics, and progression as a reaction to the more or less static models of plot structure as offered by classical narratologists. Peter Brooks's *Reading for the Plot* (1984) is a pioneering book that puts emphasis on the forward movement of plot/plotting and of reading (see also Sternberg 1978). Drawing on psychoanalysis, Brooks treats a narrative as "a system of internal energies and tensions, compulsions, resistances, and desires" in the temporal dynamics that shapes a text in the onward reading process (1984: xiv). In rhetorical narrative criticism, James Phelan sees a narrative as a "progression" built on unstable situations both in the story and in the discourse presentation. As for the story level, where the characters and/or their situations undergo some change, "the report of that change typically proceeds through the introduction, complication, and resolution (in whole or in part)" of "instabilities" within, between or among the characters (Phelan 2007: 7). In terms of discourse presentation, there exist "tensions" in the form of a discrepancy in knowledge, judgments, values or beliefs among authors, narrators, and readers (ibid., see also Phelan, 1996: 217–18). For the past twenty years or so, Phelan has taken the leading role in investigating narrative progression with his four brilliant and influential books (1989, 1996, 2005, 2007) and numerous essays. In the field of stylistics, Michael Toolan (2009) takes a computer-assisted corpus analytic approach to narrative progression, investigating how the text's lexico-phrasal patterning guides readers' expectations and responses. The investigation contributes to a fuller understanding of how words on the page give rise to "such distinct impressionistic reader judgements as ones of suspense, surprise, secrecy or gaps, mystery, tension, obscurity, and even incoherence" as the text progresses towards the end (2009: 1). The increasing interest in the dynamics

Introduction 3

of textual movement and reading activity has greatly enriched our understanding of narrative fiction, shedding much light on the functioning of the text and the communication among authors, narrators, and readers (see also Sternberg 1990, 1992, 2006; Richardson 2002).

As the definite article "the" in Brooks' *Reading for the Plot* indicates, narrative criticism so far has focused on one textual progression based on the instabilities in the plot or main line of action, although various attempts have been made at discovering deeper layers of meaning of this progression.[2] But in many fictional narratives, especially shorter ones, there exist two textual movements that still need to be distinguished. One is plot development, a major focus of attention since Aristotle. As we know, "plot" is a very elusive term in narrative theory, one that has received various definitions (see Cuddon 1979: 513–14; Dannenberg 2005: 435–39; Sternberg 1978: 10–14). In common terms, plot is the development of a narrative's sequence of events. In *Story and Discourse,* Seymour Chatman (1978: 45–48) distinguishes between the traditional "plot of resolution" and the modern "plot of revelation." In the former, events are causally related and progress towards the denouement, marked by a completed process of change of a certain kind (Crane 1952a). In the latter, by contrast, it is "not that events are resolved (happily or tragically), but rather that a state of affairs is revealed" (Chatman 1978: 48).

However, behind the plot development—no matter whether the events are connected by causality and resolved in the end or linked by contingency and created to display a state of affairs (often character-oriented)—there may exist a parallel textual movement that runs throughout. The latter conveys a different thematic import and often contains various textual details that appear peripheral or irrelevant to the themes of the plot. This complication of the textual dynamics gives rise to the complication of the reading activity when the covert textual movement gradually comes into view.

The present inquiry is concerned with the ethically oriented and aesthetically created kind of covert progression, which may be defined as:

> The covert textual progression is an ethical-aesthetic undercurrent running throughout the text behind the overt plot development. The relation between the ethical significance generated by the covert progression and the overt plot varies from narrative to narrative, ranging from supplementation to subversion, which complicates the audience's response in various ways.

Two things should be noted here. First, I follow Wayne C. Booth, the founder of contemporary rhetorical study of narrative fiction, in using the term "ethics" or "ethical" in a broad and flexible sense, making it carry the weight of political criticism as "a rough synonymy" for ideological criticism (1988: 12) and, moreover, treating it as covering both "good" and "bad" qualities (1988: 8).[3] An "ethical" message or choice, that is to say, can paradoxically be bad or "unethical." Second, the covert ethical progression foregrounds

4   Style and Rhetoric of Short Narrative Fiction

the connection between ethics and aesthetics in that it is characteristically created by the implied author with subtle stylistic and structural devices. The process of uncovering the covert progression is a process of revealing the intricate relationship between artistic techniques and ethical concerns. In other words, it highlights how ethical issues can be non-didactically, finely, and uniquely conveyed by the literary writer.

The chapters that follow all try to reveal, through stylistic analysis among other methods, a covert textual progression, its relation to the hidden ethical stance of the implied author, its rich aesthetic value, and the subtle way in which it complicates the audience's response. For the convenience of discussion and illustration, I will offer here brief sketches of the covert textual progressions uncovered in the later chapters, where attention will also be directed to the complicated readerly dynamics corresponding to the complicated textual dynamics. As regards the covert textual movements sketched here, any point that falls short of clarity may gain substantiation and clarification from the detailed discussion in the latter part of the book.

Edgar Allan Poe's "The Tell-Tale Heart" (discussed in detail in Chapter 1)

Overt plot: A neurotic character narrator who insists on his sanity tells the story of his conceiving the idea of killing an old man with a "vulture eye," his careful execution of the murder, his hiding the dismembered corpse under the floor, and finally, when three policemen come to search the house, his hearing the increasingly loud beating of the old man's heart which leads to his admitting his crime.

Covert textual progression: Throughout the text, there are two ironic undercurrents, one main and the other subsidiary. The main one, created primarily with stylistic choices showing the protagonist-narrator's continuous dissemblance and his taking unethical delight in it, centers on his unwitting self-condemnation: He unconsciously projects his own dissemblance onto the policemen, condemns the projected dissemblance as immoral and finds it extremely unbearable, which leads to the exposure of his crime. The subsidiary one, resting on the interaction between the stylistic choices depicting the unreliable narrator's continuous insistence on his being sane and the insanity debate in that historical context, centers on the narrator's unwitting self-conviction. The two undercurrents form an overall dramatic irony, implicitly conveying a moral—how one's self-satisfying hypocrisy can lead to one's downfall.

Stephen Crane's "An Episode of War" (discussed in detail in Chapter 2)

Overt plot: An unnamed lieutenant is wounded in the right arm during the intermission of a battle. He goes to a field hospital to have the wound

Introduction 5

treated, perceiving a battle going on in the distance, and at the end he arrives home with only one arm.

Covert textual progression: There is a sustained ironic undercurrent to deprive the wounded lieutenant of manhood and dignity, which joins forces with the strategies of replacing fighting against enemy with internal conflicts and rendering the battle scene meaningless to form an overall satirical covert progression against war and romanticized notions of heroism.

Kate Chopin's "Désirée's Baby" (discussed in detail in Chapter 3)

Overt plot: Désirée is a foundling adopted by the Valmondés. After growing to womanhood, she is wooed and wed by Armand Aubigny, a neighboring planter and bearer of one of the finest names in Louisiana. She gives birth to a son who looks to be of mixed race. Armand spurns both mother and child for the black blood, and Désirée, carrying her baby, commits suicide.[4] At the ending of the narrative, Armand gets to know that the son's African features come from himself instead of Désirée. This overt textual progression primarily forms an indictment of the Southern racist system.

Covert textual progression: Primarily through the interaction between subtle stylistic choices and a surprise ending, there is created an undercurrent building up a fictional world where all (really) white characters never perpetrate racial discrimination and racial oppression, making life gay for enslaved blacks and happy for free blacks, and where, in contrast, (really) black characters are guilty of racial discrimination and the only person who oppresses black people in a cruel manner is a black planter. There is thus implicitly created a dual vision of slavery: positive slavery under white masters and negative slavery under a black master. This dual vision implicitly attributes the sufferings of the blacks to the black blood and unobtrusively mythologizes and endorses the white-dominated Southern racist system.

Katherine Mansfield's "Revelations" (discussed in detail in Chapter 4)

Overt plot: Monica Tyrell always suffers terribly from her nerves in the morning. This morning she is awakened by a strong wind, and then she flies into a rage after receiving Ralph's well-intended invitation to lunch at Prince's. Upon getting her first revelation concerned with freedom, she races off to her hairdresser's. She snaps at the hairdresser George for his unusual absent-mindedness. Then George tells her that his daughter—a first child— died that morning. Monica rushes out to take a taxi to Prince's. On the way she sees a flower shop and wants to buy flowers for the little girl, but the driver fails to hear her tap at the window and she finds herself at Prince's

6 *Style and Rhetoric of Short Narrative Fiction*

already. The overt plot is regarded by many critics as an exposure of the weaknesses of the female protagonist.

Covert textual progression: Through the use of free indirect discourse among other stylistic devices, there is created a continuous undercurrent that indicates how patriarchal forces reduce the upper-middle-class Monica to a mere "doll" of men and deprive her of all her worth except youth and beauty that she no longer possesses as a 33-year-old woman. This largely accounts for her suffering from her nerves and other weaknesses. The covert progression doubles the object of authorial irony: both the protagonist's "feminine" weaknesses and the Western hegemonic structure of patriarchy or masculinist domination, the latter forming the most important reason underlying the former.

Katherine Mansfield's "The Singing Lesson" (discussed in detail in Chapter 5)

Overt plot: Miss Meadows, a thirty-year-old spinster, is in a very bad mood on her way to teach a singing lesson. When in the classroom, she treats her girl pupils coldly and wickedly because her fiancé Basil has broken off their engagement. Then she is summoned to the school office where she receives from Basil a telegram to promise marriage again. This transforms her into a warm, joyful and kind woman.

Covert textual progression: Primarily through the subtle manipulation of focalization (point of view), there is created a continuous undercurrent which indicates that what Miss Meadows dreads most is not losing Basil the man, but other people's prejudice in the phallocentric society against a woman unwanted by men. The phallocentric discrimination implicitly threatens her job, even her room for survival in society, and it therefore reduces her to behaving in an abnormal and wicked way. The text progresses to show Miss Meadows' great joy and her returning to her usual kindness when being (temporarily) free from that kind of social prejudice. The covert progression forms a veiled yet highly dramatic protest against patriarchal discrimination against women.

Katherine Mansfield's "The Fly" (discussed in detail in Chapter 6)

Overt plot: Mr. Woodifield, who retired after having a stroke, makes his weekly visit to his old boss in the office. He tells the boss about the graves of his own son and the boss's son, who were both killed in the war. After Woodifield leaves, the boss recalls his son in pain. Then he notices that a fly has fallen into his inkpot and is struggling to get free. The boss first lifts the fly out of the inkpot, then he changes his mind and keeps dropping blots of ink on the fly until it is killed, which leaves the boss wretched, frightened, and forgetful.

Introduction 7

Covert textual progression: There is an undercurrent that secretly unifies various stylistic choices which appear digressive to the main line of action. This undercurrent forms an overall irony against the boss's vanity and self-importance. The enfeebled Woodifield (whose frailness gives the boss self-satisfaction), the boss's newly decorated office (which he keeps showing off to his friends), the boss's son (the boss's pride and a tool to carry on his business), and the fly (with which the boss increasingly identifies) successively and implicitly function as a vehicle to bring out the boss's vanity and self-importance. Ironically, when the son is killed in the war and the fly by the boss himself, the boss becomes (before he can find other means to help regain his self-importance) similarly broken and wretched.

IRONY IN COVERT PROGRESSION VERSUS OTHER TYPES OF IRONY

As the above sketches indicate, the covert textual progression in prose fiction is often ironic in nature. Irony is usually classified into two basic categories: verbal and situational. The former involves a discrepancy between the literal/ostensible meaning and the intended/implied meaning of a statement, while the latter typically concerns an incongruity between the expected outcome of an action and its actual (unexpected or undesired) outcome. Classical examples of situational irony include that in *Troilus and Cressida* (Shakespeare 2007b) where "the fine speeches and grandiose ideas eventually produce nothing," or the tragic irony in *King Lear* (Shakespeare 2007a) where Lear rejects the daughter who loves him most (Cuddon 1979: 335–40; see also Booth 1974; Colebrook 2004; Fowler 1973: 101–2; Muecke 1982). The ironic covert progression studied in this book has two distinctive characteristics. First, it is a sustained ironic movement from the beginning to the end of the text, and local elements often become ironic only in relation to other elements in the covert progression. It thus differs from the more local "verbal" and "situational" irony. Second, it is an additional ironic layer behind the irony of the plot development (see Chapters 1, 4, and 5) or behind a plot development that is basically not ironic (see Chapters 2 and 6).

The New Criticism movement is well known for its concern with irony in prose fiction as well as in poetry (C. Brooks 1948, 1968, 2005). In *Understanding Fiction*, Cleanth Brooks and Robert Penn Warren set store by irony, but their attention is limited to the irony of one textual movement—that of the plot development itself. Concerning Guy de Maupassant's "The Necklace," they ask a hypothetical question: "Would there be an irony in the story even if she [the female protagonist] had never learned the true nature of the jewels?" (Brooks and Warren 1979: 72). They likewise direct attention to the facts that the irony of the plot in John Collier's "De Mortuis" is "based on a general view of life, the surprising and comic way in which things happen," and that the irony of the plot of Nathaniel Hawthorne's

8   *Style and Rhetoric of Short Narrative Fiction*

"Young Goodman Brown" rests on another generality, "the doubleness of human nature" (Brooks and Warren 1979: 73). Brooks and Warren's discussion is quite representative of traditional investigations on irony in prose fiction.

In rhetorical studies, starting from Booth's *The Rhetoric of Fiction* (1961), critics have paid much attention to narrative or "structural" irony (Abrams and Harpham 2009: 166). Instead of focusing on the events themselves, rhetorical critics are concerned with the "secret communion" between the implied author and the implied/authorial reader at the expense of the narrator: "We travel with the silent author, observing as from a rear seat the humorous or disgraceful or ridiculous or vicious driving behavior of the narrator seated in front" (Booth 1961: 300). But attention is usually devoted only to one level of irony, especially that against an unreliable narrator's misreporting, misinterpreting, and misevaluating (Phelan 2005). By contrast, this book directs attention to two levels of irony, one explicit and the other implicit. In Chapter 1, for instance, apart from the irony against the unreliable narrator's misreporting that has attracted previous critical attention, there is revealed a hidden overall dramatic irony centering on the unreliable narrator's unconscious self-condemnation and self-conviction. This kind of ironic undercurrent increases the distance between the narrator and the author/reader. In Chapters 4 and 5, behind the irony against the protagonist in the overt plot, there is uncovered a deeper ironic progression against social forces which largely account for the weaknesses of the protagonist. This kind of ironic undercurrent shortens the distance between the protagonist and the author/narrator/reader.

When the present project is only concerned with one level of irony, it is a level that has remained hidden behind a non-ironic overt textual movement, such as in Chapters 2 and 6. In Chapter 2, the hidden irony is directed not so much against the characters as against romanticized notions of war and heroism, to which the characters fall victim. In this light, this kind of ironic undercurrent shares an essential similarity with that in Chapters 4 and 5, but the distance between the characters and the author/narrator/reader is somewhat increased rather than shortened as compared with that in the non-ironic overt textual movement. In Chapter 6, by contrast, the protagonist himself forms the butt of irony in the covert textual movement, and the distance as such is much increased.

COVERT PROGRESSION VERSUS OTHER
TYPES OF COVERT MEANING

As we know, ironic meaning is covert meaning. Having seen the difference between irony in covert progression and previously discussed irony, we now come to the question: What is the difference between covert progression and other types of covert meaning? I would like to start answering this question

Introduction 9

by considering the relation between covert progression and what Armine Kotin Mortimer (1989: 276–98) calls "second story" beneath the surface of various short stories.

On the face of it, "second story" bears a striking similarity to covert progression in that "a second story that is not told outright" is also "an undercurrent of suggested meaning" (276) essential to a fuller and more accurate reading of the work as a whole. But in fact second story is drastically different from covert progression. The primary example of second story Mortimer (278–83) offers is from Maupassant's "Room 11." At the end of the narrative, the extramarital affair in room 11 between the wife of Magistrate Amandon and her lover is discovered by a police commissioner. The tale ends with the words the police commissioner "gave them their liberty, but [he] was not discreet. The next month, Magistrate Amandon received an advancement with a new residence." So there arises the "riddle": Why is the magistrate promoted? The answer is unknown to the magistrate himself. To this riddle, Mortimer (280) claims, "only a second story will supply the correct answer." In the given text sequence, the second story hides between the "indiscretion" of the police commissioner and the promotion and new residence of Amandon. The second story, which readers have to infer to make sense of the plot development, "establishe[s] the connection between the downfall of the wife and the elevation of the husband": the indiscreet police commissioner has informed Amandon's boss of the extramarital affair, and the boss has taken advantage of Amandon's wife, who "has so well pleased her husband's boss" that he rewarded her by promoting her husband (280–81). Likewise, the other second stories Mortimer (283–93) discusses invariably take the shape of an untold "secret" which the reader has to infer in order to have a complete plot line.

The essential difference between the second story and the covert progression lies in the following four aspects. First, while the second story relates to a *local gap* in the action, the covert progression is a *continuous* undercurrent running from the beginning to the end of the narrative. Second, Mortimer's second story, in the shape of "an adulterous love affair, murder, incest, [or] perversion," is an *indispensable constituent* of the plot, while the covert progression is another textual movement which runs parallel to the plot development and goes in a contrastive thematic direction. Third, while the second story, as a missing link in the plot itself, is what the reader "is actively solicited" to supply (276), the covert progression, as an undercurrent behind the plot development, tends to elude the reader's conscious attention. Fourth, while the second story, as an untold "secret" in the plot, "risks platitudes as soon as it is exposed" (ibid.), the discovery of the covert progression is aesthetically appealing and ethically thought provoking, and the effect increasingly intensifies in the process of gradual discovery.

Another type of covert meaning is discussed by Mary Rohrberger in *Hawthorne and the Modern Short Story* (1966). Inspired by such New Critical works as Richard H. Fogle's (1952) study of imagery patterns in

10 Style and Rhetoric of Short Narrative Fiction

Hawthorne's fiction, Rohrberger (1966: 105–23) draws a distinction between "simple narrative" and "short story." The former is a tale whose "total interest lies on the surface level," with "no depths to be plumbed" (106). A case in point is Somerset Maugham's "The Colonel's Lady," where "by no stretch of the imagination could either the situation, the action, or the characters be taken as symbols" (109). In contrast, the "short story" has a deeper level of meaning (106). An example is Katherine Mansfield's "The Fly," whose plot development is marked by rich symbolic meaning, with the fly functioning "as a symbol for all the characters in the story" (Roheberger 1966: 71).

On the face of it, the deeper level of meaning Rohrberger discusses is quite similar to covert progression in that it not only enriches the thematic dimension of the text but also leads to the reader's complicated response. But in fact the two essentially differ, since Rohrberger's deeper meaning hinges on whether the plot or situation itself has symbolic implications, whereas my concern is primarily with a non-symbolic covert textual movement that parallels the plot or situation. This difference emerges from our contrastive views of Poe's "The Tell-Tale Heart." The tale is dismissed by Rohrberger (1966: 120–21) as "a simple narrative" because "everything contributes to it [the plot] and to the final effect of terror" and there is "no suggestion given within the framework of the story to direct the reader to meaningful implications." But I have singled out the tale for investigation (see Chapter 1) since it has a covert progression centering on the protagonist-narrator's unconscious self-condemnation and self-conviction as mentioned above. Interestingly, both Rohrberger and I find Mansfield's "The Fly" valuable but for very different reasons. Rohrberger sets store by the narrative because its plot is marked by rich symbolic meaning. In contrast I attach importance to the narrative particularly because it has a covert progression conveying irony against the boss's vanity and self-importance, a non-symbolic undercurrent behind the symbolic plot development.

A distinction made by Clare Hanson in *Short Stories and Short Fictions, 1880–1980* is also relevant here, one between "those works in which the major emphasis is on plot and those in which plot is subordinate to psychology and mood" (1985: 5). The latter type, as pioneered by Edgar Allan Poe (e.g. "The Fall of the House of Usher" or "Ligeia"), contains "static works in which images and stylised dramatic scenes act as 'objective correlatives' for states of mind or feeling" (Hanson 1985: 4). What is relevant is the stress Hanson lays on the stylistic aspect of the "static works" characterized by symbolic or expressive images. Indeed, in the field of short fiction studies, many critics, at least from the times of New Criticism and prior to the reign of cultural studies, have placed great interpretive weight on stylistic choices in symbolic or imagist works. The basic assumption is that this kind of short story, like poetry, is "a concentrated form, wrought out of an intensification of thought and feeling and demanding an equivalent stylistic intensity" (Hanson 1985: 3). However, the investigation of style here, as in the case

Introduction 11

of Mansfield's "The Fly," has usually not led to the discovery of a covert progression behind the "psychology and mood."

Although Mortimer, Rohrberger, and Hanson are all concerned with the short story, what they investigate—a gap or missing link in the plot, a symbolic structure or an imagery pattern of the plot—is not exclusive to this genre. Even less exclusive are the ironic implications of plot as investigated by Brooks and Warren in *Understanding Fiction*, a book that only uses short stories as illustrations. In the introduction to *The New Short Story Theories*, Charles E. May summarizes the debate on whether the short story is a unique narrative form. Positioning himself in the "family resemblance" camp, May acknowledges that, except for brevity, there are no "exclusionary characteristics" that distinguish the short story from the novel, but there is "a network of similarities and relationships within examples" of the short story as a genre (xvii–xviii). I subscribe to this position. Like Rohrberger's symbolic structure (which is also found in novels such as Virginia Woolf's *To the Lighthouse* or Joseph Conrad's *Heart of Darkness*), the covert progression the present project explores is not confined to short stories.

In the field of short fiction, as in the field of the novel, existing investigations of covert meaning—no matter whether they deal with the ironic, the "secret," the symbolic, or the imagist aspect of meaning, and no matter how much interpretive weight is placed on style—have usually not paid attention to the narrative's covert progression as such. This neglect may be largely accounted for by the extent to which, starting from Aristotle, critical attention has focused on plot development—whether on the multiform significance and dynamics of the instabilities in the traditional plot of resolution or on the symbolic meaning of the modern "plot of revelation." Poe's "The Tell-Tale Heart," for instance, has appealed to numerous critics, including many psychoanalytic ones in the latter half of the twentieth century. Such analysts have focused on its plot (the premeditated murder and the exposure of the crime) or the inner drama developing along the plot, though they have approached it from various angles and often revealed a deeper level of meaning in it. To uncover the covert progression, however, we need to look behind the plot for an alternative, complementary development, which centers on the narrator-protagonist's self-satisfying dissemblance culminating in his unconscious self-condemnation, and which is joined by a subsidiary undercurrent centering on the narrator's unconscious self-conviction in that historical context (see Chapter 1). Here we may even claim that the narrative has three parallel progressions, one overt and the other two covert, instead of viewing the two as branches of a single covert progression constituting an overall dramatic irony.

In terms of the modern symbolic or imagist texts, to unveil the covert progression, we also need to find out whether there is an undercurrent that is alternative or parallel to the symbolic structure or imagery pattern of the plot or the state of affairs represented there. In Mansfield's "The Fly," unless we open our minds to two thematic progressions, we are hard put to discover

12   Style and Rhetoric of Short Narrative Fiction

the covert one centering on the boss's vanity and self-importance behind the overt one concerned with war, death, grief, helplessness, victimization, and so forth (see Chapter 6). In Mansfield's "Revelations" or "The Singing Lesson," we also need to search for the possible existence of an alternative undercurrent in order to discover the covert progression focusing on social forces, which runs contrastive or counter to the overt one focusing on the protagonist's own behavior (see Chapters 4 and 5).

In some cases, if we free ourselves of the bondage of the plot development and consciously search for the possible existence of a covert textual progression, we may perceive what we have already experienced without being aware of it. As we will see in the survey of existing criticism in the later chapters, when we think that the text only has one progression, we tend to map onto the themes of that progression whatever textual elements we find relevant in order to have the thematic unity of the text. But some elements may pertain to the covert textual progression that runs contrastive or even counter to the thematic implications of the plot. On the other hand, when we believe that the text only has one progression, we may also dismiss various textual details as unimportant or irrelevant to it, but these details may play a very important role in the covert progression. In such a process of sorting out textual elements for the one progression we have in mind, we may suppress or distort various effects of the "covert" textual elements we originally experienced. To recognize the covert progression therefore is in a sense to restore the suppressed or distorted effects. However, it would be going too far to claim that the revelation of the covert progression always functions to spell out what readers have already experienced. As we will see in the later chapters, the covert progression is characteristically based on very subtle stylistic patterning, which requires conscious and careful exploration of the text. Indeed, this book aims not only at directing attention to the covert textual progression as a significant principle of narrative structure, but also at contributing, from a fresh angle, to a better understanding of narrative techniques, especially of the relation between artistic stylistic patterning and a continuous ethical undercurrent.

It seems redundant to assert that in those narratives marked by a dual dynamics as such, to have a proper understanding of the implied author's rhetorical purposes and to get closer to the authorial norms, it is crucial to uncover the covert progression. To succeed in this attempt, it is very important, as I will argue and show below, to integrate stylistic analysis, contextual consideration, and intertextual comparison into rhetorical criticism.

IMPORTANCE OF INTEGRATING STYLE INTO RHETORICAL CRITICISM

Contemporary rhetorical narrative criticism has been shedding significant light on the relation among the implied author, narrator, character, and

Introduction 13

audience. Wayne C. Booth and James Phelan have successively figured as leaders of its two stages of development, first from the 1960s to the 1980s, and then from the 1990s up to the present. Booth and Phelan are respectively representatives of the second and third generations of the neo-Aristotelian Chicago School of literary criticism. Although the latter generations of the neo-Aristotelians differ from the first in significant ways, such as moving from the primary concern with the poetic (the text) to a concern with the rhetorical (author-audience communication) or with the rhetorical-poetic (Phelan 2007: 79–94), in some important aspects they both bear the imprint of the first generation as represented by R. S. Crane. The early neo-Aristotelians, on the one hand, marked off their approach from other branches of criticism and, on the other, advocated pluralism or the coexistence of different approaches. The disciplinary boundary has enabled the Chicago School to take on its own characteristics and contribute to the study of literature in its unique ways. But the boundary has also brought certain limitations. There are two self-imposed preclusions that have very much persisted up to the present in the rhetorical study of literary narrative: first, the preclusion of style or language, and second, the preclusion of the context of creation.

Continuous Exclusion of Style or Language

The first generation of Chicago critics followed Aristotle in subordinating literary language to the larger structure of the work in a given genre. The basic assumption is that disregarding style or language enables them to focus on the "architecture" of literary works, or more specifically, to concentrate on "how fully a given poem exemplifies the common structural principles of the genre to which it has been assigned" (Crane 1952b: 1–2). Moreover, the early Chicago critics engaged in a fierce polemic against New Critics whose exclusive concern with language and irony they found excessively limiting (see Phelan 2007: 79–87). The antagonism of the Chicago School towards the language-oriented New Criticism added to the preclusion of the analysis of style.

This tendency was inherited by contemporary rhetorical critics. In the afterword to the second edition of *The Rhetoric of Fiction* (1983 [1961]), Booth very much persists with his underplaying language or style in the first edition because of "the non-verbal basis of fictional effects" (1983: 461). To him, the earlier Chicago critics' development of Aristotle's method provides "the most helpful, least limiting view of character and event—those tough realities that have never submitted happily to merely verbal analysis" (1983: 460). He subscribes to Joseph E. Baker's view (1947: 100) that the "aesthetic surface" of fiction is found, not in words, but in the "world" of character, event, and value "concretely represented and temporally arranged" (quoted in Booth 1983: 480).

The preclusion of language is reinforced through rhetorical critics' drawing on structuralist narratology. Many rhetorical critics today have adopted

14 *Style and Rhetoric of Short Narrative Fiction*

the narratological distinction between story and discourse (see Shen 2005a; 2002). "Discourse" is defined in narratology as "the signifier" (Genette 1980: 27) or "the expression, the means by which the content is communicated" (Chatman 1978: 19), which seems to form the whole level of presentation. But in effect narratology's "discourse" only covers structural techniques, very much to the exclusion of style or verbal techniques, except for some overlapping areas such as focalization/point of view or speech presentation (see Shen 2005b). Let us compare the following two observations made by Michael Toolan in his *Narrative* (2001) and *Language in Literature* (1998) respectively:

> (1) That is to say, if we think of histoire/story as level 1 of analysis, then within discourse we have two further levels of organization, those of text and of narration. At the level of text, the teller decides upon and creates a particular sequencing of events, the time/space spent presenting them, the sense of (changing) rhythm and pace in the discourse. Additionally, choices are made as to just how (in what detail, and in what order) the particularity of the various characters is to be presented. . . . At the level of narration, the [structural] relations between the posited narrator and the narrative she tells are probed. (2001: 11–12)
>
> (2) So one of the crucial things attempted by Stylistics is to put the discussion of textual effects and techniques on a public, shared, footing. . . . The other chief feature of Stylistics is that it persists in the attempt to understand technique, or the craft of writing. If we agree that Hemingway's short story "Indian Camp," and Yeats's poem "Sailing to Byzantium," are both extraordinary literary achievements, what are some of the linguistic components of that excellence? Why these word-choices, clause-patterns, rhythms, and intonations, contextual implications [of conversation], cohesive links [among sentences], choices of voice and perspective and transitivity [of clause structure], etc. etc., and not any of the others imaginable? (1998: ix)

It is not hard to find that narratology's "techniques" (structural choices) in the first quotation are drastically different from stylistics' "techniques" (verbal choices) in the second.[5] Although the term "rhythm" appears in both quotations, it means entirely different things in the two different contexts. In the stylistic context, "rhythm" means *verbal movement* resulting from the features of words and their combination (e.g. poetic meter, sentence length, or the use of punctuation), whereas in the narratological context, "rhythm" refers to the *structural* relations between textual duration and event duration, such as detailed scenic presentation versus brief summary or ellipsis of events.

In *Story and Discourse: Narrative Structure in Fiction and Film* (1978), Seymour Chatman observes, "My primary object is *narrative* form rather than the form of the surface of narratives—verbal nuance, graphic design,

Introduction 15

balletic movements. 'Style' in this sense, the properties of the texture of the medium, is fascinating, and those who have read my work know that I have spent many hours on it. Here, however, I am concerned with stylistic details only insofar as they participate in or reveal the broader, more abstract narrative movements" (10–11). This preclusion of style is carried over into his more rhetorical *Coming to Terms: The Rhetoric of Narrative in Fiction and Film* (1990).[6]

In his ongoing effort to offer a comprehensive account of the rhetorical theory of narrative, James Phelan has published five books (1981, 1989, 1997, 2005, 2007). The first *Worlds From Words: A Theory of Language in Fiction* presents an admirable analysis of fictional style, but the author's basic position is that "language, though it varies in importance from one work to the next, will always remain subordinate to character and action, which he views as essentially nonlinguistic elements of fiction."[7] Not surprisingly, Phelan's second book is entitled "Reading People, Reading Plots: Character, Progression, and the Interpretation of Narrative." However, being highly competent in verbal analysis, Phelan has paid some attention to style in his later work especially in discussions of voice and unreliability. In general, rhetorical critics focus on character and action, more or less to the neglect of various stylistic details in their investigation of author-audience communication.

Why Should Style be Integrated into Rhetorical Criticism?

As distinct from cognitive criticism that aims at accounting for the interpretation of conventional/generic audience or actual readers, the most important task of rhetorical criticism is to try to carry out authorial reading—to try to enter the position of the implied reader or authorial audience so as to investigate the communication between the implied author and his/her ideal, hypothetical addressee.[8] The degree of success of this effort depends on how accurately the critic can infer the implied author's norms. In *The Rhetoric of Fiction*, Booth says,

> "Style" is sometimes broadly used to cover whatever it is that gives us a sense, from word to word and line to line, that the author sees more deeply and judges more profoundly than his presented characters. But, though style is *one of our main sources of insight into the author's norms*, in carrying such strong overtones of the merely verbal the word style excludes our sense of the author's skill in his choice of character and episode and scene and idea. (1983: 74; italics added)

Although Booth sees style as an important channel to get access to the author's norms, he leaves it out because "merely verbal" analysis does not allow us to gain a good understanding of character and event. I fully agree with Booth and other critics that an exclusive concern with style or language

16   *Style and Rhetoric of Short Narrative Fiction*

is limiting. But why not pay attention to both aspects? Starting from the early neo-Aristotelians, there has appeared a self-imposed unhappy choice: Either paying attention to character and event while neglecting style or paying attention to style while neglecting character and event. Making either choice may lead to a partial or distorted picture of the author's norms since, as pointed out by Booth (1983: 73–75), the norms are to be inferred from the "artistic whole" or "the sum" of the implied author's choices. Booth observes,

> If everyone used "technique" as Mark Schorer does, covering with it almost the entire range of choices made by the author, then it might very well serve our purposes. But it is usually taken for a much narrower matter, and consequently it will not do. (1983: 74)

Booth's "it will not do" applies to the exclusion of style, a very important aspect of technique. Indeed, if examining style can bring out that "the author sees more deeply and judges more profoundly than his presented characters," neglecting style may easily result in a misunderstanding of the author's norms. In terms of the dual dynamics of narrative fiction, the covert progression often rests on subtle stylistic choices that function to shape character and event in significant ways. In Chapter 2, for instance, various stylistic choices form a continuous undercurrent directing irony at romanticized notions of war and heroism, behind a somewhat non-satirical description of "an episode of war." In Chapter 6, for another example, subtle stylistic choices interact to direct sustained irony at the protagonist's vanity and self-importance behind a plot development concerned with very different thematic issues. In such cases, only by integrating style into rhetorical criticism can we more successfully enter the position of the authorial audience and carry out authorial reading. Nevertheless, it is not sufficient merely to integrate style. In order to make rhetorical criticism more powerful, persuasive, and shareable, it is also necessary to integrate relevant contextual and intertextual matters.

IMPORTANCE OF INTEGRATING CONTEXT INTO RHETORICAL CRITICISM

Continuous Exclusion of Context of Creation

The rhetorical study of fictional narrative is in general marked by the preclusion of the sociohistorical context of creation, especially the biographical information of the "real author." This preclusion can be traced back to the first generation of Chicago critics, who unequivocally precluded sociohistorical context in the neo-Aristotelian tradition seeing literary works as imitations. In his landmark essay "History versus Criticism in the Study

Introduction 17

of Literature," Crane, after pointing out the limitations of the historical approach on the aesthetic side, privileges literary criticism as "reasoned" discourse "about the works themselves and appropriate to their character as productions of art" (1967 [1935]: 11).

If the first generation of Chicago critics, like other formalist schools in the early twentieth century, ruled out sociohistorical context as a reaction against long-term prevalent and privileged historical approach to literature, the second generation started working at a time when formalist criticism had already gained the upper hand and hence the preclusion of context was more or less taken for granted. In the preface to *The Rhetoric of Fiction* (1961), Booth unequivocally asserts, "in pursuing the author's means of controlling his reader I have arbitrarily isolated technique from all of the so-cial and psychological forces that affect authors and readers." Indeed, when Booth was writing, the centrality of the text was so firmly established that it was even difficult to talk about the communication between the author and the reader. Faced with the formalist climate, the rhetorical Booth puts forward the concept of the "implied author," which on one hand makes the author text-based and on the other enables the rhetorical critic to talk about the means the author uses to persuade the reader. Although the "implied author" (the second self) is connected with the "real author" (the first self) in various ways, Booth, with his neo-Aristotelian orientation and in that extremely formalist climate, emphasized the importance of paying sole at-tention to the role-playing "implied author" on the occasion of writing, to the exclusion of the "real author" in daily life outside the writing process (see Shen 2011, 2013).

When the second edition of *The Rhetoric Fiction* was published in 1983, the academic climate had shifted from the formalist to the sociohistorical and political, and the book's ahistorical position had been subject to much critique. In the afterword to the second edition, Booth takes a partially de-fensive and partially concessive stance. He insists on his "transhistorical" (not antihistorical) position in studying the rhetoric of fiction versus study-ing its political history (413), but he praises Bakhtin for his ideological and historical criticism of literary works (414–15). Subscribing to the distinction made by Peter J. Rabinowitz (1977, 1987) among the "authorial audience," the "narrative audience," and the actual readers, Booth on the one hand em-phasizes shared response among "the relatively stable [authorial] audience postulated by the implied author—the readers the text asks us to become" across historical contexts (420), and on the other acknowledges that dif-ferent actual readers with different critical presuppositions—such as male versus female readers—tend to come up with different readings.

If the contexts of literature basically fall into two kinds—that of creation and that of reception, the latter, as Booth's 1983 afterword indicates, has found its way into rhetorical criticism through the distinction between the authorial audience and actual readers. Under the influence of contextualist approaches and in order to account for the difficulties actual readers have

18   *Style and Rhetoric of Short Narrative Fiction*

in entering the authorial audience, many rhetorical critics have investigated how flesh-and-blood readers' different experiences, knowledge, and socio-historical positioning lead to divergent readings.

As regards the context of creation, some rhetorical critics have paid attention to the historical development of techniques or genres, or to the sociocultural norms the text reflects, follows, or transgresses for certain effects (see, for instance, Booth 1983: 414–15; Rabinowitz 1987: 68–74; Chatman 1990: 198–99; Phelan 2007: 89–90). But such investigation is scanty, and with some exceptions (especially Ralph W. Rader, who challenges Crane's ahistorical position), what has remained absent from rhetorical criticism or the Chicago School in general is attention to the biographical information of the real author.[9] This persistent preclusion has to do with reasons both internal and external to rhetorical criticism.

Externally, contextualist narrative studies also tend to overlook the biographical information of the real author because of, among other things, disciplinary orientation and/or the long-term impact of the "intentional fallacy" argument. Cultural studies have focused on the relation between literature and various aspects of culture, such as politics, law, business, or other arts. Cognitive narratology, because of its primary concern with readers' cognition, when paying attention to context, has focused on the context of reading. Bakhtinian critics, when paying attention to context, have concentrated on the influence of social discourses or cultural forces on the text. Since the contextualization in rhetorical criticism is very much a result of the influence of contextualist approaches, the latter's leaving out the biographical information of the real author has lent itself to the former's preclusion in this aspect.

Internally, rhetorical criticism's preclusion of the real author has much to do with Booth's concept of the "implied author." From the first edition of *The Rhetoric of Fiction* to the recent essay "Resurrection of the Implied Author" (2005), Booth draws a sharp distinction between the "implied author" and the "real author" or "the flesh-and-blood person" (the FBP), and he stresses that only the former is relevant to rhetorical criticism.[10] No matter in what sense the "implied author" is understood (see Shen 2011), rhetorical critics in general have confined the consideration of author-audience communication to the text-based implied author on the one hand and various kinds of present-day audience on the other. Even in his attempt to historicize the narrative communication diagram, Harry Shaw (2005) still leaves out the "real author" and only argues for the historicization of the narrator.

Why Should Context of Creation be Integrated into Rhetorical Criticism?

In rhetorical criticism, we try to enter the position of the authorial audience—"the hypothetical ideal audience for whom the [implied] author constructs the text and who understands it perfectly" (Phelan and Rabinowitz 2005: 543). To enter more successfully the authorial audience, we need to infer as accurately as possible the intention, purposes, and norms of the implied

Introduction 19

author. As I discussed in detail elsewhere (Shen 2011, 2013), although later theorists have much mystified Booth's "implied author," in the encoding process the implied author is no other than the person "who writes in this manner" (Booth 1961: 71). Insofar as the encoding process is concerned, the difference between the "real author" and the "implied author" is in fact that between the person in daily life and the *same* person in the process of writing in a particular manner or assuming a particular stance, which may be contrastive or even opposed to that the "real author" takes in daily life. Our knowledge about the "real author" (involving the experiences of the person over the whole span of her life) comes from various biographical and historical materials, while our knowledge about the implied author (on the occasion of writing that particular text) comes from the text itself—the implied author's image is to be inferred from the "completed artistic whole" of that particular text (Booth, 1961: 73).

Nevertheless, in order to enter successfully the position of the authorial audience, we often need to take account of the historical context and the biographical information of the real author. As regards the historical context, the implied author writing at a given historical time may have in mind an authorial audience with access to certain historical knowledge that is indispensable to our correct understanding of the textual norms (Rabinowitz 1977: 126, 1987: 21). When Henry Fielding was writing *Tom Jones* in eighteenth-century England, he had in mind an authorial audience with knowledge of the latitudinarians and eighteenth-century thought, and our failing to pay attention to the cultural context may lead to a partial understanding of the authorial norms (see Rader 1999). When Edgar Allan Poe was writing "The Tell-Tale Heart" in nineteenth-century America, he was writing for an authorial audience with knowledge of the insanity debate in that historical context, a knowledge that is indispensable for perceiving the ironic undercurrent centering on the narrator-protagonist's unconscious self-condemnation (see Chapter 1). Similarly, when Katherine Mansfield was writing "The Singing Lesson" in early twentieth-century England, she intended the text for an authorial audience who knew that Victorian England regarded a woman who could not catch a husband as worthless, a kind of social knowledge necessary for discerning the covert textual progression as an implicit protest against phallocentric social forces (see Chapter 5).

In terms of biographical information, if the fictional narrative is somewhat autobiographical, gaining access to the real author's relevant experiences may shed light on the implied author's textual norms and rhetorical purposes.[11] When the implied author's textual choices are not modeled on the real author's experiences, if the authorial stance on the occasion of writing is linked with or affected by the real author's experiences prior to the writing process, taking account of the real author's relevant experiences will enable us to understand better the implied author's rhetorical purposes and thematic design.

To take "Désirée's Baby" for an example, previous critics have put this narrative in the anti-slavery tradition as represented by *Uncle Tom's Cabin*.

20 *Style and Rhetoric of Short Narrative Fiction*

But Kate Chopin, both before and after her marriage, showed firm and continuous support for the Confederate cause and strong objection to the abolition of slavery. Her husband was a racist, her father-in-law a harsh slave owner, and her half-brother fought for the Confederate army. This formed a sharp contrast with the background and experience of Harriet Beecher Stowe (see Hart 1983: 642). The biographical information of the historical Chopin can shed much light on the intention and purpose of the implied Chopin in creating the racist covert progression in "Désirée's Baby" (see Chapter 3).

However, in investigating the relation between text and context for inferring more accurately the implied author's norms, we must keep in mind that the text is always primary and we need to respect the text fully. The primacy of the text can be seen in the following aspects. First, if one fails to respect the text fully, the emphasis on cultural context may lead to severe distortions of textual facts (see Chapter 3 for a critique of Bauer's imposition of context on text). Second, acquiring information about the real author is not sufficient for an adequate understanding of the implied author's textual choices. Some critics have a good knowledge about the racist family background and personal experience of the historical Chopin, but without examining the stylistic and structural choices of "Désirée's Baby" itself in a careful and comprehensive way, they still have missed the racist undercurrent and misinterpreted the implied author's norms (see Chapter 3). Third, as pointed out by Booth when expounding the concept of the implied author, "just as one's personal letters imply different versions of oneself, depending on the differing relationships with each correspondent and the purpose of each letter, so the writer sets himself out with a different air depending on the needs of particular works" (1961: 71). Although bearing the same name, the different implied authors of different narratives may take divergent stances due to different thematic designs. Given such differences, to gain a better understanding of the authorial stance of a particular narrative, we must, in the first place, carry out carefully a stylistic-structural analysis of the text itself and take the contextual information only as supplementary.

IMPORTANCE OF INTEGRATING INTERTEXTUAL COMPARISON INTO RHETORICAL CRITICISM

In order to unveil the covert progression and infer the implied author's norms more accurately, we also need to integrate into rhetorical criticism the consideration of relevant intertextual matters. It should be noted that, following Aristotle's emphasis on genre, neo-Aristotelian rhetorical critics have paid much attention to the function of generic conventions, norms, and deviations (see, for instance, Booth 1983: 432; Rabinowitz 1987: 70–75). But apart from generic issues, there are other intertextual matters that need to be taken into account in inferring the implied author's norms of a specific text. What I see as especially important to rhetorical criticism is the

Introduction 21

comparison of stylistic features between the text under investigation and other related texts. The relations between the two basically fall into two kinds: intertextual contrast and intertextual similarity.

Intertextual Contrast

In investigating "An Episode of War," for instance, if we pay attention to the contrast in stylistic choices between this narrative and another war narrative by Stephen Crane—"A Mystery of Heroism"—we may gain a much better understanding of the ironic covert progression in question (see Chapter 2).

Intertextual Similarity

Not only intertextual contrast but also intertextual similarity can shed light on the text under investigation. To take Mansfield's "Revelations" for an example, a stylistic analysis of Mansfield's depiction in "Prelude" of Beryl's conscious awareness of the opposition between her false self and her real self can cast much light on how patriarchy imposes a false self on the female protagonist in "Revelations." Further, if we compare "Revelations" with Ibsen's *A Doll House* and examine carefully the similarity as well as contrast between the two texts in depicting the female protagonist, we may see much better how Mansfield is directing implicit irony against patriarchal discrimination and subjugation of woman through a covert textual progression (see Chapter 4).

For the past eighty years or so, generations of neo-Aristotelians consciously precluded, to different extents, style/language and context of creation in order to be better critics of the text or better rhetorical critics of author-audience communication. The present project argues and tries to show that integrating style, context of creation, and intertextual comparison can help us become better critics of the text or better rhetorical critics of author-audience communication since the integration enables us to interpret more accurately the norms and functions of the text and the rhetorical purposes of the implied author.

In order to uncover the covert progression in rhetorical criticism, we also need to bear in mind that the textual undercurrent is not immediately noticeable, and we need therefore make a conscious effort to search for it. This is especially so when the undercurrent is made up largely by textual elements that appear to be digressive or peripheral to the plot development. When we gradually discern the covert textual progression, our response will in various ways become more complicated.

COMPLICATED RESPONSE

In discussing readers' responses in the genre of narrative fiction, two issues should first of all be clarified. One is the distinction between responding as

22 Style and Rhetoric of Short Narrative Fiction

a professional critic and responding as an ordinary reader, and the other is what standard we should use for measuring the worth of a given text.

While an ordinary reader reads a fictional narrative, like reading a newspaper report, usually only once from the beginning to the end, a professional critic tends to read the chosen text over and over again, both forward and "backward" (to explore the connection of a later element to earlier elements), until having more or less grasped a deeper level of meaning or a covert progression of the text. When discussing the (authorial) audience's response to the textual progression in a critical essay or a book, professional critics are usually not talking about the initial response but the response out of more than one reading. The more complex or ambiguous the textual movements or the more deep-going the response, the more times of reading may be involved. This forms a contrast to experimental investigations that record actual readers' first response to a text. While we should be fully aware of the somewhat hypothetical nature of non-experimental discussions of textual progression, we should also acknowledge that it is the legitimate and proper way to do it. After all, when we talk about the dynamic textual structures in literary criticism, we are always talking about the findings out of more than one reading. As regards the covert textual progression, it usually requires more readings (both forward and "backward") to discover than the overt. The process of discovery will vary from critic to critic and is therefore hard to share, but the covert textual progression itself, once brought to light, should be sharable if the analysis is on solid and persuasive ground.

As regards the second issue, I find the tripartite distinction made by Phelan (2007) among the interpretive, ethical, and aesthetic judgments very helpful since it enables us to approach the response to narrative fiction in a more balanced manner than many previous critics. Even Booth seems to use ethics alone as the gauge: when a work initially much appreciated is later found to be ethically problematic, it is then deemed "worthless" despite its aesthetic value such as "genuine qualities of humor and imaginative vitality" (ibid.: 75–76). There is no doubt that our ethical judgment will affect our aesthetic appreciation, but it seems to go too far to use ethics as the sole criterion in evaluating narrative fiction. Phelan's model helps us to see how our interpretive, ethical, and aesthetic judgments interact and affect each other (as well exemplified by Phelan's *Experiencing Fiction*).

The following chapters will each explore the particular response to the specific covert textual progression in question, and here I shall discuss in a general manner how we may respond to the different types of relation of the covert textual progression to the overt plot development. Such relations fall into two basic categories: the subversive and the supplementary. In one category, we can further distinguish different subtypes, each inviting our response in a certain way. I would like to discuss here two subtypes of the subversive category and two subtypes of the supplementary.

Introduction 23

Category A: The Covert Progression Subverts the Overt Plot

When the covert textual progression subverts the overt plot development, it is always in the shape of a deeper dynamic meaning structure subverting, in part or in whole, a superficial one. But the covert is not always to be accepted.

Subtype (a): The Covert Progression Is Ethically Problematic or Unacceptable

A good case in point is Chopin's "Désirée's Baby," which might be regarded as being marked by what Rabinowitz (1994) calls "rhetorical passing": a racist text passing off as an anti-racist text. When anti-slavery modern readers discern the racist covert progression behind the overt anti-racist plot, they will refuse to enter, or will rather retreat from, the "authorial" reading position and will enter instead a resistant and critical reading position. It is significant to note that modern readers, when discovering the racist textual progression, may not totally dismiss the work. "Désirée's Baby" has been widely regarded as a literary masterpiece not only because of its (superficial) moral thematics but also, perhaps more importantly, because of its highly aesthetic/dramatic quality. The racist covert progression is created with remarkable ingenuity, which is aesthetically appealing. The process of uncovering the covert textual progression is a process of the interaction among complicated interpretive judgment, growing ethical objection, and ambivalent aesthetic judgment. The interpretive judgment is complicated partly because we feel at once regret (at having been deceived by the textual appearance earlier on) and delight (at now being cognizant of the true stance of the narrative). The aesthetic judgment is ambivalent in that our objection to the author's ethical stance reduces our aesthetic appreciation on the one hand, but the exploration of the covert textual progression leads to the discernment of more ingenious aesthetic skills on the other. Significantly, because of the subversiveness of the covert textual progression, its discovery characteristically leads to drastic changes in our perception of various textual details and in our emotional reaction to the characters, who are now seen as serving different or opposite ethical ends.

Subtype (b): The Covert Progression Is Ethically Agreeable

"An Episode of War" and "Revelations," for instance, belong to this subtype, but the relations between the covert progression and the overt plot involve different kinds of contrast (and hence may be further divided into hypo-subtypes). "An Episode of War" has to do with the contrast between *satiric and* (non-satirically) realistic: the overt plot seems to represent an episode of war in a realistic and non-satirical way, but the covert progression conveys the author's anti-war stance by satirizing romanticized notions of heroism. "Revelations" has to do with the opposition between *social and*

24 Style and Rhetoric of Short Narrative Fiction

personal: the overt plot seems to show the protagonist's personal weaknesses while the covert progression indicates that the weaknesses are largely to be accounted for by social factors. No matter along what line of development, the covert textual progression, being subversive in nature, will significantly alter the ethical import of the whole narrative in the reader's eye and lead to a drastic change in the reader's perception of various local details and reaction to the protagonists, who are now "transformed" either from an ordinary army man to an object of satire (who also invites the reader's sympathy as a victim of war), or from a morbid being in herself into a victim of social forces.

Category B: The Covert Progression Supplements the Overt

If the covert textual progression supplements the overt plot development, it sometimes does not affect our response to the overt plot, but it always operates to complicate or enrich, though in a less radical way, our perception of the whole narrative, which is now seen as taking on additional ethical function and aesthetic value.

Subtype (a): The Covert and the Overt Go in the Same Direction

"The Tell-Tale Heart" is a good case in point: its overt plot goes along the crime and legal-punishment line and its covert progression more subtly in the same direction, along the line of self-condemnation coupled with self-conviction. In contrast with Category A, here the overt plot development is not seen as deceptive but as presenting a surface level of meaning, with the undercurrent conveying an additional deeper level of meaning. Because of the same direction shared by the two progressions, the perception of the covert here does not alter the perception of the textual elements associated with the overt, but it does alter the ethos of the whole narrative since the text is now seen as having more ethical depth and aesthetic ingenuity. The process of responding to the covert progression is marked by new interpretive delight (at having uncovered a deeper textual movement), growing ethical insight, and increasing aesthetic appreciation.

Subtype (b): The Covert and the Overt Go in Two Different Directions

"The Fly" belongs to this subtype, whose covert progression has an ethical concern quite different from that of the plot development. Because of the different directions the two progressions go along, the discovery of the covert will more significantly change the ethos of the whole narrative. In "The Fly," the uncovering of the covert progression increases to a notable extent the ethical irony of the text with the boss now perceived not only as a victim of war/fate and a victimizer of the fly but also as the butt of the irony directed against vanity and self-importance. Apparently, the discernment of the covert progression in this subtype will somewhat change the perception of the relevant textual details. The change in the understanding of the ethical

Introduction 25

concerns of the narrative is typically accompanied by increasing aesthetic appreciation of the author's artistry in subtly creating the dual dynamics.

DIFFERENT TYPES OF SHARED READING

While being aware that for some readers of some fictional narratives, authorial reading is very difficult or even impossible to arrive at and that no reading of a literary narrative is definitive, I hold the rhetorical assumption that a significant value of reading narrative is to share readings.[12] There are at least four kinds of shared reading. In the first kind, different actual readers recognize the dominant patterns of the authorial communication and interpret the text in similar ways. In the second kind, actual readers have experienced certain effects of the work without being fully aware of them, but when these effects are pointed out, readers recognize them as part of the authorial communication. In the third kind, different actual readers miss the same key aspects of the authorial communication and so still interpret the text in similar ways. In the fourth kind, these shared misreadings become revised; in this kind, actual readers encounter a new interpretation that they find more adequate to the authorial communication and more persuasive than their own and so they share the new reading. In this book, my arguments about covert progressions are also arguments for shared readings of the second and fourth kinds. My claims are that readers who have focused only on the overt progressions have either felt but not done justice to the covert patterns or that their attention to the overt has led them to miss these subtler patterns. In some cases, I realize that the present interpretations may at first appear more or less unexpected. But it is in the nature of the covert not to be initially noticed, and I hope that my attention to "overall" patterns of style and structure and to intertextual and contextual matters will lead my readers to share these readings. This kind of shareability is particularly valuable in testifying to the usefulness and advantageousness of the approach adopted in arriving at the new reading. Despite the fact that literary texts often contain gaps, ambiguity, or indeterminacy, and that actual readers often face a range of obstacles to entering the authorial audience, the rhetorical approach the present project advocates and practices remains committed to the principle that our efforts to seek shared readings not only can help resolve critical controversy but also can enhance our appreciation of the communicative achievements of the authors whose works we love to read and to teach.[13]

The chapters that follow will explore in detail the covert textual progressions and the ethical-aesthetic effects they generate in six short fictional narratives. The chapters fall into two parts. Part One, comprising Chapters 1 to 3, deals with three short narratives by the American authors Edgar Allan Poe, Stephen Crane, and Kate Chopin. They not only are famous short fiction writers but also characteristically create short fiction with complicated

26 *Style and Rhetoric of Short Narrative Fiction*

dynamics. Part Two, consisting of Chapters 4 to 6, probes into the different ways of progressing covertly in three narratives by Katherine Mansfield. These six narratives span nearly a century from the 1840s to the 1920s and represent different period-styles: romanticism (Poe), realism (Crane), regionalism (Chopin), and modernism (Mansfield).

There are three reasons why Part Two should concentrate solely on an author like Mansfield. First, Part One is devoted to American authors, and it is right and proper for Part Two to be devoted to the works by the (New Zealand-born) British author Mansfield, so as to present a somewhat balanced picture of Anglo-American narratives. Second, while it is important to see how dual narrative dynamics function differently in the narratives by different writers, it may also be helpful to see how they function in different ways in the narratives by the same writer and, moreover, even for conveying similar ethical significance. Chapters 4 and 5 unravel two covert progressions in Mansfield's narratives that convey a somewhat feminist ethical import but in very different ways. Third, the present project focuses on short narrative fiction, a genre in which Mansfield figures as a most prolific and prominent writer. Mansfield is well-known for her depiction of female experiences, and Chapters 4 and 5 investigate two short narratives respectively portraying an upper-middle-class lady and a school teacher, while Chapter 6, as a way to offer some balance, explores a short narrative where male characters take center stage.

Because of the limited space, the present project can only uncover the covert progressions in a handful of short fictional narratives. But the following point involving three interrelated aspects should become clear: If a fictional narrative has dual dynamics but we only pay attention to the overt, we will either get a partial picture (if the covert supplements the overt) or a false picture (if the covert subverts the overt) of the ethical import of the text; we will only see a more flat or a distorted image of the characters involved; and we can only appreciate the narrative's aesthetic value in a limited and one-sided way. The process of experiencing the covert progression is a process of gaining a relatively fuller, more balanced, or more accurate understanding of the ethical import and artistic quality of the whole work.

Part I

Style and Covert Progressions in American Short Fiction

1 Style, Unreliability, and Hidden Dramatic Irony
Poe's "The Tell-Tale Heart"

Of the three short stories by American authors investigated in Part One, Edgar Allan Poe's "The Tell-Tale Heart" (1843) was published earliest, and it is the only one in character narration. I will start with revealing an ethically oriented covert progression in this narrative, primarily through analyzing the stylistic patterning in the tale's structural unity. This covert progression has much to do with Poe's ingenious use of narratorial unreliability, especially the complex interplay between the unreliable and the reliable as encoded in the same words of the narrator, which helps convey an overall dramatic irony with implicit ethical import. I anticipate immediate objection to my attempt at unraveling the hidden ethical import of this narrative since generations of critics have believed that Poe is not concerned with ethics but aesthetics (see, for instance, Buranelli 1961; Cleman 1991; Polonsky 2002). In view of this, I will first offer a discussion of Poe's theory of prose fiction to pave the way for the analysis.

POE'S THEORY OF PROSE FICTION

The current ethical turn in narrative studies suggests a congenial context in which to clear up a long-term misunderstanding about Poe's view on prose fiction. Critics widely held that Poe's aestheticism covers prose fiction as well as poetry (see below), but in effect, Poe holds a non-aesthetic view of the subject matter of prose fiction. In this genre, Poe makes an unequivocal distinction between structural design and subject matter. While putting the structural design of prose fiction completely on a par with that of poetry (both confined to the aesthetic trajectory), Poe treats the subject matter of prose fiction as different in nature from that of poetry—as often based on Truth and diametrically opposed to Beauty. Commenting on Nathaniel Hawthorne's *Twice-Told Tales* (1842), Poe observes:

> We have said that the tale has a point of superiority even over the poem. In fact, while the *rhythm* of this latter is an essential aid in the development of the poem's highest idea—the idea of the Beautiful—the

30   *Style and Rhetoric of Short Narrative Fiction*

artificialities of this rhythm are an inseparable bar to the development of all points of thought or expression which have their basis in *Truth*. But Truth is often, and in very great degree, the aim of the tale. . . . The writer of the prose tale, in short, may bring to his theme a vast variety of modes or inflections of thought and expression—(the ratiocinative, for example, the sarcastic or the humorous) which are not only antagonistical to the nature of the poem, but absolutely forbidden by one of its most peculiar and indispensable adjuncts; we allude of course, to rhythm. It may be added, here, *par parenthèse*, that the author who aims at the purely beautiful in a prose tale is laboring at great disadvantage. For Beauty can be better treated in the poem. (Poe 1984a: 573)

According to Poe, it is in effect the genre-specific "rhythm" that makes Beauty "the sole legitimate province of the poem" (Poe 1984b: 16), while the prose tale is open to a wide range of thematic materials that "have their basis in Truth" and are "antagonistical" to Beauty.[1] Poe's "Truth," though, has a much wider application than "Truth" in what Poe calls "the heresy of *The Didactic*"—the assumption "that the ultimate object of all Poetry is Truth" and that "Truth" simply means the inculcation of a moral (Poe 1984c: 75). For Poe, however, "Truth" constitutes the basis for a wide range of modes of thought and expression, including but not confined to the ethical.

This non-aesthetic thematic conception has been blocked from critical view by Poe's consistent aesthetic conception of formal design.[2] For Poe all works of literary art should achieve the most important "unity of effect" (Poe 1984a: 571). In order to obtain structural unity, the writer of a prose narrative, like the writer of a poem, should preconceive a single effect and then invent and combine events for this "pre-established design." Moreover, in order to preserve unity of effect, a prose narrative, like a poem, should be fairly short, able to "be read at one sitting" (1984a: 572).

Since behind Poe's consistent emphasis on aesthetic formal design lies his non-aesthetic conception of the tale's subject matter, Poe regards Hawthorne's work as an exemplar of good prose writing, and he readily stresses Hawthorne's ethical concerns (Poe 1984a: 574–75). One tale by Hawthorne that Poe (ibid.: 574) particularly appreciates and praises is "Wakefield," which is marked by strong ethical concerns. The omniscient narrator welcomes the reader "to ramble with [him] through the twenty years of Wakefield's vagary" in order to find the "moral" of Wakefield's marital delinquency (Hawthorne 1974: 131). The narrator, from an ethical position superior to that of the protagonist, persuades his reader of the morbid vanity, selfishness, and ruthlessness that underlie Wakefield's folly. Although Poe, out of a strong concern for dramatic effects, avoided such explicit moral teaching by an omniscient narrator, he has in some of his tales, such as "The Tell-Tale Heart," implicitly and subtly conveyed a moral through subtle stylistic choices in a unified structural design.

Style, Unreliability, and Hidden Dramatic Irony 31

Poe's insistent emphasis on aesthetic structural unity has caused many critics to overlook his non-aesthetic and ethically related conception of the subject matter of prose fiction. This underlies the widely held view of Poe as being closely associated, in the domain of prose fiction as well as that of poetry, with "Art for Art's sake." Critics have argued that "Poe banished 'the didactic' from the proper sphere of art" and that there is "an apparent lack of interest in moral themes throughout Poe's work" (Moldenhauer 1968: 285; Cleman 1991: 623). Vincent Buranelli more specifically asserts that "sin and crime are absent from" Poe's fictional world, because "Poe does not touch morality" and "the terrible deeds that abound there are matters of psychology, abnormal psychology, not of ethics" (1961: 72).

John Cleman extends Poe's "aesthetic" of poetry to prose narrative and then differentiates between the two genres only in terms of aesthetic concerns: "To some degree, this seeming indifference to moral issues can be explained by Poe's aesthetic in which the 'Moral Sense,' 'Conscience,' and 'Duty' have, at best, 'only collateral relations' with the primary concerns: for poetry 'The Rhythmical Creation of Beauty,' and for prose fiction 'the unity of effect or impression' " (Cleman 1991: 623–24).[3] Such differentiation between the two genres is undesirable since, in Poe's view, "the unity of effect or impression" is as important for poetry as for prose fiction. The real difference between the two genres lies in aim or subject matter: Beauty for poetry, and Truth for prose fiction.

When critics acknowledge Poe's concern with "Truth" in prose narrative, they tend simply to drag it into the aesthetic trajectory. John S. Whitley, for instance, writes: "While the highest idea of a poem is the idea of the Beautiful, Poe argues that the aim of the tale is Truth. . . . but perhaps by 'Truth' he really meant the working of every part of the story—rhythm, plot, character, language, references—towards a denouement which ends the story logically, consistently and satisfactorily" (2000: xii). Thus, Poe's separation of the structural design and subject matter of the tale is unwittingly transformed into a unified conception hinging solely on the unity of effect. Joseph J. Moldenhauer, even as he challenges the traditional view that Poe disregarded morality, is still confined to structural unity: "According to Poe, the supreme criterion for the literary performance is not truthfulness, moral or otherwise, but rather unity" (1968: 286). Like many other critics, Moldenhauer puts the genre of prose fiction completely on a par with poetry, and, in challenging the traditional view of Poe's disregard for morality in literature, he limits his discussion to what Poe means by "Beauty," treating the subject matter of poetry as the subject matter of literature in general (ibid.: 286–89). As a result, Moldenhauer's effort to bring morality back to Poe's theory of literature—through "aesthetic supermorality" (ibid.: 289)—only adds to the misunderstanding of Poe's view on the subject matter of prose fiction.

Keeping Poe's non-aesthetic conception of the tale's subject matter in mind, I now proceed to an investigation of the "The Tell-Tale Heart."

32   *Style and Rhetoric of Short Narrative Fiction*

COVERT PROGRESSION AND OVERALL DRAMATIC IRONY

As mentioned in the Introduction, "The Tell-Tale Heart" presents a neurotic narrator's account of his premeditated murder of an old man and finally his compelled admission of the crime because he hears his victim's relentless heartbeat in front of the policemen.[4] This plot development has attracted the attention of numerous critics, who have discussed its various aspects through diversified approaches, especially psychoanalysis since the mid-twentieth century (see below). I approach the tale from a different angle, attempting to reveal, through tracing the stylistic patterning in the narrative's structural unity, a covert progression marked by an overall dramatic irony with significant ethical import.

In expounding his theory of the "unity of effect," Poe stresses the importance of the dénouement of the literary work. The writer should have the dénouement constantly in view, and every plot "must be elaborated to its *dénouement* before any thing be attempted with the pen" (Poe 1984b: 13). In view of Poe's emphasis on the dénouement, I start with the ending of "The Tell-Tale Heart":

No doubt I now grew *very* pale; but I talked more fluently, and with a heightened voice. Yet the sound [the heartbeat of the victim] increased— and what could I do? It was *a low, dull, quick sound—much such a sound as a watch makes when enveloped in cotton.* I gasped for breath—and yet the officers heard it not. I talked more quickly—more vehemently; but the noise steadily increased. I arose and argued about trifles, in a high key and with violent gesticulations; but the noise steadily increased. Why *would* they not be gone? I paced the floor to and fro with heavy strides, as if excited to fury by the observations of the men—but the noise steadily increased. Oh God! what *could* I do? I foamed—I raved— I swore! I swung the chair upon which I had been sitting, and grated it upon the boards, but the noise arose over all and continually increased. It grew louder—louder—*louder!* And still the men chatted pleasantly, and smiled. Was it possible they heard not? Almighty God!—no, no! They heard!—they suspected!—they *knew!*—they were making a mockery of my horror!—this I thought, and this I think. But anything was better than this agony! Anything was more tolerable than this derision! I could bear those hypocritical smiles no longer! I felt that I must scream or die! and now—again! —hark! louder! louder! louder! *louder!*— "Villains!" I shrieked, "dissemble no more! I admit the deed!—tear up the planks! here, here!—It is the beating of his hideous heart!" (Poe 1984d: 559, italics original and underlining added)[5]

After killing the old man, the protagonist dismembers the corpse and hides it under the floorboards. Three policemen come to search the house and the protagonist answers their questions "cheerily" and feels "singularly at

Style, Unreliability, and Hidden Dramatic Irony 33

ease" (559). They are now at the very spot where the corpse is buried. As regards the plot development, in this climactic title scene, attention tends to be focused on the underlined words. These words show that the protagonist is pursued by his victim's heart as a tool or symbol of revenge (see below), a fantastic heart that dramatically starts beating again when the murderer is in a most confident, triumphant, and cheery mood. The heart, by beating louder and louder, deprives the cold-blooded and marble-hearted murderer of his after-murder ease in front of the policemen, making him increasingly irritated and horrified. The sound eventually compels the murderer to admit his crime ("again!—hark! louder! louder! louder! *louder!* . . . I admit the deed! . . . It is the beating of his hideous heart!"). The final sentence of the narrative—"It is the beating of his hideous heart!"—echoes its title, "The Tell-Tale Heart."

But if we open our minds to more than one textual progression and examine carefully the stylistic choices in this passage and in the structural unity of the narrative as a whole, we may descry that what we have here is also the dénouement of a covert progression behind the plot development: The narrator-protagonist is the only dissembling person in the whole textual sequence and he keeps gloating over his own immoral dissimulation. In this final scene, he unconsciously projects his own dissemblance onto the policemen and finds the projected dissemblance increasingly unbearable, which leads to his downfall ("Anything was more tolerable than this derision! I could bear those hypocritical smiles no longer! I felt that I must scream or die! . . . 'Villains!' I shrieked, 'dissemble no more! I admit the deed!' "). In this light, the protagonist's condemnation of the unsuspecting policemen— "Villains! . . . dissemble no more!"—amounts to unwitting self-condemnation. That is to say, the covert progression is marked by dramatic irony with a significant ethical dimension: implicitly telling us how one's self-satisfying dissemblance leads to one's downfall.

Within the crucial ending of the narrative, we can discern the stylistic patterning at the dénouement of the covert progression in three steps. At the first step, a series of verbal processes and their adjuncts interact to represent the protagonist's increasingly intensive efforts to cover up the victim's heart beating in order to dissemble innocence: "talked more fluently, and with a heightened voice," "talked more quickly—more vehemently," "argued about trifles, in a high key and with violent gesticulations," "I foamed—I raved—I swore!" This is reinforced by three action processes and their adjuncts, "I paced the floor [where the victim is buried] to and fro with heavy strides, as if excited to fury . . . and grated [the chair] upon the boards." At the second step, we have the stylistic choices describing the narrator-protagonist's ungrounded suspicion about the policemen's dissemblance, including his self-questioning "Was it possible they heard not?" and his exclamatory assertion in free indirect discourse: "Almighty God!—no, no! They heard!—they suspected!—they *knew!*—they were making a mockery of my horror!—this I thought, and this I think." At the last step, we have

34 *Style and Rhetoric of Short Narrative Fiction*

the stylistic choices depicting the narrator-protagonist's reaction to what he takes to be the policemen's hypocrisy: "Anything was more tolerable than this derision! I could bear those hypocritical smiles no longer! I felt that I must scream or die!" " 'Villains!' I shrieked, 'dissemble no more! I admit the deed!' " The last shriek functions as a boomerang against the narrator-protagonist who is the only "hypocritical" "villain" in the whole narrative.

In contrast with the plot development where the underlined words in the above quotation are of most significance, in the covert progression only the stylistic choices singled out here receive emphasis, and the underlined words become much less important with the exception of "I admit the deed!" which is significant both to the covert progression and to the plot development.

Our perception of the covert textual progression significantly changes our interpretive, ethical, and aesthetic judgments as based on the plot development. Interpretively, we come to see more thematic relevance of the stylistic choices that depict the narrator's gloating over his own dissimulation and his wrong perception and reporting of the policemen's "dissemblance." This helps us gain a fuller and better view of his unreliable narration on all the three axes: facts, values, and perception (see Phelan 2005; see also Shen "Unreliability" in *The Living Handbook of Narratology*). In terms of our ethical judgment, instead of seeing the narrator-protagonist only as a psychological figure, we come to discern him as a butt of implicit ethical irony, which greatly increases the narrative distance between him and us. Aesthetically, we newly perceive the artistic value of various textual details behind their trivial or digressive appearance as they gradually fall into place in the covert progression.

Now, with the crucial ending in mind, we come to explore the earlier stages of the covert progression. The character narrator begins to tell the murdering process by arguing, "You fancy me mad. Madmen know nothing. But you should have seen how wisely I proceeded—with what caution— with what foresight—with what dissimulation I went to work!" (555). Previous critics have taken the last sentence only as the narrator's assertion of his being sane (see, for instance, Robinson 1965: 369; Nesbitt 2000: 239) or as indicating the need for the protagonist to be "cautious" in his Oedipal revenge on "the father" (Bonaparte 1949: 492). But if we open our minds to a textual undercurrent, we may discover that this is the beginning of the covert progression towards the narrator-protagonist's unconscious condemnation of his own dissemblance. In this sentence, the words "wisely," "caution," and "foresight" (referring partly to his well-prepared concealment of the corpse) all point to the narrator-protagonist's belief in his own cunning. Further, the term "dissimulation," which functions to define the preceding words, more explicitly refers to his dissemblance.

In what follows, behind the plot development focusing on the three-step murdering process —preparing for the killing, the killing act, and hiding the corpse—the covert textual progression centers on the murderer's

Style, Unreliability, and Hidden Dramatic Irony   35

dissemblance and his taking delight in it throughout. After he makes up his mind to carry out the murder, the protagonist becomes "never kinder to the old man" and he keeps this mask of kindness "during the whole week" when seeking an opportunity to kill the old man. The tension between his trying to murder the old man and his being "never kinder" to his intended victim highlights his hypocrisy. He very "cunningly" spies on the sleeping old man for this whole week without being detected (555). At daybreak, he would hypocritically go into the old man's chamber, "calling him by name in a hearty tone, and inquiring how he has passed the night" (556). On the night of killing the old man, he can "scarcely contain [his] feelings of triumph" and "fairly chuckle[s]" at heart because he is extremely proud of his "sagacity" in dissembling—"the extent of my own powers [of dissembling]," "[the old man] not even to dream of my secret deeds or thoughts" (556). After killing the old man, he takes "wise precautions" to hide the corpse and he does it "so cleverly, so cunningly" that he well conceals the dismembered body under the floor without leaving any trace: "no human eye—not even his—could have detected any thing wrong. There was nothing to wash out—no stain of any kind—no blood-spot whatever. I had been too wary for that. A tub had caught all" (557). When the police officers come to search the house after a neighbor reports hearing a shriek during the night, he dissemblingly bids the policemen "welcome" and invites them to "search—search *well*" (558). At the dénouement, as we have just seen, there is a strong ironic tension between the protagonist's dissemblance in trying to cover up his crime and his intolerance of what he takes to be the policemen's dissemblance.

Now, two questions arise: Are the policemen dissembling? Has the protagonist heard his victim's heart beating in the first place? To answer these questions, I want to examine several passages in the textual sequence. The first passage is from the very beginning:

> True!—nervous—very, very dreadfully nervous I had been and am; but why *will* you say that I am mad? The disease had sharpened my senses—not destroyed—not dulled them. Above all was the sense of hearing acute. I heard all things in the heaven and in the earth. I heard many things in hell. How, then, am I mad? Hearken! and observe how healthily—how calmly I can tell you the whole story. (555)

The second passage occurs in the middle of the tale:

> And now have I not told you that what you mistake for madness is but over-acuteness of the senses?—now, I say, there came to my ears a low, dull, quick sound, such as a watch makes when enveloped in cotton. I knew *that* sound well, too. It was the beating of the old man's heart. . . .
> It grew louder, I say, louder every moment! . . . But the beating grew louder, louder! . . . In an instant I dragged him to the floor, and pulled

36 *Style and Rhetoric of Short Narrative Fiction*

the heavy bed over him. I then smiled gaily, to find the deed so far done. But, for many minutes, the heart beat on with a muffled sound. This, however, did not vex me; it would not be heard through the wall. At length it ceased. The old man was dead. I removed the bed and examined the corpse. Yes, he was stone, stone dead. I placed my hand upon the heart and held it there many minutes. There was no pulsation. He was stone dead. (557–58)

The final passage is from the end:

> Yet the sound increased—and what could I do? It was *a low, dull, quick sound—much such a sound as a watch makes when enveloped in cotton.* I gasped for breath—and yet the officers heard it not. . . . It grew louder—louder—*louder!* And still the men chatted pleasantly, and smiled. (559)

Many readers regard the narrator's claims to supernatural powers of hearing only as evidence of his madness. It is of course likely that Poe is using the structural consistency to show the continuity and coherence of the narrator-protagonist's madness as manifested by the "over-acuteness" of his hearing.[6]

But there is another possibility: Poe seems to use stylistic patterning in the structural unity to suggest that the over-acute hearing is a fantastic fictional fact. The words at the beginning of the tale emphatically present the narrator's claim that his "sense of hearing" is inhumanly or superhumanly "acute." This is echoed by the middle of the tale, which stresses the protagonist's "over-acuteness of the senses," enabling him to hear the increasingly loud beating of the old man's heart. After the protagonist has pulled the bed over the old man, the description of his behavior lends credibility to his claim of hearing the old man's heart beating in two ways. First, his feeling satisfied without being vexed by the heart beating ("I then smiled gaily . . . This, however, did not vex me") rules out the possibility that he is hearing his own heart beating out of guilt or nervousness, a point that gains continuous support in the following textual sequence. Second, although one person's hearing another person's heart beating with a heavy bed in between sounds impossible in reality, the description of the protagonist's examining the corpse is perfectly in keeping with our experiences of the world: "I placed my hand upon the heart and held it there many minutes. There was no pulsation" (558), which functions to make believable the preceding description of the protagonist's hearing the old man's heart beating. In other words, Poe makes a fantastic fictional fact credible through related realistic details. This move paves the way for the crucial dénouement, in which the protagonist's hearing the beating of the old man's heart is repeated virtually verbatim, and in which the fact that the old man is dead (no matter now in heaven or in hell) echoes with the narrator's claim at the beginning of the tale: "I heard all things in the heaven and in the earth. I heard many things in hell." In Poe's fantastic

Style, Unreliability, and Hidden Dramatic Irony 37

fictional world, for the man whose sense of hearing is "over acute," it seems to make no difference whether the sound is on earth or in heaven/hell.

It is interesting that critics readily accept Poe's fantastic fictional facts in "The Black Cat" and "The Fall of the House of Usher," as well as Franz Kafka's fantastic transformation of the protagonist into a monstrous verminous bug in "Metamorphosis" (1915).[7] Yet many critics have refused to accept that the protagonist of "The Tell-Tale Heart" hears the (alive or dead) old man's heart beating—in Zimmerman's words, "it would have been impossible for him to hear such a noise unless his ear were against the old man's chest" (1992: 40). These critics take the noise as the sound of an insect in the wall (Reilly 1969: 5–7); or as the heartbeat of the protagonist himself, associated with his conscience or sense of guilt (Tucker 2001: 115; Shelden 1976: 77; Hoffman 1972: 227; Robinson 1965: 374; cf. Alber et al. 2010); or as a matter of the mad protagonist's auditory hallucinations (Zimmerman 1992: 40–41; Phillips 1979: 128–30). But Poe's fantastic fictional world seems to defy real-life criteria (cf. Todorov 1975: 24–27), and the structurally unified textual sequence seems to suggest that the protagonist, with his "over-acute" sense of hearing, is able to hear the dead man's heart beating.

Significantly, in this fictional world the "over-acuteness of the sense," which is a typical symptom of insanity in reality, is made to appear as a characteristic of sanity. As the narrator argues, based on a criterion that he apparently shares with his narratee: "The disease had sharpened my senses—not destroyed—not dulled them. Above all was the sense of hearing acute. I heard all things in the heaven and in the earth. I heard many things in hell. How, then, am I mad? . . . And now have I not told you that what you mistake for madness is but over-acuteness of the senses?" At the crucial dénouement, the protagonist's process of hearing also seems to suggest his being sane in this aspect:

> My head ached, and I fancied a ringing in my ears: but still they [the policemen] sat and still chatted. The ringing became more distinct:—it continued and became more distinct: I talked more freely to get rid of the feeling: but it continued and gained definiteness—until, at length, I found that the noise was *not* within my ears.
>
> No doubt I now grew *very* pale;—but I talked more fluently, and with a heightened voice. Yet the sound increased—and what could I do? (559)

The protagonist's rational realization that he "fancied a ringing in [his] ears," his conscious effort "to get rid of" the fantasy, and his final discovery that the noise, which "continued and gained definiteness," was "*not* within [his] ears," all point to his being "sane" in this aspect in this fictional world.

This description, which moves from the fancied ringing in the protagonist's ears to the final discovery that the noise is external to his body, also rules out the possibility that the protagonist is hearing his own heart beating.

38 *Style and Rhetoric of Short Narrative Fiction*

Indeed, one does not need an over-acute sense of hearing to hear one's own heart beating—one feels rather than hears the beating of one's own heart. If Poe's purpose were to suggest that what the protagonist hears is his own heart beating, the above-quoted interaction among the beginning, middle, and end of the textual movement concerned with the protagonist's over-acute hearing would be not only unnecessary but also out of place. Besides, Poe's description of the narrator-protagonist does not suggest any trace of his conscience/guilt:

> In an instant I dragged him to the floor, and pulled the heavy bed over him. I then smiled gaily, to find the deed so far done. But, for many minutes, the heart beat on with a muffled sound. This, however, did not vex me; it would not be heard through the wall. . . .
>
> If still you think me mad, you will think so no longer when I describe the wise precautions I took for the concealment of the body. . . . First of all I dismembered the corpse. I cut off the head and the arms and the legs. . . .
>
> There was nothing to wash out—no stain of any kind—no blood-spot whatever. I had been too wary for that. A tub had caught all—ha! ha! (558)

The self-satisfying "smiled gaily," "did not vex me," and "ha! ha!" betray the narrator-protagonist's cold-bloodedness and go against the interpretation that the narrative represents "the voice of a guilty conscience" (Ward 1924: 35) or "[g]uilt is a major theme of the tale" (Tucker 2001: 115). This narrator-protagonist is a man who is simply beyond the sense of guilt.[8] Moreover, this man, who at the beginning of the tale claims to have been "dreadfully nervous," is "singularly at ease" in front of the policemen:[9]

> . . . they [the policemen] had been deputed to search the premises.
>
> I <u>smiled</u>,—for *what* had I to fear? I <u>bade the gentlemen welcome.</u> The shriek, I said, was my own in a dream. The old man, I mentioned, was absent in the country. I took my visitors all over the house. I <u>bade them search— search *well.*</u> I led them, at length, to his chamber. I showed them his treasures, secure, undisturbed. In <u>the enthusiasm of my confidence,</u> I brought chairs into the room, and desired them *here* to rest from their fatigues, while I myself, in <u>the wild audacity of my perfect triumph,</u> placed my own seat upon the very spot beneath which reposed the corpse of the victim.
>
> The officers were satisfied. My *manner* had <u>convinced them.</u> I was <u>singularly at ease.</u> They sat, and while I answered <u>cheerily,</u> they chatted of familiar things. (558–59, italics original and underlining added)

The words underlined point at once to the narrator-protagonist's dissemblance and his gloating over it. The contrast between the protagonist's being

Style, Unreliability, and Hidden Dramatic Irony 39

"dreadfully nervous" as a rule and his being "singularly at ease" in front of the policemen ironically and dramatically underscores the point that he is absolutely beyond the sense of guilt.

As we know, usually after hiding the corpse, a murderer, in fear of discovery, would try hard to prevent other people—especially policemen—from getting to the spot. But for the sake of creating dramatic irony, Poe depicts the murderer as stupidly inviting the policemen to sit in the very room where he hid the corpse, and, moreover, as most stupidly sitting himself "upon the very spot beneath which reposed the corpse of the victim," out of his enthusiastic confidence and "perfect triumph." The stupidity arises from the protagonist's immoral behavior since it is essentially a matter of his gloating over his dissemblance. But he falls victim to his own dissemblance: His sitting upon the heart of the victim makes it very natural for him to be chased by the victim's revengeful heart in this fantastic fictional world.

Now, a significant point to note is that even if the sound is a matter of the protagonist's hearing his own heart beating associated with his conscience/guilt, or even if it is a matter of his insane auditory hallucinations, a crucial fact will remain unchanged: The policemen with normal hearing cannot hear the heart beating and are therefore not dissembling. That is to say, by making the textual movement continuously convey, from the beginning through the middle to the end, the "overt-acute" hearing of the protagonist, Poe frees the policemen of the charge of dissemblance and invites us to see the unreliability of the narration.

The narrator concludes that the policemen's inability to hear the heart beating really cloaks a pretense that mocks his own horror. This unreliable interpretation and reporting arise from his own immoral behavior, and what he suspects the policemen to be doing to him is precisely what he has done to others:

> To think that there I was, opening the door, little by little, and he [the old man] not even to dream of my secret deeds or thoughts. I fairly *chuckled* at the idea. . . .
> Presently I heard a slight groan, and I knew it was the groan of mortal terror. . . . I knew what the old man felt, and pitied him, although I *chuckled* at heart. (556, italics added)

Later, when the policemen come to search the house, the narrator reports: "I smiled,—for *what* had I to fear? I bade the gentlemen welcome" (558). The stylistic choices "chuckled at the idea," "chuckled at heart," and "I smiled," which appear to be unimportant in the plot development, become thematically significant in the covert progression, since they lend themselves to the implicit overall dramatic irony. Compare the narrator's final pleadings:

> They heard!—they suspected!—they *knew!*—they were making a mockery of my horror!—this I thought, and this I think. But anything was

40   Style and Rhetoric of Short Narrative Fiction

better than this agony! Anything was more tolerable than this derision!
I could bear those hypocritical smiles no longer! I felt that I must scream
or die! (559)

In retrospective character narration, usually the narrating self is better-in-
formed, more knowledgeable and ethically improved as compared with the
experiencing self. That is why Rimmon-Kenan compares the retrospective
Pip in Charles Dickens's *Great Expectations* to traditional omniscient narrators for being "a higher narratorial authority in relation to the story which
he narrates" (2002: 96). But in the covert progression of "The Tell-Tale
Heart," Poe invites us to see that this retrospective narrator shares the same
limitation in knowledge and the same immorality with the experiencing self.
By making the narrator utter "this I thought, and this I think," Poe shows
that the narrating self shares the experiencing self's wrong interpretive judgment on the policemen, just as the two selves share the same unethical delight in his own dissemblance. Through the subtle echoing among words
(the repeated "chuckled at" with "making a mockery of"; "I [hypocritically]
smiled" with "those hypocritical smiles"), Poe guides us to see that precisely
because the murderer mocks at the old man's horror and treats the policemen with hypocritical smiles, he suspects that the policemen are mocking at
his horror and treating him with hypocritical smiles as well.

While the narrator-protagonist gloats over his own dissemblance and en-
joys his mockery and hypocritical smiles at others, he finds the same behavior from others to be most intolerable ("I felt that I must scream or die!").
But, as mentioned above, what he finds most intolerable, in effect, is only his
own immoral behavior unwittingly projected onto the policemen. His shriek
"Villains! dissemble no more! I admit the deed!" intends to call to a stop
the policemen's "dissemblance" but only ironically and unconsciously calls
to a stop his own dissemblance. His unwitting self-condemnation, which is
foregrounded as the only direct speech in the tale and which is given more
prominence by paragraph division and the textual end-focus position, culminates the structurally unified dramatic irony in the covert progression.[10]

The covert progression has so far eluded critical attention. Apart from the
traditional focus on one textual progression—that of the plot development,
there may be other reasons underlying the critical neglect. As discussed in
the previous section, many critics take Poe's aestheticism as covering both
poetry and prose fiction, and so they have overlooked the ethical dimension
of the tale. Besides, many critics are led by the narrator's words to believe
that he is giving his account of his cunning and dissimulation only to prove
that he is not mad. In this vein, if critics find the narration problematic or
unreliable, they only take it as an indication of the narrator's madness (see,
for instance, Silverman 1991: 208–9; Wilson and Lazzari 1998: 345–47;
Zimmerman 2001).

Interestingly, one critic, William Freeman, while paying attention to the
protagonist's over-acuteness of hearing, perceives it as a matter of getting an

Style, Unreliability, and Hidden Dramatic Irony 41

excess of unwanted knowledge. He says, "To see, to feel, to sense too much is to suffer the punishment of destructive knowledge. . . . The closing of the old man's eye and the silencing of the seemingly jeering detectives is the plotted equivalent of Poe's less lethal efforts to dim our own perception and weaken our assumptions about meaning and intent" (2002: 102). Freeman's words, especially the expression "the silencing of the seemingly jeering detectives," point to the fact that missing the covert progression may lead to a misinterpretation of the plot development. Another critic, Paul Witherington tries to show how "the narrator seduces the listener by getting him to participate vicariously in the crime, an accomplice after the fact" (1985: 472). As for the ending, Witherington argues that here the reader is prompted to identify with the police officers and indeed to become one of the "Villains!" To Witherington, the reader is "a villain for wanting to listen to the recreation of a tale of horror, and he's a naïve hypocrite for imagining that he can do so with impunity" (ibid.: 474). From this point of view, the narrator-protagonist is justifiably leveling a moral condemnation against the policemen and the reader. But in fact, in the covert progression behind the overt plot, Poe has implicitly turned the butt of the moral condemnation from the policemen to the narrator-protagonist himself, who is the only hypocritical "villain" in the narrative. Witherington's interpretation illustrates especially well this point made by Booth: Narratorial unreliability, which conveys the implied author's stance in an indirect way, may involve costs, such as the failure of "transcending the limits of the immediate scene," especially the limits of the unreliable narrator (1961: 174–75). But if we can transcend the limits and descry the narratorial unreliability in the covert progression, we may gain, in Booth's words, a sense of pleasure "compounded of pride in [our] own knowledge, ridicule of the ignorant narrator, and a sense of collusion with the silent author" (ibid.: 304–5).

It is significant that, in investigating character narration, we may need to pay attention not only to what is unreliable but also to the conflict between the reliable and the unreliable as encoded by the implied author in the same words of the narratorial discourse. In "The Tell-Tale Heart," the narrator asserts, "You fancy me mad. Madmen know nothing. But you should have seen me. You should have seen how wisely I proceeded—with what caution—with what foresight—with what dissimulation I went to work!" (555). Previous critics have focused on the gap between the narrator's unreliable claim of his being sane and the textual elements displaying his insanity to a certain extent (see below). They have overlooked the narrator's assertion of his dissemblance partly because it is in keeping with his deeds. But the assertion is at once factually reliable and ethically unreliable (taking immoral delight in his dissemblance). This reliable reporting and unreliable evaluation, as noted above, marks the beginning of the covert progression towards ironic self-condemnation. At the ending, the narrator-protagonist's accusation of the policemen's "dissemblance" as being immoral sounds reliable in terms of ethical evaluation and is therefore either overlooked or

42 *Style and Rhetoric of Short Narrative Fiction*

endorsed in existing criticism. But the accusation, in effect, is not only factually unreliable but also ethically problematic—the narrator-protagonist takes delight in his own dissemblance throughout and the double standard renders his ethical judgment questionable.

It should be stressed that the covert progression in "The Tell-Tale Heart" does not rest with the main line of action—it is not a deeper level of meaning of the plot development. Let's take a look at two representative plot summaries. The first was given at the beginning of the twentieth century:

> The Tell-Tale Heart is one of the most effective parables ever conceived. Shorn of its fantastic details regarding the murdered man's vulture-like eye, and the long-drawn-out detail concerning the murderer's slow entrance into his victim's room, the story stands as an unforgettable record of the voice of a guilty conscience. Beneath the floor lies the victim's body; the police-officers sit chatting pleasantly with the murderer, who has met them with perfect outward calm and apparently satisfied them that the old man whom he had killed is absent in the country. Then, above the cheery talk of familiar things, he begins to hear "a low, dull, quick sound—much such a sound as a watch makes when enveloped in cotton"—the sound of the ceaseless beating of the tell-tale heart. By its insistent pulsation he is driven into a state of increasing terror and frenzy, until he tears up the flooring-boards and reveals his crime (Ward 1924: 35–36).

As far as the murdering process is concerned, we lose sight of the murderer's dissemblance and his gloating over it, since what is relevant to the main line of action is only "the murderer's slow entrance into his victim's room." When it comes to the ending, we likewise lose sight of the murderer's projecting his own dissemblance onto the policemen and his finding the projected dissemblance most unbearable, since what is relevant to the main line of action is the "insistent pulsation" of "the tell-tale heart" itself. Unless we open our minds to another textual movement paralleling the main line of action, the covert progression will not come into view no matter what efforts we make in trying to uncover a deeper level of meaning of the plot development.

Nearly one century later, in her summary of the tale's plot in *Short Story Criticism*, Anna Sheets Nesbitt (2000: 239) writes:

> After again declaring his sanity, the narrator proceeds to recount the details of the crime. Every night for seven nights, he says, he had stolen into the old man's room at midnight holding a closed lantern. Each night he would very slowly unlatch the lantern slightly and shine a single ray of light onto the man's closed eye. As he enters the room on the eighth night, however, the old man stirs, then calls out, thinking he has heard a sound. The narrator shines the light on the old man's eye as usual, but

Style, Unreliability, and Hidden Dramatic Irony 43

this time finds it wide open. He begins to hear the beating of a heart and, fearing the sound might be heard by a neighbor, kills the old man by dragging him to the floor and pulling the heavy bed over him. He dismembers the corpse and hides it beneath the floorboards of the old man's room.

At four o'clock in the morning, the narrator continues, three policemen come asking to search the premises . . . He soon begins to hear a heart beating, much as he had just before he killed the old man. It grows louder and louder until he becomes convinced the policemen hear it too. They know of his crime, he thinks, and mock him. Unable to bear their derision and the sound of the beating heart, he springs up and, screaming, confesses his crime.

In this plot summary, we also fail to see the murderer's dissimulation and his taking unethical delight in it during the eight-night murdering process. As for the ending, although Nesbitt pays attention both to the policemen's "derision" and the old man's beating heart, we still lose sight of the murderer's *projecting* his own dissemblance onto the unsuspecting policemen and his finding the *projected* dissemblance most unbearable. The dramatic irony of the murderer's unwitting self-condemnation will not become visible unless we consciously search for a hidden textual progression throughout the text, one that parallels the plot development.

For over one-and-a-half centuries, "The Tell-Tale Heart" has attracted the attention of numerous critics who have focused on the plot development, though approaching it from various angles and often reaching a deeper level of meaning. Not surprisingly, in existing interpretations of the themes of the tale there is no mention of the implicit moral as conveyed by the covert progression—how one's self-satisfying dissemblance leads to one's downfall:

> critics agree that there are two primary motifs in the story: the identification of the narrator with the man he kills and the psychological handling of time. The narrator says he understands his victim's terror just as he is about to murder him, and the beating heart he mistakes for the old man's may well be his own. Throughout the story the narrator is obsessed with time: the central image of the heart is associated with the ticking of a watch, the nightly visits take place precisely at midnight, and time seems to slow and almost stop as the murderer enters the old man's chamber. Another major theme is that of the eye, which some critics consider to have a double meaning, as the external "eye" of the old man is seen in contrast to the internal "I" of the narrator. Several commentators have pointed out that the symbolism in the work is highly structured and intertwined, so that the various themes—of death, time, nature, inner versus outer reality, the dream, the heart, and the eye—work together for accumulated effect. (Nesbitt 2000: 240)

44   *Style and Rhetoric of Short Narrative Fiction*

The psychoanalytic approach dominated the scene in the latter half of the twentieth century. As summarized by Witherington (1985: 474), this approach characteristically takes the police to be "the murderer's super-ego," the narrator's admitting his crime a matter of "the narrator's compulsion to unmask and destroy himself" and the entire inner story (corresponding to the instabilities in the plot) "a psychodrama of compulsions and counter compulsions" (see also Bonaparte 1964; Davidson 1966: 189–90; Canario 1970; Davis 1983; Kennedy 1987: 132–34; Zimmerman 2001). No matter what approaches critics adopt, when attention is focused on the plot development, the covert progression as such will remain unseen, since it is a textual undercurrent paralleling the plot development. The various stylistic details that are important to the covert progression as shown above tend to appear to be trivial and digressive when measured with the gauge of the plot development and therefore tend to be overlooked.

If we explore the ethically oriented dramatic irony of "The Tell-Tale Heart" further, we may find that it extends to the narrator's "sanity defense," which is closely related to the cultural context of the narrative.

UN/RELIABLE SANITY DEFENSE AND HISTORICAL CONTEXT

In "The Tell-Tale Heart," the character narrator uses his narration in the service of self-defense:

> True!–nervous–very, very dreadfully nervous I had been and am; but why *will* you say that I am mad? . . . Hearken! and observe how healthily— how calmly I can tell you the whole story. (555)

In the narrative, we see the conflict between the narrator's protestations about his sanity and various symptoms of his insanity: his "dreadful" nervousness, the lack of a rational motive for killing ("[The old man] had never wronged me. He had never given me insult" [555]), his irrational fear of the old man's eye (which he regards as an "Evil Eye"), and his obsession with a queer idea ("It is impossible to say how first the idea entered my brain; but once conceived, it haunted me day and night" [555]).[11] As the tale ends with the protagonist's admitting his guilt to the policemen, critics tend to agree that this defense is made by the narrator in the process of legal justice. The narration, however, is less an effort to defend his innocence from a murder charge than an effort to prove that he is sane. In order to account for the deviant direction of the defense, which goes against conventional expectations, and to account for the contradiction between claimed sanity and actual symptoms of insanity, it is necessary to look into the cultural context of Poe's tale.

"The Tell-Tale Heart" was produced in the context of the increasing controversy in the mid nineteenth century over the "insanity defense" (see

Style, Unreliability, and Hidden Dramatic Irony   45

Cleman 1991; Maeder 1985). Before the end of the eighteenth century, the most common test of exculpatory insanity was the loss of reason and the "knowledge of good and evil" (Cleman 1991: 628; Maeder 1985: 7–12). As John Cleman writes, with "the equation between reason and the moral sense, any sign of rationality—such as appearing calm and reasonable in court, premeditating or planning the crime, or seeking to hide or avoid punishment—demonstrated the presence of an indivisible conscience and concomitant moral responsibility" (Cleman 1991: 628; see also Maeder 1985: 9–12). To qualify for legal exemption, the defendant had to be, in the words of Judge Tracy in 1774, "a man that is totally deprived of his understanding and memory, and doth not know what he is doing, no more than an infant, than a brute, or a wild beast."[12]

At the turn of the century, however, Benjamin Rush, the father of American psychiatry, distinguished the moral faculties from the intellectual faculties (represented by different areas in the brain) and developed a new theory of insanity—"moral derangement"—in which insanity was considered a disease affecting the moral faculties alone without disordering the intellect (see Rush 1972; Ray 1962; Bynum 1989: 141). In the 1830s, James Cowles Prichard further developed and popularized the discussion, making what he called "moral insanity" the "focus of psychological studies and polemical arguments until replaced by the category of psychopathic personality at the end of the century" (Carlson 1972: xi; Bynum 1989: 142–44). The courts in the nineteenth century began to accept arguments for an exculpatory "moral insanity," or partial insanity, and with the increasing use of the insanity defense for defendants who did not fit the commonsense image of insanity, the defense became an object of ridicule and led to the suspicion that the defense was undermining civil order (see Maeder 1985; Cleman 1991: 625–27). Some judges believed "that moral insanity was, in Baron Rolfe's words, 'an extreme moral depravity not only perfectly consistent with legal responsibility, but such as legal responsibility is expressly invented to restrain'" (Bynum 1989: 144).[13] The claim of moral insanity also met serious opposition within the profession of psychiatry, and "by the late 1840s even some distinguished asylum superintendents began denying the existence of a 'moral' insanity" (ibid.). The public at that time "tended to suspect deception in defense pleas of insanity, and newspapers often fanned these feelings" (ibid.).

The asylum reforms of the period also "contributed to the public view that to be acquitted on the grounds of insanity was to avoid punishment" (Cleman 1991: 625). Before the end of the eighteenth century, the insane were treated very much like criminals, subjected to similar confinement and corporal punishments (see Foucault 1988: 38–64). As Cleman writes, "with the reforms, the insane were housed apart from criminals and, to some degree, treated with . . . compassion and care" (1991: 625). Poe explicitly satirizes these reforms in his tale "The System of Doctor Tarr and Professor Fether" (1844), in which he depicts in a highly dramatic manner the adoption of the

46   Style and Rhetoric of Short Narrative Fiction

"soothing system" at the *Maison de Santé*, a system that frees the insane from all punishments and, in most cases, from confinement. But the lunatics in the *Maison de Santé* take over, imprison the keepers in underground cells, and treat them inhumanly until the lunatics are subdued again.

In "The Tell-Tale Heart," the narrator-protagonist displays typical symptoms of partial insanity or "moral insanity." On the one hand, he retains his rationality in "calmly" telling the story, premeditating the crime, cunningly carrying it out and trying to hide it; but on the other hand, as just mentioned, he displays "dreadful" nervousness, the lack of a rational motive for killing, his irrational fear of the old man's eye, and his obsession with a queer idea. It is significant that, although the narrator-protagonist is morally insane according to the social standards at that time, Poe implicitly denies the existence of "moral insanity" in this fictional world by using the loss of rationality as the sole criterion for determining insanity—a criterion established through the narrator's own words (e.g. "Madmen know nothing"). Interestingly, even according to the narrator's own criterion of sanity (a criterion that obtains in this textual world), his sanity defense is still somewhat unreliable since he is marked by various symptoms of irrationality. Yet he is rational enough to be convicted of murder according to the criterion in this textual world.

As for the thematic relation between the "The Tell-Tale Heart" and the cultural context, it is arguable that Poe is purposefully making use of the social controversy to extend the ethically oriented dramatic irony in the textual undercurrent. Closely linked with the ironic covert progression as such, we have an implicit textual movement towards the narrator's unwitting yet firm self-conviction:

> True!–nervous–very, very dreadfully nervous I had been and am; but why *will* you say that I am mad? . . . Hearken! and observe how healthily— how calmly I can tell you the whole story. (555, at the very beginning of his narration)
>
> You fancy me mad. Madmen know nothing. But you should have seen me. You should have seen how wisely I proceeded—with what caution—with what foresight—with what dissimulation I went to work! (555, at the start of narrating the murdering process)
>
> It took me an hour [every night] to place my whole head within the opening so far that I could see him as he lay upon his bed. Ha! would a madman have been so wise as this? (555, when describing in detail his seven-night spying on the old man at midnight)
>
> If *still* you think me mad, you *will think so no longer* when I describe the wise precautions I took for the concealment of the body. (558, italics added)

Many critics see these claims only in terms of the narrator's madness itself. Alfred C. Ward says: "From the very first sentence his madness is apparent

Style, Unreliability, and Hidden Dramatic Irony   47

through his desperate insistence upon his sanity; and the preliminaries of his crime go to prove that madness" (1924: 36). Similarly, Marie Bonaparte observes, "Thus the narrator—whom Poe evidently wishes to show as mad, or, at least, the victim of the Imp of the Perverse—begins by denying his madness like the 'logical' lunatic he is" (1949: 491). E. Arthur Robinson also writes, "Poe's 'The Tell-Tale Heart' consists of a monologue in which an accused murderer protests his sanity rather than his innocence. The point of view is the criminal's but the tone is ironic in that his protestation of sanity produces an opposite effect upon the reader" (1965: 369). Robinson concludes that "since such processes of reasoning tend to convict the speaker of madness, it does not seem out of keeping that he is driven to confession by 'hearing' reverberations of the still-beating heart in the corpse he has dismembered, nor that he appears unaware of the irrationalities in his defense of rationality" (ibid.). Quoting the narrator's "How, then, am I mad? Hearken! And observe how healthily—how calmly I can tell you the whole story," Daniel Hoffman comments: "When a narrator commences in *this* vein, we know him to be mad already. But we also know his author to be sane. For with such precision to portray the methodicalness of a madman is the work not of a madman but of a man who truly understands what it is to be mad" (1972: 222). In the same vein, Elizabeth Phillips (1979: 128–30) offers a detailed discussion of how the narrator-protagonist resembles the homicidal maniacs.

Some recent critics have paid attention to the cultural context of Poe's tale, and they regard the narrator-protagonist as morally insane. One is Paige Matthey Bynum, who tries to show that "Poe's narrator in 'The Tell-Tale Heart' is a morally insane man, and Poe would have expected his readers to locate the symptoms of that condition in the language of his narration" (1989: 141). Similarly, John Cleman observes, "Even the narrator's insistent denial of the charge of insanity fits the pattern of symptoms of the homicidal maniac, so that the act of the tale's telling and its self-defensive posture constitute evidence in a determination of partial insanity" (1991: 632). Another critic Brett Zimmerman, taking into account both the historical context of Poe's time and the sociocultural context of contemporary time, argues that the narrator in "The Tell-Tale Heart" not only is morally insane but also "corresponds with current psychoanalytic profiles of the 'paranoid schizophrenic' personality" (1992: 39). Zimmerman finds the narrator's "vehement insistence" of his sanity, like his "brag[ging] and boast[ing]" of his "brilliant circumspection" and "finesse" in the murdering process, a most important source of irony in the tale. But he only sees it as the narrator's "inflated opinion of himself," which is "in keeping with the current view that a 'common delusion among paranoid schizophrenics involves exaggerated grandiosity and self-importance'" (1992: 41). Along this line of thinking, Zimmerman argues that "Poe's madman" confesses his crime "because he suffers from delusions of persecution," a typical symptom of paranoid schizophrenia (1992: 44).

48 *Style and Rhetoric of Short Narrative Fiction*

But in effect, Poe has subtly precluded the issue of moral insanity from this fictional world through the narrator's insistent claim, directly or indirectly, that the loss of reason is the only criterion for determining sanity, a criterion the narrator shares with his narratee ("You fancy me mad. Madmen know nothing. . . . would a madman have been so wise as this? . . . If still you think me mad, you will think so no longer when . . ."). If we not only consider the historical context but also carefully examine the stylistic details, and, more importantly, open our minds to a textual undercurrent behind the plot development, we will discern that, while Poe subtly uses a structurally unified covert progression to turn the protagonist's condemnation of the policemen into the protagonist's unconscious self-condemnation, he likewise resorts to contextual relations to turn the narrator's progressive "sanity defense" in the process of legal justice into the narrator's unconscious yet firm self-conviction. Poe seems to make the protagonist's unconscious self-condemnation and unconscious self-conviction reinforce each other in order to convey the implicit moral in a highly dramatic and ironic manner.

If Poe's "The System of Doctor Tarr and Professor Fether" forms an explicit satire on the asylum reforms of the period, "The Tell-Tale Heart" functions as an implicit social satire, ridiculing the "insanity defense" through the unexpected, opposite, and ironic "sanity defense." While greatly increasing the dramatic effects by depicting a murderer who appears to be partially insane, Poe, faced with the social controversy, uses the ironic "sanity defense" in order to convey the ethical lesson in question and to prevent readers from absolving the murderer of his guilt and treating him with compassion and pity.

It should have become clear that Poe's "The Tell-Tale Heart" is marked by strong ethical concerns. A substantial part of the tale's ethical import is aesthetically conveyed through a veiled double-layer movement towards the narrator-protagonist's unconscious self-condemnation coupled with his unwitting self-conviction. This double-layer undercurrent rests with the narrator-protagonist's multiple unreliability. Indeed, Poe's ingenious use of unreliability may function to enrich our understanding of this narrative technique. In "The Tell-Tale Heart," we see multiple interplays between the unreliable and the reliable. First, the narrator is factually reliable in telling the narratee about his dissemblance and cunning, but is ethically unreliable in taking delight in his immoral behavior, a delight as conveyed by the same words. Second, the narrator-protagonist is interpretively and factually unreliable in interpreting and reporting the policemen to be dissembling, but is ethically reliable in deeming the "dissemblance" to be a villainous act, a reliability that is, however, undermined by the narrator-protagonist's taking pride in his own dissemblance. These two kinds of unreliability join hands in contributing to the overall dramatic irony culminating in the narrator-protagonist's self-condemnation. Third, the narrator is factually somewhat unreliable in claiming that he is sane since he displays notable features of insanity, and meanwhile he is factually somewhat reliable in making this claim

Style, Unreliability, and Hidden Dramatic Irony 49

since he retains enough rationality in calculatingly executing the murder, and his partially reliable claim ironically amounts to unwitting self-conviction, which justifies the legal arrest at the crucial dénouement. Poe makes the two aspects of the overall dramatic irony interact with and reinforce each other in order to convey, in a highly aesthetic way, ethical effects to readers.

Subtle and indirect as Poe's techniques are, if we consciously search for a possible undercurrent behind the plot development and combine a careful structural-style analysis with extratextual (e.g. the historical insanity debate) and intertextual (e.g. "The System of Doctor Tarr and Professor Fether") considerations, we will be able to descry the ethically oriented overall dramatic irony based on the complex use of narratorial unreliability. In existing theoretical discussions of unreliability, attention has not yet been paid to the multiple interplay between the unreliable and the reliable, nor to the interaction between the unreliable and the reliable along the same axis, nor to the chaining interaction among three kinds of unreliability (e.g. misreporting arising from the misinterpretation of other people's behavior, which in turn is associated with the misevaluation of one's own behavior). The investigation of the covert progression in Poe's "The Tell-Tale Heart," that is to say, may help broaden our perspective on the ingenuity and complexity of a literary writer's use of narratorial unreliability.

Primarily because of the critical tradition to pay attention only to one textual movement in prose fiction, the ethical-aesthetic covert progression in "The Tell-Tale Heart" has eluded generations of critics. No matter how well we understand other significance or implications of the text, missing the double-layer covert progression will necessarily result in the loss of the most subtle part of the tale's ethical import and the most ingenious aspect of the tale's artistry. Like Hopkins's underthought, Poe's covert progression presents a great challenge to interpretation. But precisely because of the challenge, the process of uncovering it is marked by a particularly keen intellectual delight, an unexpected gain in ethical understanding, and an un-hoped-for increase in aesthetic appreciation. As we shall see in later chapters, the same holds for other covert progressions no matter in what unique way each moves aesthetically forward and no matter whether the undercurrent supplements or subverts the overt plot development in ethical significance.

2 Style and Unobtrusive Emasculating Satire

Crane's "An Episode of War"

While the covert progression in Poe's "The Tell-Tale Heart" has much to do with the unreliability of the character narrator, in Stephen Crane's "An Episode of War," the narration is extradiegetic and the narrator is a reliable mouthpiece of the implied author. To discover the covert progression in such a narrative, instead of exploring various hidden gaps between the narrator's words and the fictional facts, we try to find out how the author creates an undercurrent through reliable stylistic and structural choices for certain ethical purposes. In "An Episode of War," behind the (non-satirical) realist plot development, there is created a satirical emasculating undercurrent against war and traditional notions of heroism.

Regarded as a "best" or an "archetypal" Crane story (Wolford 1989: 68; Stallman 1976: 373; Nagel 1975: 11), "An Episode of War" has attracted much critical attention. Critics tend to treat it as a (non-satirical) realistic or naturalistic narrative (see the Introduction for a summary of the overt plot development).[1] Challenging existing criticisms which "have consistently viewed 'An Episode of War' as a narrative whose sole purpose is to describe war realistically," Mary Shaw offers a reading that sees the tale as a satirical narrative, "whose primary purpose is not simply to present commendable, realistic portrayals of traditional heroism, but to comment or criticize" since it confronts "portrayals of idealized heroic attitudes" with "dramatizations of actual repercussions of the fruition of these attitudes [referring to the protagonist's amputation in the end]" (1991: 26–30). Critics on both sides have overlooked a covert satirical progression, which Crane creates primarily through subtle stylistic choices, to subvert implicitly "idealized heroic attitudes" or "commendable, realistic portrayals of traditional heroism" from the beginning to the end of the textual movement. In terms of the covert progression, Crane implicitly invites very different judgments from his readers. Interpretively, Crane unobtrusively asks readers to judge the protagonist and other army men as emasculated figures (who, as victims of war, also invite readers' compassion), made weak and powerless, which goes against romanticized notions of heroism. Ethically, Crane secretly calls for readers to share his negative judgment on war. Aesthetically, Crane invites readers to appreciate his verbal and structural devices that satirize war and contemporary heroics in a highly artistic way.

MAIN UNDERCURRENT TO DEPRIVE
THE SOLDIERS OF MANHOOD

The narrative begins with the protagonist's rationing out his company's supply of coffee:

> The lieutenant's rubber blanket lay on the ground, and upon it he had poured the company's supply of coffee. Corporals and other representatives of the grimy and hot-throated men who lined the breastwork had come for each squad's portion.
>   The lieutenant was frowning and serious at this task of division [compare: serious at the division]. His lips pursed as he drew with his sword various crevices in the heap, until brown squares of coffee, astoundingly equal in size, appeared on the blanket. He was on the verge of a great triumph in mathematics [compare: He was about to finish his very precise division], and the corporals were thronging forward, each to reap a little square [compare: and the corporals were just going to get their portions], when suddenly the lieutenant cried out and looked quickly at a man near him as if he suspected it was a case of personal assault. The others cried out also when they saw blood upon the lieutenant's sleeve.[2]

As regards referring expressions, the nominal phrase "the lieutenant," which refers to the protagonist, appears three times without naming the person involved. Significantly, the lieutenant, the corporals and all the other military persons are kept anonymous throughout the narrative. By means of anonymity in referring to the characters, the military ranks are foregrounded, leading us to expect a fierce battle, an expectation initially aroused by the title "An Episode of War." The words "task," "triumph," and "assault" in a military context are usually associated with fighting against the enemy. But such conventional expectations are defeated by the transitivity patterning.[3] The lieutenant uses his sword—the only weapon of his described in the narrative—not to fight against the enemy, but to divide coffee, and he is very "serious" at this so-called "task." Similarly, instead of referring to a remarkable war victory, "a great triumph" is used to refer to the protagonist's precision in dividing coffee, a precision that has no connection with any military activity in the narrative, thus appearing digressive and irrelevant to "an episode of war." And the corporals, instead of charging against the enemy, are thronging forward only to "reap a little square of coffee." When the lieutenant is hit by a bullet, he does not suspect it to be from the enemy, but a "personal" assault from a fellow soldier. Moreover, instead of showing bravery and endurance, both the lieutenant (as an experienced soldier) and the corporals "cried out" at the result of the sniper's shot. That is to say, the pattern of transitivity, or the realized action, mental, relational and behavioral processes, conflicts with what is conventionally expected of military men in such a situational context, producing much textual tension and ironic effect.

52 Style and Rhetoric of Short Narrative Fiction

This narrative was originally entitled "The Loss of an Arm,"[4] an unpublished title that tallies perfectly with the narrator's summary at the ending of the published text: "And this is the story of how the lieutenant lost his arm" (272). When the narrative was published, the title was changed to "An Episode of War." This title leads readers to expect the plot to center on a fighting scene, but at the opening of this short narrative, Crane unexpectedly focuses our attention on the protagonist's dividing coffee for the company. Here we can get a glimpse of how discoursal stylistic choices "work on" story events and change their effects. With the original title "The Loss of an Arm," there is hardly any satirical effect in reading the protagonist's dividing coffee (when he gets wounded), but with the title "An Episode of War," a certain amount of tension and satirical effect may arise from the clash between readers' expectations for a fighting scene and the story facts Crane has selected to present (see below for why the title is changed to a more satirical one in the published text). And Crane's other stylistic choices implicitly reinforce the satirical effect, which will gradually increase through Crane's skilful choice of story facts and stylistic techniques in the later textual movement. Not surprisingly, the thematic function of such textual elements, which appear to be unimportant or digressive to the plot development, tends to elude critical attention unless we make a conscious effort to explore a possible hidden dynamic.

A later description goes: "At the roadside a brigade was making coffee and buzzing with talk like a girl's boarding school" (271). According to the traditional division of labor between the two genders, dividing coffee or making coffee is a feminine task. But of course army men at the front can only rely on themselves, and Hemingway's narratives of men doing manly things also at times turn to coffee-making. However, it is significant that Crane gives unusual prominence to the soldiers' performing this traditionally feminine task within the limited space of this short narrative: Not only opening the story with the protagonist's dividing coffee, making his getting wounded while dividing coffee the title event of the story, but also depicting a brigade's making coffee and explicitly comparing the army men to "girls" in authorial commentary. Since the explicit comment "like a girl's boarding school" drastically goes against readers' expectations of male soldiers, the stylistic choices have the function of highlighting the related story fact of the soldiers' "making coffee."

On a wider scope, according to traditional conception of heroic male soldiers, they are typically brave, active, calm, broad-minded, and physically strong. Significantly, manliness as such forms the very foundation of traditional heroism, and fictional narratives in favor of heroism characteristically depict a protagonist as full of such manhood. A careful examination of the stylistic choices among other techniques in "An Episode of War" reveals that, behind the appearance of presenting "commendable, realistic portrayals of traditional heroism," there is an undercurrent that goes in the opposite direction—it continuously deprives the protagonist and other soldiers of manhood.

Style and Unobtrusive Emasculating Satire 53

In the following passage, Crane shows the army men's passivity or inaction with various choices of transitivity. The wounded lieutenant "*looked sadly,* mystically, over the breastwork at the green face of a wood" where the bullet has come and "the men about him *gazed statue-like* and *silent, astonished* and *awed* by this *catastrophe*" (268, italics added). In the traditional conception, heroic soldiers, in contrast with ordinary guys, would treat a wound in the arm just as an injury rather than a "catastrophe," and would face it calmly and bravely rather than being "astonished and awed" into helplessness and incapacity to act. Crane spares no ink in foregrounding the army men's passivity or inaction: "As the lieutenant stared at the wood, [his comrades] too swung their heads, so that for another instant all hands, still silent, contemplated the distant forest" (268) and when the lieutenant is departing for the hospital, "the men *in silence stared at* the woods, *then at* the departing lieutenant; *then at* the wood, *then at* the lieutenant" (270, italics added). The consistent choice of mental processes, the repetition of "then at" (conveying a sense of mechanicalness), and the circumstantial elements showing the army men's sadness and inactivity interact to deprive the army men of any heroic quality. What is more, the stylistically wrought undercurrent also conveys the protagonist's utmost physical weakness and helplessness:

> The orderly-sergeant took the sword and tenderly placed it in the scabbard. At the time, he *leaned nervously backward,* and did not allow even his finger to brush the body of the lieutenant. A wound gives strange dignity to him who bears it. Well men shy from his new and terrible majesty. It is as if the wounded man's hand is upon the curtain which hangs before the revelations of all existence—the meaning of ants, potentates, wars, cities, sunshine, snow, a feather dropped from a bird's wing; and the power of it sheds radiance upon a bloody form, and makes the other men understand sometimes that they are little. His comrades look at him with large eyes thoughtfully. Moreover, they fear vaguely that the weight of a finger upon him might send him headlong, precipitate the tragedy, hurl him at once into the dim, gray unknown. *And so* the orderly-sergeant, while sheathing the sword, *leaned nervously backward.*
> There were others who proffered assistance. One timidly presented his shoulder and asked the lieutenant if he cared to lean upon it, but the latter waved him away mournfully. He wore the look of one who knows he is the victim of a terrible disease and understands his helplessness. He again stared over the breastwork at the forest, and then, turning, went slowly rearward. He held his right wrist tenderly in his left hand as if the wounded arm was made of brittle glass. (269–70, italics added)

Many critics treat the description as investing the protagonist with dignity or glory.[5] Shaw shares this view but takes it that the description that attributes

54   Style and Rhetoric of Short Narrative Fiction

"strange dignity" to the protagonist "solely reflects the point of view of the soldiers, who are still deluded by the romantic notion of war" (1985: 96).[6] This kind of reading is supported by the noticeable words like "dignity," "majesty," "the curtain which hangs before the revelations of all existence," "power," "radiance." But if we examine Crane's stylistic choices very carefully, we may discover that, behind the dignified, "romantic" picture, there is an ironic undercurrent where the lieutenant's wound is used both as a vehicle to convey Crane's nihilistic view of the world and as a means to dramatize the lieutenant as an extremely weak and vulnerable person. Superficially, the lieutenant is dignified by "majesty," but in what precedes, Crane puts "a trident" on a par with "a spade" (269) and at the present stage, he juxtaposes "potentates" with "ants" and "a feather dropped from a bird's wing," thereby rendering the former as unimportant as the latter. These stylistic arrangements subtly undermine the significance of "majesty," a word ironically modified by "terrible" just as "dignity" by "strange." In a similar fashion, the fact that the power of "the revelations of [the insignificance of] all existence" "sheds radiance upon" the lieutenant's "bloody form" only makes his comrades understand the insignificance and meaninglessness of all human beings (and of course of all wars).

Particularly worth noticing is the verbatim repetition of the orderly-sergeant's "lean[ing] nervously backward." At the former appearance of the expression, we are given the impression that the leaning backward is due to the lieutenant's having acquired "strange dignity," but this impression turns out to be false with the appearance of the conjunction "so" ("And so the orderly-sergeant, while sheathing the sword, leaned nervously backward"), which indicates to the careful reader that actually it is the lieutenant's utmost vulnerability that makes the orderly-sergeant "lean nervously backward." Significantly, the orderly-sergeant's not allowing "even his finger to brush the body of the lieutenant," which caricatures the lieutenant's vulnerability, is reinforced by his comrades' not allowing "the weight of a finger" upon the lieutenant for fear that it may "send him headlong" and "hurl him" immediately into death. The deplorable weakness of the lieutenant is further dramatized in the following paragraph. Although when one of the soldiers offered the wounded lieutenant a shoulder to lean on, "the latter waved him away," the action is modified by "mournfully." And the following sentence continues to present a woeful picture of the lieutenant who wears "the look of one who knows he is the victim of a terrible disease and understands his helplessness."

An intertextual comparison with Crane's "A Mystery of Heroism" (1895) and "The Open Boat" (1898) may shed much light on Crane's emasculating stylistic choices in "An Episode of War." In "A Mystery of Heroism," there is also a description of a wounded lieutenant:

> A lieutenant of the battery rode down and passed them, holding his right arm carefully in his left hand. And it was as if this arm was not at all a part of him, but belonged to another man. His sober and reflective charger went slowly. The officer's face was grimy and perspiring, and his

Style and Unobtrusive Emasculating Satire 55

uniform was tousled as if he had been in direct grapple with an enemy. He smiled grimly when the men stared at him. He turned his horse toward the meadow. (Crane 1965: 260)

The following diagram may help clarify the picture:

"A Mystery of Heroism"	"An Episode of War"
as if he had been in direct grapple with an enemy	a case of personal assault;
smiled grimly;	sadly; mournfully; helplessness;
carefully; the officer's face was grimy and perspiring	tenderly; the victim of a terrible disease
as if this arm . . . belonged to another man	as if the wounded arm was made of brittle glass; the weight of a finger upon him might . . . hurl him at once into the dim, gray unknown

While in "A Mystery of Heroism," the stylistic choices suggest that the lieutenant may have grappled bravely with an enemy, in "An Episode of War" the lieutenant suspects the enemy's assault to be from his own comrade. Further, the stylistic choices in "A Mystery of Heroism" depict a manly lieutenant, who remains calm and active after getting wounded. By contrast, in "An Episode of War," the stylistic choices put the wounded lieutenant in an extremely passive and deplorable position. Notice the contrast between the adverbs "carefully" and "grimly" in "A Mystery of Heroism" and the more or less emasculating adverbs "tenderly," "sadly," and "timidly" (describing a fellow soldier) in "An Episode of War." In terms of the wounded arm, we also have the contrast between "belonged to another man" and the emasculating "made of brittle glass," which dramatizes the lieutenant as being extremely weak. The lieutenant in "An Episode of War" is only in the position of the goal, and the actor is either "a terrible disease" or "a finger." A finger upon him can immediately cause his death, which caricatures his being deplorably weak. Such intertextual comparison helps us perceive the hidden satirical dynamic in "An Episode of War," and to see that the implied authors of the two narratives actually hold contrastive ethical stances towards, and invite readers' different judgments on, war and heroism (see below).

In Crane's "The Open Boat," the captain is also injured, but like the case in "A Mystery of Heroism," the picture is very different from that in "An Episode of War":

The injured captain, lying in the bow, was at this time buried in that profound dejection and indifference which comes, temporarily at least, to even the bravest and most enduring when, willy nilly, the firm fails,

56 Style and Rhetoric of Short Narrative Fiction

the army loses, the ship goes down. The mind of the master of a vessel is rooted deep in the timbers of her, though he command for a day or a decade, and this captain had on him the stern impression of a scene in the grays of dawn of seven turned faces, and later a stump of a top-mast with a white ball on it that slashed to and fro at the waves, went low and lower, and down. Thereafter there was something strange in his voice. Although steady, it was deep with mourning, and of a quality beyond oration or tears.

"Keep'er a little more south, Billie," said he.

"'A little more south,' sir," said the oiler in the stern. (Crane 1984: 885–86)

This is the initial description of the injured captain. Although he is having "that profound dejection," the sadness or depression does not have to do with his injury but with the loss of his ship (the "mind of the master of a vessel is rooted deep in the timbers of her"). It is a professional loss ("the firm fails, the army loses, the ship goes down") that "even the bravest and most enduring" man with professional dedication or sense of responsibility would find difficult to bear. It is true that the captain's voice is "deep with mourning," but in contrast with the lieutenant in "An Episode of War," his mourning is not associated with his own injury, but with the death of his fellow crewmen and the sinking of his ship. The captain remains calm, continuing to give professional orders in a "steady" voice. Besides, the captain remains amiable:

Then the captain, in the bow, *chuckled* in a way that expressed *humor*, contempt, tragedy, all in one. "Do you think we've got much of a show, now, boys?" said he.

Whereupon the three were silent, save for a trifle of hemming and hawing. To express any particular optimism at this time they *felt to be childish and stupid*. . . . On the other hand, the ethics of their condition was decidedly *against any open suggestion of hopelessness*. So they were silent.

"On, Well," said the captain, soothing his children, "we'll get ashore all right." . . . The hurt captain, lying against the water-jar in the bow, spoke always in a low voice and calmly, but he could never command a more ready and swiftly obedient crew than the motley three of the dingey. (1984: 887–88, italics added)

Like the lieutenant and other soldiers in "An Episode of War," the captain and his crew in "The Open Boat" remain anonymous, and so their professional identity is made prominent. But while the injured captain and the motley crew of the dinghy behave in a calm and brave sailorly manner in the face of great danger, the injured lieutenant and his comrades are satirically depicted as being unsoldierly, with the lieutenant showing uttermost fragility and "helplessness," like "the victim of a terrible disease." For the authorial

Style and Unobtrusive Emasculating Satire 57

reader of "An Episode of War," the process of descrying the satirical undercurrent is a process of gaining increasing interpretive delight, growing negative ethical judgment on war, and increasing aesthetic appreciation of Crane's stylistic techniques.

At a later stage of the textual movement, Crane uses the device of what we may call "childization" in portraying the protagonist as a way to reinforce the overall emasculating undercurrent. Before reaching the hospital, the lieutenant meets an officer who "appropriated the lieutenant and the lieutenant's wound" (271). Crane's ingenious technique of putting both the lieutenant and his wound in the "goal" position of the officer's action process "appropriate" functions to deprive the lieutenant of both his dignity and subjectivity. The officer binds up the lieutenant's wound, "scolding away in the meantime," his tone suggesting that the lieutenant is "in the habit of being wounded every day" (271). The adjunct "in the habit of being wounded every day" both depreciates the wound to a trivial daily fault and attributes the "fault" to the lieutenant's own inclination. Under the officer's "parental" treatment, the lieutenant "hung his head, feeling, in this presence, that he did not know how to be correctly wounded" (271), which somewhat ascribes the wound to the lieutenant's ignorance, reinforcing the stylistic strategy of making the injury appear as a fault of the lieutenant himself. With such expressions bordering on caricature, Crane implicitly invites us to see the lieutenant as a timid and naïve child. This forms a striking contrast with the picture in "The Open Boat" as quoted above, where the captain, who remains calm and dignified after getting hurt, treats his crew like a loving father ("soothing his children") and the crewmen themselves consciously guard against "childish and stupid" behavior.

The lieutenant in "An Episode of War" then meets the doctor who operates on him. The doctor also treats him like a dominating parent, in whose presence the lieutenant at first remains "very meek" (272). When the doctor asks him to come along for the operation, his face "flushed," saying "I guess I won't have it amputated" (272). The doctor reacts rudely:

> "Nonsense, man! Nonsense! Nonsense!" cried the doctor. "Come along, now. I won't amputate it. Come along. *Don't be a baby.*"
> "Let go of me," said the lieutenant, holding back wrathfully, his glance fixed upon the door of the old school house, as sinister to him as the portals of death.
> And this is the story of how the lieutenant lost his arm. When he reached home, his sisters, his mother, his wife, sobbed for a long time at the sight of the flat sleeve. "Oh, well,' he said, standing *shamefaced* amid these tears, "I don't suppose it matters so much as all that." (272, italics added)

This is the very end of the narrative. The rhetorical strategy of "childization" is made explicit with the doctor's asking the lieutenant not to behave

58   Style and Rhetoric of Short Narrative Fiction

like "a baby" and the doctor fools the lieutenant into amputation like a parent fools a child for medical treatment. Earlier in the textual movement, when the lieutenant first meets the doctor, Crane goes even further in humiliating him through the use of narratorial comment, treating him as an offender for getting wounded:

> "Good-morning," [the doctor] said, with a friendly smile. Then he caught sight of the lieutenant's arm, and his face at once changed. "Well, let's have a look at it." He seemed possessed suddenly of a great contempt for the lieutenant. This wound evidently placed the latter on a very low social plane. . . . When the wound was disclosed the doctor fingered it disdainfully. "Humph," He said. "You come along with me and I'll tend to you." His voice contained the same scorn as if he were saying: "You will have to go to jail." (271–72)

While in romantic notions of heroism, getting wounded is glorious (with "gloriously wounded" as a set phrase), Crane, through the joint function of the doctor's change in attitude and the narrator's conjectural comments ("seemed," "evidently," "as if"), makes it appear as a criminal offence, thereby scathingly satirizing contemporary heroics. Although the authorial reader will not go so far as to place the lieutenant "on a very low social plane," judging him "disdainfully" or with "great contempt" like the doctor, there is no doubt that the authorial reader will not see the protagonist as "commendable" since the interaction between story facts and stylistic techniques has implicitly placed him into the position of a deplorable butt of satire. Of course the real target of Crane's satire is not the protagonist himself, but war and romanticized notions of heroism. And Crane invites his readers to cherish a certain degree of compassion for the protagonist as a victim of war through depicting his extreme physical weakness and his losing one arm. Indeed, as quoted above, Crane depicts the wounded lieutenant as "the victim of a terrible disease," who "understands his helplessness."

Some critics take it that the protagonist's last utterance "I don't suppose it matters so much as all that" manifests his courage and fortitude (see, for instance, Nagel 1975: 11, Knapp 1987: 169–70). However, behind this superficially courageous picture, there in effect exists a continuation of the satirical undercurrent. It is significant that Crane uses the word "shamefaced" to qualify the protagonist's behavior ("he said, standing shamefaced amid these tears"). Before the amputation, the protagonist, like a child, is marked by excessive fear, viewing the door of the hospital "as the portals of death." But the amputation is after all not that horrible and the protagonist is now ashamed of his earlier childish fear, which is set off by the narrator's placid summary "And this is the story of how the lieutenant lost his arm." But of course the last utterance of the protagonist has other implications, such as reflecting the indifference of war (Nagel 1975: 13; Wolford 1989: 68), or indicating the insignificance of human beings (Gibson 1968: 96; LaFrance

Style and Unobtrusive Emasculating Satire   59

1971: 103). But a careful consideration of the subtle stylistic choices enables us to discern that the last part of the narrative forms the final phase of the satirical undercurrent that, from the very beginning of the narrative, continuously emasculates the protagonist among other soldiers behind the realistic overt plot development.

The fact that the overall emasculating undercurrent has eluded generations of critics may be accounted for by the following factors. First, as far as prose fiction is concerned, although critics do often try to find out various kinds of deeper meaning concerning the instabilities in the main line of action, the critical tradition tends to neglect an undercurrent that appears to be digressive or unimportant to the main line of action. This can easily lead to the neglect of covert strategies like Crane's emasculating devices that lie peripheral to or outside of the main line of action. Second, there is a lack of attention to the interaction among related textual elements in different parts of the text. The protagonist's dividing coffee with his sword becomes an important emasculating device only in relation to various other emasculating devices permeating the textual movement (including the explicit comparison of army men to girls). It is significant that, in this narrative, there is no description of the protagonist's fighting with the enemy, and his dividing coffee is the only place he is seen as using his weapon—his only weapon mentioned in the narrative.

Moreover, to descry the emasculating undercurrent in "An Episode of War," we also need to break free from the bondage of certain interpretive frames concerning Crane's literary creation. H.S.S. Bais says that "assertion of manhood is one of the most important themes in the novels of Stephen Crane" (1988: 23) and Hoffman observes that Crane's "theme of grace under pressure in a masculine world of conflict provided Hemingway with a model" (1979: 290). Such observations apply to Crane's narratives like "A Mystery of Heroism" and "The Open Boat" but do not apply to "An Episode of War." But such views tend to form more or less fixed interpretive frames that can easily lead to the neglect of Crane's emasculating strategy, including that of "childization" (not to mention "criminalization") in "An Episode of War." Stanley Wertheim, for instance, goes no further than seeing that "the lieutenant of 'An Episode of War' resembles Hemingway's shattered heroes, who can never recover from their physical and emotional wounds" (1997: 190–91). As I will emphasize in Chapter 3, in writing different fictional narratives, the same writer may hold contrastive stances and depict drastically different characters. Far from contributing to the "theme of grace under pressure in a masculine world of conflict," the protagonist of "An Episode of War" very much goes in the opposite direction according to this narrative's rhetorical design.

Although Shaw tries to reveal the satirical nature of the narrative, due to the lack of attention to a possible undercurrent, as well as insufficient attention to the interaction among subtle stylistic devices in different parts of the text, she fails to discern the satirical emasculating undercurrent and

60 Style and Rhetoric of Short Narrative Fiction

still sees the lieutenant as a "representative of traditional heroism" (1985: 100) or as "an embodiment of contemporary heroics" (1991: 26), thus still misunderstanding the ethical import of the tale and missing a large part of Crane's masterful technique.[7]

As mentioned above, the protagonist and other characters in this tale remain anonymous, only referred to in terms of their military ranks or identities, and there is no specification as to when and where the events take place. Many critics hold that the narrative depicts an episode of the American Civil War (see, for instance, Geismar 1953: 131; Wolford 1989: 61; Schaefer 1996: 115), but there is no textual clue as to which war is depicted. One may argue that Crane used "blue" to refer to the color of the uniform of an infantry, but in Crane's "The Kicking Twelfth" (1900) published at about the same time, the army of the imaginary Spitzenberg empire is also in blue uniform, so the color of the uniform alone cannot function as hard evidence. Thus, in contrast with Crane's *The Red Badge of Courage: An Episode of the American Civil War,* "An Episode of War" may represent an episode of any war from the early or middle nineteenth century when long-distance sharpshooting was developed, and the anonymous characters may represent army men in general. It is in this somewhat allegorical narrative that Crane creates the emasculating undercurrent, which therefore takes on a wider relevance, inviting readers to see war as meaningless and romanticized notions of heroism as illusory in general.

SUBSIDIARY UNDERCURRENT CENTERING ON INTERNAL CONFLICTS

If the emasculating undercurrent functions to undermine the most important cornerstone of heroism, Crane subtly reinforces the ethical import by creating a subsidiary undercurrent that centers on internal conflicts as a satirical replacement for fighting against the enemy—a related cornerstone. The whole textual movement of the narrative, which goes in a chronological way, roughly falls into four phases: first, the protagonist's getting wounded; second, his going to the field hospital; third, his arrival at the field hospital; and finally, his returning home. If we examine the stylistic choices carefully, we shall discover that, except for the very short last phase comprising only two sentences, all the preceding three phases of the textual movement contain internal conflicts that appear digressive or peripheral to the main line of action and that implicitly and satirically take the place of fighting against the enemy.

At the beginning of the narrative, upon being hit by a bullet, the protagonist does not look in the direction of the enemy, but at one of his own comrades, and the epithet "personal" in "as if he suspected it was a case of personal assault" explicitly invites readers to see the conflict between the two warring sides as a case of internal strife. More importantly, Crane makes the wounded protagonist appear as only struggling with his own weapon:

Style and Unobtrusive Emasculating Satire 61

[the wounded] officer had, of course, been compelled to take his sword into his left hand. He did not hold it by the hilt. He gripped it at the middle of the blade, awkwardly. Turning his eyes from the hostile wood, he looked at the sword as he held it there, and *seemed puzzled as to what to do with it.* In short, this weapon had of a sudden become *a strange thing to him.* He looked at it in a kind of *stupefaction,* as if he had been endowed with a trident, a *scepter, or a spade.*

Finally he tried to sheathe it. To sheathe a sword held by the left hand, at the middle of the blade, in a scabbard hung at the left hip, is a feat worthy of a sawdust ring. This wounded officer engaged in a desperate struggle with the sword and the wobbling scabbard, and during the time of it he breathed like a wrestler. (269, italics added)

It is not fortuitous that in this short narrative, Crane devotes two paragraphs to the protagonist's sheathing his sword, his only weapon mentioned in the whole text. As we know, the "sword" is a traditional synecdoche for the military, and traditionally a soldier is supposed to be most familiar with his sword. The protagonist, as a lieutenant, is an experienced soldier, and the wound in his right arm cannot really justify his estrangement from his sword to such a degree that he looks "at it in a kind of stupefaction as if he had been endowed with a trident, a scepter, or a spade." This is radical defamiliarization for a satirical rhetorical purpose. In Crane's time, a trident can only catch fish, and a scepter or a spade is also not a military weapon. In the authorial comment led by "as if," the protagonist's sword is compared to these non-military items, and, further, the tongue-in-cheek syntactic juxtaposition of these items involves an antithetical movement from elevation ("trident" → "scepter") to debasement ("scepter" → "spade"), thereby unobtrusively yet mockingly deconstructing the military function of the sword. More significantly and satirically, the protagonist is "engaged in a desperate struggle with" his own weapon, which is the only "struggle" he carries out in the whole narrative. It is surely for the sake of satire that Crane makes the protagonist grip his sword "at the middle of the blade" and engage in "a desperate struggle" with it. As regards the attribute of the relational process "was a feat worthy of a sawdust ring," the head noun "feat" in the war context usually refers to the heroic feat of defeating the enemy, but the postmodifier "worthy of a sawdust ring" turns it into a feat of a non-military circus show and somewhat reduces the protagonist to a clown.

Viewing the description non-satirically, James Nagel observes that the protagonist "at the opening, is very much a creature of his status as soldier," able to handle his weapon "with appropriate dexterity, dividing the coffee into heaps 'astoundingly equal in size,'" but after being wounded "he undergoes a change of role, no longer displaying his prowess of swordsmanship" (Nagel 1980: 11; see also Holton 1972: 144; Gibson 1968: 95). In fact, behind this overt textual movement, there exists a satirical undercurrent. Indeed, if the "prowess of swordsmanship" of a "soldier" lies at

62 Style and Rhetoric of Short Narrative Fiction

the root of traditional heroism, it is precisely what Crane aims at satirizing both by making the sound protagonist use his sword merely to divide coffee and by making the wounded protagonist struggle with his sword instead of fighting against the enemy. Many other critics also take a non-satirical view. Stanley Wertheim, for instance, comments that after the protagonist is wounded, the "sword becomes an encumbrance that he transfers awkwardly to his left hand and that someone else must sheath for him. It is a symbol of his transformation from competence and mastery to ineffectuality and dependence" (1997: 95). Such views make sense but are confined to the surface textual movement, failing to see the covert satirical progression underneath.

On his way to the hospital, the wounded protagonist perceives the activity of a battery, which, as we shall see in the following section, also implicitly conveys internal conflict. When the protagonist arrives at the hospital, what comes into his sight is a scene of internal strife:

> The low white tents of the hospital were grouped *around* an old schoolhouse. *There was here a singular commotion.* In the *foreground* two ambulances interlocked wheels in the deep mud. The drivers were tossing the blame of it back and forth, gesticulating and berating, while from the ambulances, both crammed with wounded, there came an occasional groan. An interminable crowd of bandaged men were coming and going. Great numbers sat under the trees nursing heads or arms or legs. *There was a dispute of some kind raging* on the steps of the schoolhouse. (271, italics added)

After the accident happens, the drivers should work together to solve the problem in order to save the wounded. But from Crane's satirical pen, the drivers are only engaged in fighting selfishly and narrow-mindedly against each other with words and gestures, to the neglect of the pain and danger of the wounded crammed in the ambulances. As we know, the field hospital is a place to cure the wounded and to save lives, where, of course, quarrels and disputes sometimes may also occur. But through the stylistic repetition of "There was . . ." among other means, Crane more or less focuses the reader's attention on the "commotion" and the "dispute," the former taking place "in the foreground" and the latter "raging" on the steps of the schoolhouse as the centre of the hospital (the tents are grouped around this building where the protagonist undergoes amputation).[8] For the rhetorical purpose of satirizing war, Crane foregrounds the internal strife, making what is peripheral occupy the center of the stage. This case well shows how the author's stylistic choices may function to shape the story, changing to a certain extent the nature of the entity involved. The focus on the internal conflicts is indeed implicitly satirical since there is no close-distance description of any fighting against the enemy in the whole narrative. However, as far as the main line of action is concerned, the cases of internal strife that Crane

Style and Unobtrusive Emasculating Satire 63

subtly foregrounds only appear to be insignificant or digressive details in the war setting. Not surprisingly, like the main emasculating undercurrent, the subsidiary undercurrent of replacing fighting against the enemy with internal conflicts has also eluded generations of critics. This critical neglect is also primarily to be attributed to the critical tradition of concentrating on the plot development, a tradition that also underlies misinterpretations of the following battle scene.

RENDERING BATTLE AGAINST ENEMY MEANINGLESS

The only battle against the enemy is a scene the protagonist watches in the distance on his way to the hospital:

> As the wounded officer passed from the line of battle, he was enabled to see many things which as a participant in the fight were unknown to him. He saw a general on a black horse gazing over the lines of blue infantry at the green woods which veiled his problems. An aide galloped furiously, dragged his horse suddenly to a halt, saluted, and presented a paper. It was, for a wonder, precisely like an historical painting.
>
> To the rear of the general and his staff a group, composed of a bugler, two or three orderlies, and the bearer of the corps standard, all upon maniacal horses, were working like slaves to hold their ground, preserve their respectful interval, while the shells boomed in the air about them, and caused their chargers to make furious quivering leaps.
>
> A battery, a tumultuous and shining mass, was swirling *toward the right*. The wild thud of hoofs, the cries of the riders, shouting blame and praise, menace and encouragement, and, last, the roar of the wheels, the slant of the glistening guns, brought the lieutenant to an intent pause. The battery swept in curves that stirred the heart; it made halts as dramatic as the crash of a wave on the rocks, and when it fled onward this aggregation of wheels, levers, motors had a beautiful unity, as if it were a missile. The sound of it was a war-chorus that reached into the depths of man's emotion.
>
> The lieutenant, still holding his arm as if it were of glass, stood watching this battery until all detail of it were lost, save the figures of the riders, which rose and fell and *waved lashes over the black mass*.
>
> *Later, he turned his eyes toward the battle*, where the shooting sometimes crackled like bush-fires, sometimes sputtered with exasperating irregularity, and sometimes reverberated like the thunder. He saw the smoke rolling upward and saw crowds of men who ran and cheered, or stood and blazed away *at the inscrutable distance*. (270, italics added)

What first comes into the protagonist's sight is a general who gazes at the green woods "which veiled his problems." Crane's stylistic choice of "his

64 Style and Rhetoric of Short Narrative Fiction

problems," which sounds personal and vague, is devoid of any suggestion of a heroic or patriotic battle. As for the bugler and the bearer of the corps standard, they are traditionally symbolic of glory and valor, leading and encouraging the army to charge forward at the enemy. But from Crane's satirical pen, they work "like slaves" only to preserve their respectful interval from their own general. In this way, Crane subtly invites us to see the simile "like an historical painting" in an ironic light.

The third paragraph focuses on a battery, which some critics take to be "in an exchange with an unseen enemy" (Nagel 1980: 101). But a close examination of the adjuncts in this paragraph in relation to those in the fifth reveals that the battery, instead of being engaged in fighting, is moving away from the battle ("A battery . . . was swirling *toward the right*. . . . The lieutenant . . . stood watching this battery until all detail of it were lost. . . . *Later,* he turned his eyes *toward the battle*"). The battle is taking place in front of the protagonist, but the battery is "swirling toward the right," away from the battle. Moreover, Crane's masterful stylistic arrangement foregrounds the incongruity of the cries of the riders while moving away—"shouting blame and praise, menace and encouragement." The deliberately arranged antitheses contribute subtly to the undercurrent of replacing fighting against the enemy with internal conflicts. The "blame" and "menace" also seem to echo the scolding and threatening of the protagonist by the officer and the doctor as quoted above. In the present phase, we can see another dimension of the internal conflict if we consider the third and fourth paragraphs together: "A battery, a tumultuous and shining mass. . . . [the riders] waved lashes over the black mass," where Crane's stylistic repetition of the term "mass" gives us the impression that the riders are waving lashes over their own battery.

It is also significant that Crane uses "levers" instead of "barrels" and describes the whole battery as an "aggregation of wheels, levers, motors" as if it were a transport team. In this context, many words take on an ironic ring: the stirring "war-chorus" only consists of the "tumultuous" sound of the battery's swirling away from the battle; the battery's "fle[eing] onward" is not a movement towards the enemy, but "toward the right" away from the enemy (thus the verb "flee" may be taken in its primary sense of escaping); the "beautiful unity" only manifests the transporting rather than the battling function of the battery (perhaps a subtle way to emasculate the battery); and the "missile" is not aimed at killing the enemy in the front, but fleeing towards the right, away from the battle. To see Crane's satire in a clearer light, let's take a look at his poem "War is Kind":

> Do not weep, maiden, for war is *kind*.
> Because your lover threw wild hands toward the sky
> And the affrighted steed ran on alone,
> Do not weep.
> War is *kind*.

Style and Unobtrusive Emasculating Satire 65

Hoarse, booming drums of the regiment,
Little souls who thirst for fight,
These men were born to drill and die.
The unexplained *glory* flies above them,
Great is the Battle-God, *great,* and his Kingdom—
A field where a thousand corpses lie.

. . .

Swift blazing flag of the regiment,
Eagle with crest of red and gold,
These men were born to drill and die.
Point for them the *virtue* of slaughter,
Make plain to them the *excellence* of killing
And a field where a thousand corpses lie.

Mother whose heart hung humble as a button
On the *bright splendid* shroud of your son,
Do not weep.
War is *kind.*[9]

From Crane's satirical pen, words like "kind," "glory," "great," "blazing," "virtue," "excellence," and "splendid" mean just the opposite to their conventional senses, which alerts us to the fact that we cannot take Crane's words at face value and must try to find out what they really mean in the Cranean context. If Crane is here unequivocally tongue-in-cheek, his satire is very much veiled and only forms a covert progression in "An Episode of War." But both similarly call for readers to see through the superficial senses of words for what the author really means and judges underneath.

In the fifth paragraph of the above quoted passage taken from "An Episode of War," Crane describes a direct exchange with the enemy for the first and only time in the narrative. From the protagonist's perspective, we cannot see any glory or significance of the battle, not even the borderline between the warring sides. The "smoke rolling upward" should be a result of shelling, but we do not know which side is doing the shelling. And since the fighting is going on, the battery's moving away like a transport team in the previous paragraphs appears more ironic. Interestingly, what is "exasperating" is not a setback on the protagonist's side, but the irregularity of the shooting itself, as if it were a game rather than a battle. The protagonist perceives "crowds of men who ran and cheered, or stood and blazed away at the inscrutable distance." The actions of the "crowds" are incongruous: "ran" versus "stood;" "cheered" versus "blazed away," resulting in a sort of chaos and inconsequence, and the shooting is not at the enemy but at "the inscrutable distance," a masterful choice of referring expression that unobtrusively functions to undermine heroism. In sum, after the protagonist

66 Style and Rhetoric of Short Narrative Fiction

passes "from the line of battle," he is enabled to see the meaningless nature of war. Again, primarily through subtle stylistic choices, Crane invites us to subvert from a specific angle the meaning of war and romantic notions of heroism.

Many critics take the conventionally commendatory words in this passage at their face value. Eric Solomon focuses on the "lyricism" of the depiction, taking it that Crane was moved by "the sheer beauty of war" (1966: 124); Bettina Knapp is impressed by "the melodic and visual beauty" of the description, which, in his view, renders war "as a glorious but viciously cruel experience" (1987: 169); Robert Stallman sets store by the scene's appearing "like something in 'a historical painting,' or fixed and statue-like" (1952: 262). Milne Holton makes a comparison between this description, which he takes to be representing the positive side of war, and the description of the hospital (e.g. an "interminable crowd of bandaged men"), which he takes to be embodying the negative side (1972: 145). Such readings of the passage are a result of the interaction of conventional interpretive frames and impressions of the surface details, overlooking Crane's satire underneath. Shaw also fails to perceive the disparity between the superficial meaning of the commendatory words and what Crane really intends them to convey in the undercurrent of the text. As a result, she only comes up with the unconvincing assertion that "this carefully contrived, idealized picture must be recognized as manifest fiction if the reader is to identify the satiric nature of this narrative" (1985: 94). In effect, what Crane offers to his readers on a deeper level is far from an idealized picture but is in itself a satirical picture with the commendatory words actually playing the function of deflating contemporary heroics.

It should have become clear that, behind the overt plot development, Crane has created an undercurrent to emasculate the soldiers. The satirical effect is reinforced by the subsidiary undercurrent to replace fighting against the enemy with internal conflicts, as well as by a related description of a meaningless battle scene. The three forces join hands to form an overall satirical covert progression against war and romantic notions of heroism.

CONTEXTUAL AND INTERTEXTUAL RELATIONS

As we know, Crane had no experience of war until 1897, and the war narratives published earlier like *The Red Badge of Courage: An Episode of the American Civil War* (1895) and "A Mystery of Heroism" were based on his reading relevant materials, interviewing veterans and on his own imagination. In 1897 Crane went to Greece to report on the Greco-Turkish war, and in 1898 to Cuba to report on the Spanish-American war. These experiences "allowed him personally to see behind war's romantic, imperialistic façade" (Shaw 1991: 29). Starting from the battle of Velestino in the Greek war, Crane was intent upon reporting the "true face" of war, whose "real

Style and Unobtrusive Emasculating Satire   67

product" was "the mutilation of human bodies" (Benfey 1992: 209). He also tried to define the product of war by a wounded soldier on the road to Volo: "Behind him was the noise of the battle: the roar and rumble of an enormous factory. This was the product. This was the product, not so well finished as some, but sufficient to express the plan of the machine. This wounded soldier explained the distinct roar. He defined it" (quoted in Benfey 1992: 210). Crane cherished sympathy for the youth deluded by romanticized notions of heroism, saying that "if from time to time he is made to look ridiculous, it is not his fault at all. It is the fault of the public" (Crane 1971: 173). He wrote in a self-mocking fashion, "We are as a people a great collection of the most arrant kids about anything that concerns war, and if we can get a chance to perform absurdly we usually seize it" (ibid.). And he goes on to say:

> I know of one newspaper whose continual cabled instructions to its men in Cuba were composed of interrogations as to the doings and appearance of various unhappy society young men who were decently and quietly doing their duty along o'Nolan [a private shot dead] and the others. The correspondents of this paper, being already impregnated with soldierly feeling, finally arose and said they'd be lamed if they would stand it. (Crane 1971: 173)

Significantly, Crane's war reporting was "a sustained and startling exception" since it moved away from conventional patriotic claims and the usual description of "victories and reverses, courage and cowardice" towards the "unmasking of war" as it is, "forever issuing correctives" on people's romanticized notions of war (Benfey 1992: 209–11). Indeed, long before anti-war writers like Wilfred Owen, Siegfried Sassoon, and Robert Graves, Crane "had confronted the chauvinism, the imperialism, the patriotic humbug of a bellicose decade that gloried in the honor and self-sacrifice of war" (Beaver 1982: 191). Thomas Gullason asserts that "none was a more ardent anti-imperialist, a more serious, defiant, sincere humanitarian than Stephen Crane" (1958: 237).

Not surprisingly, Crane's narratives about war written after he had personally experienced it tend to be more scathing in satire than those created earlier. "An Episode of War" is surely more satirical than *The Red Badge of Courage: An Episode of the American Civil War,* but scholars differ as to the dates of creation and publication of this narrative. Some hold the view that "An Episode of War" was written in 1899 and was published in England in *Last Words* in 1902.[10] But a more convincing account by some other scholars is that the narrative was created during 1895 to 1896, but for various reasons was not published until 1899 (Schaefer 1996: 114; Wertheim 1997: 143). In any case, one point is beyond dispute, that is, "An Episode of War" was in print not earlier than 1899. As indicated above, Crane in the 1897 inventory designated the narrative as "The Loss of an Arm," but in the published version, the title is changed to the much more satirical "An Episode

68 *Style and Rhetoric of Short Narrative Fiction*

of War." We have good reason to infer that after having experienced war personally, when revising the narrative for publication, Crane replaced the original title with a more satirical one and may have made other changes in the same direction.

Mary Shaw observes that a "comparison of Crane's treatment of romanticized traditional heroism in earlier works, such as 'A Mystery of Heroism' and 'An Episode of War,' to later works, such as 'The Upturned Face' and 'The Kicking Twelfth,' reveals that Crane's attack on idealized heroism is much more direct and severe in Crane's later works" (Shaw, 1991: 29). As for the similarity between "A Mystery of Heroism" and "An Episode of War," Shaw only mentions Crane's suggestion of the meaninglessness of idealized heroism "by the empty bucket in 'A Mystery of Heroism' and by the lieutenant's amputated arm in 'An Episode of War' " (ibid.). But as analyzed above, in "An Episode of War," Crane invites readers to see the lieutenant's amputated arm in relation to the satirical undercurrent throughout the narrative, which renders the satire much more scathing. We have already seen the contrast between Crane's depiction of a manly lieutenant in "A Mystery of Heroism" and that of an emasculated lieutenant in "An Episode of War." Let us now compare the description of the battery in "An Episode of War" as quoted above with a corresponding description in "A Mystery of Heroism":

> The battery on the hill presently engaged in a frightful duel. The white legs of the gunners scampered this way and that way, and the officers redoubled their shouts. The guns, with their demeanours of stolidity and courage, were typical of something infinitely self-possessed in this clamour of death that swirled around the hill. (Crane 1965: 260)

In describing a battery, the implied authors of the two Crane texts use very different stylistic choices. In "A Mystery of Heroism," the stylistic choices show a somewhat heroic battery engaged in a fierce fighting against the enemy with "stolidity and courage," while those in "An Episode of War" implicitly represent a battery that is marked by internal strife and that rapidly retreats from the battle like a transport team.

It is worth mentioning that in its satirical undercurrent that replaces fighting against the enemy with internal conflicts, "An Episode of War" comes quite close to "The Upturned Face" (1900), which similarly focuses on the internal tension and strife involved in burying the body of a comrade (with the shooting between the opposing troops merely forming the background), thus also subverting romanticized heroics. But the subversion is more noticeable in "The Upturned Face," whose title explicitly refers to the "chalk-blue face" of the corpse and whose overt plot development centers on burying the corpse. Crane's "The Kicking Twelfth" also presents an overt subversion of heroics with its ironic title and an overt plot development marked by satirical contrasts similar to what we have seen in Crane's "War is Kind." The following passage is a case in point:

Style and Unobtrusive Emasculating Satire 69

It could be said that there were only two prominent points of view expressed by the men after their victorious arrival on the crest. One was defined in the exulting use of the corps' cry ["Kim up the Kickers"]. The other was a grief-stricken murmur which is invariably heard after a hard fight: "My God, we're all cut to pieces!" . . . It was the moment of despair, the moment of the heroism which comes to the chosen of the war god. (50–51)

In the last sentence, Crane, through the juxtaposition of the repeated "the moment of," deridingly or dialectically equates "despair" with "heroism," thus reinforcing the preceding satirical device of putting exultation on a par with a grief-stricken state. Moreover, similar to the emasculation in "An Episode of War" but in a much less subtle way, Crane uses what we may call "clownization" to deprive the army men of their dignity in "The Kicking Twelfth," where we find many explicitly ridiculing descriptions, such as "A maddened and badly frightened mob of Kickers came tumbling into the trench and shot at the backs of fleeing men. And at that very moment the action was won, and won by the Kickers. . . . a hammered and thin and dirty line of figures which was His Majesty's Twelfth Regiment of the Line. . . . [The protagonist] presented himself directly [at the ending], his face covered with disgraceful smudges, and he had also torn his breeches" (51). Compared with the covert emasculation, such overt "clownization" more directly subverts the heroic images of soldiers in traditional romanticized notions. It is not surprising that, Mary Shaw, with an eye for satire, readily perceives the severe satire on the textual surface of "The Kicking Twelfth" and "The Upturned Face," but still overlooks, like other critics, the severely satirical undercurrent in "An Episode of War."

In this chapter, we have seen how stylistic choices, among other textual elements, subtly and continuously interact in "An Episode of War" to build up, behind the overt plot development, a sustained undercurrent to convey the meaninglessness of war and the illusory nature of romanticized heroism. The undercurrent can easily be overlooked, since it is not a deeper level of meaning of the main line of action but is composed mainly of textual elements that appear to be peripheral or digressive to the main line of action. It should have become clear that overlooking the satirical undercurrent may result in a distorted picture of the ethical import of the text, a partial appreciation of the aesthetic techniques, and a wrong inference of the implied author's rhetorical purposes. This is a point that will be further shown, though from different angles, by the later chapters exploring more or less subversive covert progressions.

3 Style, Surprise Ending, and Covert Mythologization
Chopin's "Désirée's Baby"

Kate Chopin's "Désirée's Baby" (1893) is widely anthologized, regarded not only as Chopin's most successful work but also as "a superb piece of short fiction" (Wolff 1978: 133), "one of the best of its kind in American literature" (Arner 1996: 145), and "one of the world's great short stories" (Reilly 1996: 73).

The narrative has a highly dramatic plot: The female protagonist Désirée is a foundling adopted by the Valmondés. After growing to womanhood, she is wooed and wed by Armand Aubigny, a neighboring planter who bears one of the finest names in Louisiana. Désirée gives birth to a son who appears to be of mixed race. Armand spurns both mother and child for their black blood, and Désirée, holding her baby, commits suicide.[1] Eventually, Armand learns that the baby's African features come from him instead of Désirée.

This narrative has attracted much critical attention. Most critics take it primarily as a story protesting against racism. However, Catherine Lundie (1994: 131) writes: "Readers and critics see the story as a tragedy of racism, of the slave system. But in fact it is something much more specific: a tragedy of the African American woman. The condition of being black and female is much more debilitating than that of being black and male." This view is shared by some other critics, who see Désirée as a victim of both racial and sexual discrimination (see, for instance, Elfenbein 1989: 126–31; Skaggs 1985: 25–26; Toth 1981: 205–7). In contrast to the race-oriented view and the concern with both race and sex, some critics take a gender-oriented view, focusing almost exclusively on the unequal relationship between Désirée as a woman and Armand as representing masculinist oppression (see, for instance, Foster and LeJeune 1997).[2] Taking into account still another issue, Ellen Peel (1990: 230) sees the narrative as lying "at the nexus of concerns of sex, race, and class." She criticizes the text for merely inviting "readers to pity the suffering caused by inequalities of power but not to wonder how those inequalities could change" (ibid.). Viewing the narrative in terms of literary history, Robert D. Arner (1996: 145) puts the story in "the *Uncle Tom's Cabin* tradition and the *Clarissa* tradition." In terms of the former tradition, Arner (ibid.: 140) thinks that, though there is no absolute distinction between white and black in the text, "the [color] line is so indelibly

Style, Surprise Ending, and Covert Mythologization 71

fixed in the white man's mind" that "acts of renunciation are difficult to perform and no single act is sufficient to redeem the South from the curse of its racial caste system." Some critics go beyond race and sex politics and take Armand's "cruelty towards the slaves, and ultimately towards his wife and child" as "not simply a product of nineteenth-century racism" but related to "the dark side of personality" (Foy 1991: 222) or the "potential for personal evil that he shares with all fellow creatures" (Wolff 1978: 129).[3]

This chapter will reveal that, behind the overt plot development, there exists a covert textual progression that implicitly conveys a racist stance and unobtrusively mythologizes the Southern racial system.[4] This covert progression depends both on the interaction among stylistic choices in different parts of the text and on the surprise ending. As I will show below, if we only look at local textual details, we will be hard put to discern the covert progression. And before reaching the surprise ending, we only have a contrast between better whites and a worse white with the latter discriminating against and oppressing the blacks. But with the surprise ending, coupled with the interaction of stylistic choices in different parts of the text, the picture is implicitly turned into a racist one, opposing superior whites to inferior blacks.

It should first be noted that the Southern racial system was marked by the "one-drop rule"—any person with one drop of black blood was deemed black (see Peel 1990: 227; Williamson 1980: 98). Accordingly, I will use "black" to refer to any person with such blood in this fictional world. If racism consists of racial discrimination and racial oppression, the implied author of this narrative has created a covert textual progression where (really) white characters never perpetrate racial discrimination and oppression but instead make life gay for enslaved blacks and happy for free blacks. By contrast, in this fictional world, (really) black characters are guilty of racial discrimination, and it is only the black planter who oppresses black people. When we come to discern the covert progression, we will realize that "Désirée's Baby" is in essence a racist text that is directed neither against the Southern racial system nor against the dark side of human nature but against the inferiority of the black blood.

RACIST COVERT PROGRESSION BEHIND
ANTI-RACIST PLOT DEVELOPMENT

At the beginning of the narrative, Madame Valmondé, Désirée's step mother, drives over to L'Abri to see Désirée and her baby. On her way, she recalls how her husband found Désirée lying asleep at the gateway of their plantation and the childless Valmondés adopted her. People had various speculations about Désirée's origin, but in time Madame Valmondé believes that it is "a beneficent Providence" (173) who has sent the child to her. Désirée's obscure origin foreshadows the later suspicion that Désirée's baby's black blood comes from Désirée.

72 Style and Rhetoric of Short Narrative Fiction

Then Madame Valmondé goes on to recall how Armand Aubigny fell in love with Désirée, with the narratorial comment: "That was the way all the Aubignys fell in love, as if struck by a pistol shot. . . . The passion that awoke in him that day, when he saw her at the gate, swept along like an avalanche, or like a prairie fire, or like anything that drives headlong over all obstacles" (173). The assertive nominal group "all the Aubignys," coupled with the forceful parallel images, foregrounds a point of similarity—the only similarity mentioned in the narrative—between the young master Armand (whom the surprise ending reveals to be black) and his white father, old Aubigny. This may lead readers to believe that the (black) young master is just like his (white) father in terms of love. But if we consider the textual details in different parts of the text and open our minds to a covert progression behind the overt plot, we will find essential difference between the father and the son in terms of racial discrimination and oppression. The white father falls in love with a *black* woman and, instead of just having an affair with her, marries her and lets his mulatto son inherit his "oldest and proudest name," making both mother and child very happy. By contrast, the (really) black Armand marries a *white* girl for love and then, having mistaken her for a woman of mixed race, spurns both her and his mulatto son, leading to their tragic death. It is not surprising that this essential contrast in the textual undercurrent has not received critical attention since the implied author is an artful ideologist, liable to mislead readers with local stylistic devices, such as those used to establish the superficial similarity between Armand and his father.

The following passage, however, explicitly introduces a contrast between the (really) black Armand and Désirée's white father, Mr. Valmondé. The latter asks the former to consider Désirée's obscure origin when the former wants to marry her: "Monsieur Valmondé grew practical and wanted things well considered: that is, the girl's obscure origin. Armand looked into her eyes and did not care. He was reminded [by Monsieur Valmondé] that she was nameless. What did it matter about a name when he could give her one of the oldest and proudest in Louisiana?" (174). In the overt plot, we see Mr. Valmondé as being marked by racial discrimination in that he is concerned about Désirée's race, while Armand does not care about it. But if we take into account relevant stylistic choices in other parts of the narrative, we will discern an opposite picture in the covert progression: the white Mr. Valmondé is free from racial discrimination since he himself does not hesitate to adopt Désirée with her obscure origin, and when she is mistaken for being colored, the Valmondés not only offer her their home but also claim her to be their "own" (see below). By contrast the black Armand is marked by strong racial discrimination, and he spurns both his wife and his son for their black blood.

Then the question arises: Why does Mr. Valmondé ask Armand to consider Désirée's obscure origin? The answer is not far to seek: Mr. Valmondé's words concerning Désirée's obscure origin function to pave the way for her mistaken identity later, which means that this is an artistic device of foreshadowing. If we merely look at the local stylistic choices, we can only see

Style, Surprise Ending, and Covert Mythologization   73

Mr. Valmondé as having the sense of racial discrimination, but if we take an "overall" view of the relevant textual details in different parts of the narrative, we will be able to perceive Mr. Valmondé as being free from racial discrimination.

When Madame Valmondé reaches Désirée's home, the L'Abri house, there appears a description of the house from her point of view:

> she shuddered at the first sight of it, as she always did. It was a sad looking place, which for many years had not known the gentle presence of a mistress, old Monsieur Aubigny having married and buried his wife in France, and she having loved her own land too well ever to leave it. The roof came down steep and black like a cowl, reaching out beyond the wide galleries that encircled the yellow stuccoed house. Big, solemn oaks grew close to it, and their thick-leaved, far-reaching branches shadowed it *like a pall*. Young Aubigny's [Armand's] rule was a strict one, *too*, and under it *his negroes had forgotten how to be gay*, as they had been during the old master's *easy-going and indulgent* lifetime. (174, italics added)

Critics focusing on the plot development have in general overlooked this description of the setting, which, however, has a very important role to play in the covert progression. In "Young Aubigny's rule was a strict one, too," the adverb "too," emphasized by the preceding comma, functions to link the (black) young master with the symbolic setting. Although what the "too" harks back is not clearly signaled, the adjective it modifies— "strict"—restricts the linkage to the harsh or forbidding quality of the setting, conveyed by such words as "steep," "solemn," and "like a pall" in the immediately preceding sentence, a simile that seems to foreshadow the tragic death of Désirée and her baby as caused by the young master (see below). This connection has been overlooked by previous critics, even when commenting on the passage. Brewster E. Fitz (2000: 85) thus focuses on "the *yellow* stuccoed house" (Fitz's italics), which leads him to speculative questions like "Is La Blanche the yellow daughter of old Monsieur Aubigny, and therefore an aunt of Armand?"[5] In the covert progression, however, we can discern a much firmer association between the harsh-looking setting and the strict rule of the (black) young master.

Significantly, although the white old master and the black young master have the same relationship to the house, in the covert progression the implied author, by using the adverb "too," links the forbidding and funereal house only with the young master, and moreover by a direct contrast between the young and the old in terms of personality, implicitly dissociates the old from any connection with the symbolic setting. And while the black young master's strict rule makes the enslaved blacks unhappy, the white old master is "easy-going and indulgent," enabling them to live a "gay" life—the term "indulgent" may even suggest an affectionate parent/

74 *Style and Rhetoric of Short Narrative Fiction*

child relationship. Through such subtle stylistic choices, the implied author implicitly invites the authorial audience to make negative ethical judgment on the black young master and positive ethical judgment on the white old master.

After Madame Valmondé enters Désirée's house, she sees Désirée and her baby lying on a couch. The day is very hot, but "the yellow nurse woman sat beside a window fanning herself" instead of the child in her charge (174), which forms a contrast with a later description of a little quadroon boy "fanning the child" in a similar situation (176). When Désirée puts a question to the light-skinned mulatto nurse, she answers it "majestically" (174), an adverb that seems to indicate her pride in front of Désirée. The abnormal behavior of the mulatto nurse appears to be of no importance to the plot development and therefore has not received any attention. But, as we will soon see, it forms an important constituent of the racist covert progression.

When Madame Valmondé notices the African features of Désirée's son, she "lifted it and walked with it over to the window that was lightest. She scanned the baby narrowly, then looked as searchingly at [the mulatto nurse], whose face was turned to gaze across the fields" (174–75). Apparently, at this time, the mulatto nurse already knows the child's being colored and she naturally believes that the black blood comes from Désirée with the "obscure origin." That is why she turns her face away—to avoid the embarrassing situation of having to confirm the suspicion of the baby's African origin. And that is why she is "fanning herself" instead of the child and why she answers Désirée's question "majestically"—she treats the colored mother and son coldly and proudly. Like Armand, the mulatto nurse is guilty of racial discrimination.

One may argue that the racial discrimination of the black nurse and the really black Armand springs from their personalities rather than from their race. We cannot rule out this possibility, but an overall consideration of the stylistic choices in the text does lead to a general picture divided by race: all white characters are free from racial discrimination and, by contrast, all black characters' racial attitude, whenever described, is guilty of racial discrimination. As regards the black characters, leaving aside the enslaved blacks working in the fields (whose racial attitudes are not described) and the little quadroon boy (who is too young to have gained a racial awareness of Désirée's baby), there are only two other black individuals mentioned in the story: Armand's late mother and an enslaved woman called La Blanche (whose invisible blackness plays a role in Armand's mistaking Désirée for being of mixed race). These two women are never put into interaction with other black characters (except of course for the mother/son relationship), and the text contains no indication of their attitude towards other blacks. That is to say, when the narrative conveys people's racial attitudes, either directly or indirectly, blacks are always—and whites, who are in the same racial situations, are never—guilty of racial discrimination against blacks. This racial divide has been blocked from view by the anti-racist overt plot development.

Style, Surprise Ending, and Covert Mythologization   75

When Madame Valmondé talks with Désirée about Armand's attitude towards the baby, Désirée, who is not yet aware of her baby's being colored, says:

> "Oh, Armand is the proudest father in the parish . . . he hasn't punished one of [the enslaved blacks]—not one of them—since baby is born. Even Négrillon, who pretended to have burnt his leg that he might rest from work—he only laughed, and said Négrillon was a great scamp. Oh, mamma, I'm so happy; it frightens me."
>
> What Désirée said was true. Marriage, and later the birth of his son had softened Armand Aubigny's imperious and exacting nature greatly. This was what made the gentle Désirée so happy, for she loved him desperately. When he frowned she trembled, but loved him. When he smiled, she asked no greater blessing of God. But Armand's dark, handsome face had not often been disfigured by frowns since the day he fell in love with her. (175)

In the overt plot, we see the happy married life of Armand, Désirée, and their son, with an emphasis set on the transforming power of love (Toth 1981: 206; Peel 1990: 236). Taking into account the tragic ending, Robert D. Arner (1996), however, draws attention to the difference between Armand and his father as well as Désirée's foster parents. He asserts that "the story makes clear that Armand does not really love Désirée; he thinks of her as a possession, a rich prize to display to his friends and to flatter his vanity," while the story depicts the real love of Armand's father and Désirée's foster parents which forms an "antidote to the poison of racial abstraction" (1996: 141). But the text does convey emphatically that Armand falls in love with Désirée "as if struck by a pistol shot" and that he loves his wife and son dearly until he discovers his son's African features and mistakes his wife for being colored.

If we open our minds to a textual undercurrent, we may see a very different picture: it is not a matter, as Arner believes, of Armand's lacking love and the other persons' having love, but a matter of (the really black) Armand's being guilty of racial discrimination and the other (white) characters being free of racial discrimination. Indeed, the drastic change in Armand's feelings towards Désirée and the baby, which forms a direct contrast with the white characters' constant feelings in similar racial situations, emphatically brings out his racial discrimination.

In the covert progression, the stylistic choices in the passage quoted above function implicitly to reinforce the contrast between superior white and inferior black slave owners. Like Armand's white father, the (really) white Désirée is by nature benevolent and indulgent to the enslaved blacks: when Armand treats the enslaved blacks kindly, she feels extremely happy ("I'm so happy," "This was what made the gentle Désirée so happy"); and when Armand again treats the enslaved blacks cruelly, Désirée is "miserable enough

76 Style and Rhetoric of Short Narrative Fiction

to die" (175). Both Désirée's happiness and her misery indicate her innate benevolence towards the enslaved blacks and function to set off Armand's imperious or satanic treatment of them. It is significant that Armand's kindness to the enslaved is merely temporary. The head noun "nature" in "Armand Aubigny's imperious and exacting nature" has a significant role to play in the covert progression. Désirée's words "it frightens me" also point to Armand's innate harshness towards the enslaved blacks.

The above quoted passage does indicate the transforming power of love, but given the racial concern of the covert progression, it also seems to imply that being in love with and close to the white blood enables the (really) black Armand to change temporarily for the better.[6] When Armand is estranged from his white wife (now mistaken for a mulatto)—his having loosened the tie with the white blood, "the very spirit of Satan seemed suddenly to take hold of him in his dealings with the slaves" (175).[7]

Missing the racist covert progression, Arner (1996: 140) sees the relation between Armand and his father as one between (white) old and young slave owners in general, observing that "the sins of the fathers are repeatedly visited upon the children, for Armand inherits not only his father's slaves but also a set of rigid social codes prescribing his attitude toward the Negro" (1996: 140). Emily Toth also puts Armand on a par with white slave owners generally. In "[Armand's] behavior to his wife and to his slaves," Toth (1981: 207) says, "the reader sees what Harriet Beecher Stowe also showed: slavery destroys not only the slave's character, but also the master's. Chopin shows that patriarchy limits the development not only of the wife, but also of the husband." Such comments unwittingly obliterate the divide the implied author has implicitly set up between the superior white and the inferior black.

When Désirée by chance notices her son's African features, she is frightened:

> Presently her husband entered the room, and without noticing her, went to a table and began to search among some papers which covered it.
>
> "Armand," she called to him, *in a voice which must have stabbed him, if he was human. But he did not notice.* "Armand," she said again. Then she rose and tottered towards him. "Armand," she panted once more, clutching his arm, "look at our child. What does it mean? tell me."
>
> He *coldly* but gently loosened her fingers from about his arm and thrust the hand away from him. "Tell me what it means!" she cried despairingly.
>
> "It means," he answered lightly, "that the child is not white; it means that you are not white."
>
> . . . "Look at my hand; whiter than yours, Armand," she laughed hysterically.
>
> "As white as La Blanche's," he returned *cruelly;* and went away leaving her alone with their child.

Style, Surprise Ending, and Covert Mythologization 77

When she could hold a pen in her hand, she sent a despairing letter to Madame Valmondé.

"My mother, they tell me I am not white. Armand has told me I am not white. For God's sake tell them it is not true. You must know it is not true. I shall die. I must die. I cannot be so unhappy, and live."

The answer that came was brief:

"*My own* Désirée: Come *home to Valmondé*; back to your mother who loves you. Come with your child." (176–77, italics added)

In the overt plot, we see the Southern racial system as the victimizer and Désirée as the victim, and we perceive Armand's behavior as being representative of that of white slave owners in general. In the covert progression, however, we discern the continued contrast between the inferior black and the superior white. The stylistic choices "if he was human," "coldly," and "cruelly" interact to convey the innate cruelty of the (really) black Armand. It is true that the implied author also uses "gently" to describe Armand's action, but the word, which merely indicates the moderateness of the action, is preceded by "coldly" and used to modify the cold action "loosened her fingers from about his arm and thrust the hand away from him." It thus does not have any power to alleviate Armand's "inhuman" cruelty in discriminating against his wife and his son (notice the contrast between Désirée's "our child" [also the narrator's "their child"] and Armand's distancing "the child"). The same applies to the word "lightly," which is followed by Armand's cold words. By contrast, Désirée's foster parents are free from racial discrimination as indicated by her foster mother's affectionate letter. Compare the original letter with a paraphrase:

"My own Désirée: Come home to Valmondé; back to your mother who loves you. Come with your child."

Paraphrase:

"My own Désirée: Come home; back to your mother who loves you.

The manor of Valmondé is owned by and named after Mr. Valmondé. The letter's spelling out "to Valmondé," which is very much redundant, functions to imply the welcome from Désirée's foster father as well. One may argue that this is just a matter of parental affection, but we should bear in mind that Armand's parental affection is, by contrast, determined by race: It totally disappears as soon as he finds his son to be colored. In the letter, the imperative last sentence "Come with your child" is also somewhat redundant—surely Désirée will take her baby with her. This sentence, which recalls the title of the narrative, functions to strengthen the contrast between the white Valmondés and the black Armand in terms of racial discrimination.

78 *Style and Rhetoric of Short Narrative Fiction*

In what follows, the text implicitly aligns the (really) black Armand with Satan and the (really) white Désirée with God:

> When the letter reached Désirée she went with it to her husband's study, and laid it open upon the desk before which he sat. She was like a stone image: silent, white, motionless after she placed it there.
>
> In silence he ran his cold eyes over the written words. He said nothing. "Shall I go, Armand?" she asked in tones sharp with agonized suspense.
>
> "Yes, go."
>
> "Do you want me to go?"
>
> "Yes, I want you to go."
>
> He thought Almighty God had dealt cruelly and unjustly with him; and felt, somehow, that he was paying Him back in kind when he stabbed thus into his wife's soul. Moreover he no longer loved her, because of the unconscious injury she had brought upon his home and his name.
>
> She turned away like one stunned by a blow, and walked slowly towards the door, hoping he would call her back.
>
> "Good-by, Armand," she moaned.
>
> He did not answer her. That was his last blow at fate. (176–77)

In the overt plot, we continue to see the Southern racial system as the victimizer and Désirée as the victim. But in the covert progression, we perceive the black Armand in his satanic spirit fighting against Almighty God,[8] with the white Désirée functioning as a martyr of sorts ("he was paying Him back in kind when he stabbed thus into his wife's soul") or perhaps even a saint ("Désirée had been sent to her [foster parents] by a beneficent Providence. . . . For the girl grew to be beautiful and gentle, affectionate and sincere,—the idol of Valmondé . . . Her hair [on her way to death] was uncovered and the sun's rays brought a golden gleam [perhaps suggesting a halo] from its brown meshes" (173–77).[9]

What is more, in the covert progression, the implied author invites the authorial audience to see Armand as the killer of Désirée with the following stylistic choices: "he stabbed thus into his wife's soul. . . . She turned away like one stunned by a blow. . . . That was his last blow." Indeed, if the (really) black Armand were a little bit like the nondiscriminating white characters or if he had a little less of the "spirit of the Satan," Désirée and her baby would have survived. Notice the implied author's stylistic choices that describe Désirée pinning her hope on Armand's keeping her and her increasing despair: " 'Shall I go, Armand?' she asked in tones sharp with agonized suspense," "walked slowly towards the door, hoping he would call her back," " 'Good-by, Armand,' she moaned." Earlier, the text emphasizes that Désirée loves Armand "desperately" ("When he frowned she trembled, but loved him. When he smiled, she asked no greater blessing of God" [175]), and now being bereft of his love simply means uttermost unhappiness and death to her.

Style, Surprise Ending, and Covert Mythologization   79

In fact, when Désirée is still in the dark about her son's African features and the racial problem has not yet surfaced for her, Armand's cold treatment of her and her son, coupled with his harsh treatment of the enslaved blacks, makes Désirée "miserable enough to die" (175), foreshadowing her final end caused by his coldness and cruelty.

Moreover, in the covert progression, we have the continued contrast between the nondiscrimination of Désirée's white foster parents (the letter inviting Désirée to go back to them) and the strong racial discrimination of the black Armand. Although Désirée's white foster parents are in a similar family situation as Armand (white foster parents in relation to colored foster daughter and white husband to colored wife), they bear no grudge against God for having sent them a mulatto because they are free of Armand's satanic spirit and racial discrimination. They only offer love and care to Désirée and her baby and claim the mulatto to be their "own." Moreover, Armand's inhuman nature and satanic spirit are set off by his loving and benevolent white father, from whom he has inherited "the oldest and proudest" name in Louisiana. It is highly ironic for the black son, who owes "his home and his name" to the nondiscrimination of his white father who marries a black wife, to discriminate against his wife and son. Through these direct contrasts between the white and black characters in similar racial situations, the implied author implicitly invites the authorial audience to see that Désirée's tragedy is caused by the ethical deficiencies of the black character himself.

It is not surprising that the implied author does not let Désirée return to her white foster parents, since the mythologization of the Southern racial system lies in attributing the severe consequences (including tragic deaths) of racial discrimination and oppression to a cruel black, who forms a stark contrast with the kind whites. It is far from fortuitous that in this fictional world, all whites are ethically perfect, but the black master and the yellow nurse are marked by ethical deficiencies. Moreover, it is not surprising that the implied author does not let any character in this narrative say anything about how unjust or otherwise flawed the racist thinking is, let alone take action against it (compare Peel 1990: 229–30), since the purpose of the narrative is to defend the Southern racial system, especially the racist assumption that the white race is superior to the black.

It is worth noting that, although Armand is of mixed race, the implied author uses various devices to indicate that his bad character comes from his black blood. First, the Maupassant-style surprise ending emphatically conveys Armand's African heritage. Second, since the outward indication of black versus white blood is usually the different color of the skin, Armand, not surprisingly, is endowed with "dark" skin (175) in contrast to the white-skinned Désirée (176–77).[10] Third, the implied author uses the setting to link the black mother and black son together. As analyzed above, although both Armand and his father bear the same relationship to the house, the implied author, through the use of subtle stylistic choices, only associates

80 *Style and Rhetoric of Short Narrative Fiction*

the symbolic house with the former, exclusive of the latter. In a similar fashion, the "sad-looking" condition of the house is only referred to Armand's mother ("had not known the gentle presence of a mistress. . . . she having loved her own land too well ever to leave it"), not to the present mistress, Désirée (who in effect should be more responsible for the present condition of the house). As a result, the ominous house functions to pair the black Armand with his black mother: The former's character is compared to the house's condition, and the latter is held responsible for that condition. It is true that for the sake of the surprise ending among other reasons, the identity of Armand's black mother has to be kept in the dark, and she therefore has to remain in Paris.[11] But the authorial narrator could have come up with a more neutral or more understandable reason (say, her having fallen ill) instead of the reason of her "having loved her own land too well ever to leave it," where the adverb "too" carries a somewhat reproaching tone.

It should have become clear that behind the anti-racist overt plot development, we have a racist textual undercurrent:

> **Overt plot:** The series of events show the extremely negative consequences of the Southern racial system, culminating in the death of the "colored" Désirée and her baby, which conveys the implied author's critical attitude toward racism. As cited above, many "readers and critics see the story as a tragedy of racism, of the slave system," and consequently, the story is placed in "the *Uncle Tom's Cabin* tradition." The color line is also seen as being "so indelibly fixed in the white man's mind" that "no single act is sufficient to redeem the South from the curse of its racial caste system."
>
> **Covert progression:** Through the interaction of textual details in different parts of the text, coupled with a surprise ending, there is created a textual undercurrent that conveys two different racial systems: one dominated by whites, and the other by a (real) black. In the former, since all whites are free from racial discrimination and racial oppression, enslaved blacks live gaily and a free black can even become the beloved wife of a white planter bearing "the oldest and proudest" name or the cherished foster daughter of the white master and mistress of another plantation. In the latter system, by contrast, not only do the enslaved suffer a great deal (from the "strict" and later "satanic" treatment by the really black master), but free persons, as represented by Désirée in her "mistaken" black identity, also meet with severe oppression. The tragic death of Désirée and her baby forms an indictment against black domination since only the (really) black persons have racial discrimination and only the (really) black planter practices racial oppression.

The covert progression implicitly undermines and subverts the anti-racist concern of the overt plot development, and the narrative is in essence a mythologization of the white-dominated Southern racial system and it is

Style, Surprise Ending, and Covert Mythologization   81

only against an imaginary racial system where the black becomes the master of society.

If we examine the stylistic choices at the end of the text carefully, we will find that in the covert progression, Armand continues his persecution of Désirée even after her death:

> Some weeks later there was a curious scene enacted at L'Abri. In the centre of the smoothly swept back yard was a great bonfire. Armand Aubigny sat in the wide hallway that commanded a view of the spectacle; and it was he who dealt out to a half dozen negroes the material which kept this fire ablaze.
>
> A graceful cradle of willow, with all its dainty furbishings, was laid upon the pyre, which had already been fed with the richness of a priceless layette. Then there were silk gowns, and velvet and satin ones added to these; laces, too, and embroideries; bonnets and gloves; for the corbeille had been of rare quality.
>
> The last thing to go was a tiny bundle of letters; innocent little scribblings that Désirée had sent to him during the days of their espousal. There was the remnant of one back in the drawer from which he took them. But it was not Désirée's; it was part of an old letter from his mother to his father. He read it. She was thanking God for the blessing of her husband's love:—
>
> "But above all," she wrote, "night and day, I thank the good God for having so arranged our lives that our dear Armand will never know that his mother, who adores him, belongs to the race that is cursed with the brand of slavery." (177–78)

In this final passage of the narrative, there are two different spatiotemporal frames, one is the present time in the back yard, where Armand deals out the things for burning, and the last thing he hands out is a bundle of letters. Then there comes an analepsis, going back to the room where Armand collected the letters: "There was the remnant of one back in the drawer from which he took them." Toth (1981: 205) observes, "After burning Désirée's effects, Armand finds a letter from his dead mother to his dead father." But surely, the discovery of the remnant of the letter occurred not after the burning in the yard but in the room when Armand was collecting the letters.[12] Moreover, after discovering the remnant—which is not in an envelope, nor within the bundle of letters—Armand "read it."[13] If we omit the post-modifying and explanatory words involved, we may see the textual movement more clearly: "There was the remnant of one back in the drawer. . . . He read it."

When Armand considered himself white and his wife and son black, it was natural for him to try to get rid of the things they left behind. But since he has discovered the remnant of his mother's letter and gets to know that his son's African features come from himself, why is he still burning those

82 Style and Rhetoric of Short Narrative Fiction

things? In a situation like this, any person with human feeling would be tortured by guilt and regret, and would cherish the things of the deceased. But there are simply no such indications, only a description of Armand's cold-blooded burning of the things left by his wife and son. One may argue that, to strengthen his false identity as a white, Armand is putting up a show of purifying his house from the traces of the "black" wife and son. But the burning takes place in the "back yard," where the only persons present are Armand and his own black slaves. A more plausible interpretation is that the black Armand is again engaged in his satanic fighting against God by continuing the persecution of Désirée as God's martyr. We recall that, when Armand discovered his son's African heritage and mistook his wife for a mulatto, he "thought Almighty God had dealt cruelly and unjustly with him; and felt, somehow, that he was paying Him back in kind when he stabbed thus into his wife's soul." The present discovery that he himself is, contrary to his firm belief, actually born black and Désirée born white surely makes him in his satanic spirit all the more resentful at God's treatment and all the more eager to pay Him back.[14] In the Bible and in literature, Satan is closely associated with fire, and here the black Armand seems to use satanic fire to continue the persecution of the white martyr Désirée both physically (burning her dresses, bonnets, laces, gloves) and spiritually (burning her "innocent little scribblings").[15] In terms of the physical aspect, the "silk gowns" and the rest of the clothes now burned look back to the fatal departure: "Désirée [on her way to commit suicide as God's martyr] had not changed the thin white garment nor the slippers which she wore. . . . She did not take the broad, beaten road which led to the far-off plantation of Valmondé. She walked across a deserted field, where the stubble bruised her tender feet, so delicately shod, and *tore her thin gown to shreds*" (177, italics added). Désirée's "thin gown" is a metonymy of her fragile body, and the stubble tearing it "to shreds" invites the authorial audience's strong sympathy since it implicitly symbolizes the destruction of this delicate (really white) woman as a martyr of God. In the covert progression, what we have in the final scene is a picture of the satanic black master joining hands with his black workers to continue the persecution, now with fire, of the white martyr Désirée and her son (whom Armand has disowned and who accompanies Désirée in her martyrdom).

Ellen Peel (1990: 230) observes that "through the traumas experienced by Armand, the story invites readers to pity the sufferings caused by inequalities of power" between the sexes and between the races.[16] But when Armand discovers his son's African features, the text only presents his harsher handling of the slaves, his inhuman treatment of his "black" wife ("if he was human") and his satanic defiance of God while depicting at length Désirée's traumatic suffering (176–77). And when Armand discovers his own black identity, the text likewise merely presents him as a cold-blooded master: "Armand Aubigny sat in the wide hallway that commanded a view of the spectacle; and it was he who dealt out to a half dozen negroes the

Style, Surprise Ending, and Covert Mythologization 83

material which kept this fire ablaze." The verb "command" and the emphatic syntactic pattern "it was . . . who . . ." underscore Armand's dominance, control, and agency. By examining the stylistic choices in a careful and overall way, we can see that the implied author is only inviting sympathy to the delicate white victim Désirée and not to Armand the victimizer with inferior black blood.

Catherine Lundie (1994: 131) correctly perceives where the text locates the trauma but fails to discern its racist implications: "The condition of being black and female is much more debilitating than that of being black and male. We see this in the final picture that we have of Armand, a grand Southern slaveholder, sitting in lonely state in his mansion, directing those darker skinned than he to destroy all that would remind him of his tragedy." Later in her argument Lundie (ibid.: 134) also points out that Désirée is in effect "a white woman" persecuted by a villainous "black man." But without discovering the racist covert progression, she is only concerned with the issue of miscegenation:

[The black Armand] will pass as white for the rest of his days, but even if he did not, even if his heritage were made known, it would do the (white) woman he married no good; she "may be vindicated by the discovery that she is not responsible for the racial characteristics of their child, but she will be forever stigmatized socially by the fact that she has been possessed by a black man and has borne his son." [Elfenbein 1989: 127] (Lundie 1994: 134)

Not surprisingly, Lundie still sees the narrative as an indictment against the Southern racial system, with "the particular powerlessness of women caught within that system" (ibid.), and she takes the fact that Désirée turns out to be white and Armand black as a contradiction to the narrative's general concern with "the particular plight of the African American woman or the doubly damning effects of being black and female" (ibid.: 133).

These comments indicate that missing the covert textual progression will unavoidably result in a misunderstanding of the implied author's rhetorical purposes and thematic design. When we gradually discern the racist covert progression, we will resist more and more strongly the ethical norms of the narrative. Booth (1961: 157) says, "A bad book . . . is often most clearly recognizable because the implied author asks that we judge according to norms that we cannot accept." The case is much more complicated with "Désirée's Baby," which has an ethically unacceptable covert progression hidden behind an ethically agreeable overt plot. When the covert progression gradually comes into view, we will become increasingly critical of the implied author's ethical stance, but, as mentioned in the introduction, we may not totally dismiss the narrative as being bad and worthless. As we have seen, the covert progression is created with remarkable stylistic and structural ingenuity, which is aesthetically appealing. But of course, we do

84 *Style and Rhetoric of Short Narrative Fiction*

feel deeply regretful for the implied author's using artistry for unacceptable ethical ends.

Now with the covert progression in mind, we turn to a consideration of the life experiences of the flesh-and-blood Chopin and other fictional narratives related to "Désirée's Baby."

EXTRATEXTUAL AND INTERTEXTUAL CONSIDERATIONS

From the biographies by Daniel S. Rankin (1932), Per Seyersted (1969), and Jean Bardot (1992) as well as the culturally oriented critical study by Helen Taylor (1989), the following picture emerges. When Kate Chopin was a girl of ten in St. Louis, the Civil War broke out, and her family, which owned many black slaves, took the Southern side. Although the city "was ruled with an iron Union hand," Chopin's half-brother joined the Confederates, and Chopin herself was known as the "Littlest Rebel" of St. Louis, tearing down the Union flag from the front porch at the risk of being arrested (Seyersted 1969: 20). Chopin's half-brother, with whom she had strong emotional ties, was captured in 1862 and later exchanged, but on his way to his regiment he died of typhoid fever. This caused Chopin deep and long-term grief. Her support for the Confederate cause and objection to emancipation "must have accorded well with her husband's overt racism" (Taylor 1989: 143).

Her husband, Oscar Chopin, was the son of a wealthy Louisiana planter, Dr. Victor Chopin, who bought his vast Red River plantation after the death of its owner, Dr. Robert McAlpin. Legend has it that this was the site of the plantation in *Uncle Tom's Cabin* and McAlpin was the model for the cruel Simon Legree. In popular memory, Victor Chopin is put on a par with McAlpin in terms of the extreme cruelty to slaves. Although some scholars speculate that "perhaps some of the odious traits" associated with the latter have come "to cloud the remembrance of Dr. Chopin" (Rankin 1932: 86; see also Bardot 1992: 30), it is beyond doubt that Victor Chopin did treat slaves with "great severity" (Bardot 1992: 30). Oscar Chopin himself was a member of the activist branch of the racist White League, and he and his wife lived after the Civil War in a region with strong racial tensions (Taylor 1989: 144–45). Throughout, Kate Chopin forms a sharp contrast with the flesh-and-blood author of *Uncle Tom's Cabin*. Harriet Beecher Stowe, growing up in Connecticut, was influenced by the antislavery sentiment prevailing at her father's school and, upon moving to Maine in 1850, was stirred more than ever by antislavery discussions, which prompted her to write the famous novel (Hart 1983: 642).

If *Uncle Tom's Cabin* provides a more or less realistic picture of the cruelty of the white master towards the slaves, "Désirée's Baby" presents a picture contrary to Chopin's life experiences.[17] While Chopin's father-in-law was a very harsh master, Désirée's is described as benevolent, treating his slaves in an "easy-going and indulgent" way. While Louisiana's racial caste

Style, Surprise Ending, and Covert Mythologization 85

system forbad interracial marriage by law (Dominguez 1986: 25–26), in "Désirée's Baby" the white master bearing "the oldest and proudest" name in Louisiana marries a black woman (though in Paris), and Désirée's white foster mother not only readily provides a home for the "colored" Désirée but claims the "mulatto" to be her "own" daughter.[18] Moreover, while the real-life Chopin "knew the faithful love of her negro 'mammy' " (Seyersted 1969: 21), the mulatto nurse in "Désirée's Baby" is depicted as "fanning herself" instead of the baby in her charge.

Significantly, in the Southern racial system, the "requirement for masters and slaves produces an ideology of racial superiority, with its own philosophers, legal scholars, and pseudoscientists to validate it," and "genetic and racial theories" emerged "as powerful tools of white domination" (Mullen 1994: 79–80). "Désirée's Baby," however, was written at a time (November 1892) when the South's racial system had long been abolished and the defense of that system could only be made more or less implicitly. Not surprisingly, the narrative has an anti-racist overt plot. But behind it, there exists a racist covert progression which implicitly defends the superiority of the white blood and unobtrusively mythologizes the Southern racial system. This is a disguised literary return to the earlier defense of white-dominated slavery in reality. Clearly, the extratextual information about Chopin's background and sociohistorical context throws important light on the reasons underlying the racist stance of the implied author of "Désirée's Baby."

Chopin only wrote two narratives about antebellum Louisiana, the other being "La Belle Zoraïde" (1894, one year after "Désirée's Baby"). It is a tragic love story told by an old Negress to her mistress at bedtime. The title character is Zoraïde, a beautiful enslaved mulatto maid. She falls in love with a handsome Negro working in the fields on another plantation, but her mistress wants her to marry that planter's mulatto body servant, whom Zoraïde detests. Since Zoraïde disobeys the mistress's order and "sins" with her lover, her mistress not only induces that planter to sell her lover to a far away place but also deprives Zoraïde of her baby, resulting in her becoming incurably insane. Peggy Skaggs (1985: 20) sees the narrative as an illustration of "one of Chopin's best themes: that tragedy results when a person is robbed of her right to be her own person and to love whom she will," and Per Seyersted (1969: 93) reads the narrative as "more a plea for woman's right to choose her husband than a direct condemnation of slavery." I agree that the narrative is a plea for woman's rights, but if we examine the implied author's stylistic choices in an overall way and open our minds to another textual movement behind the plot development, we will discern that, behind the overt plot as such, there is a racist covert progression aimed at mythologizing slavery which regrettably undercuts the feminist theme.

At the beginning of her narrative, the old Negress presents a very affectionate relation between the victimizing white mistress and the victimized slave girl:

86 *Style and Rhetoric of Short Narrative Fiction*

No wonder Zoraïde was as charming and as dainty as the finest lady of la rue Royale: from a toddling thing she had been brought up at her mistress's side; her fingers had never done rougher work than sewing a fine muslin seam; and she even had her own little black servant to wait upon her. Madame, who was her godmother as well as her mistress, would often say to her:

"Remember, Zoraïde, when you are ready to marry, it must be in a way to do honor to your bringing up. It will be at the Cathedral. Your wedding gown, your corbeille, all will be of the best; I shall see to that myself. You know, M'sieur Ambroise is ready whenever you say the word; and his master is willing to do as much for him as I shall do for you." (1894b: 282)[19]

The adjectives "charming" and "dainty" are usually used to depict fine upper-middle-class white girls. And the comparative "as the finest lady of la rue Royale" more explicitly puts the slave girl on a par with such white girls. This paves the way for presenting the enslaved and later victimized Zoraïde as a happy daughter of her "godmother"—her white owner and victimizer. The white mistress not only has "brought up" the enslaved Zoraïde, but also has provided her with a "servant to wait upon her," treating Zoraïde just as her own daughter. The old Negress's narratorial description is backed up by the stylistic choices in the white mistress's own words, such as "do honor to your bringing up," "at the Cathedral," "will be of the best," and "I shall see to that myself." Similarly, the enslaved servant Ambroise is depicted very much as a beloved "son" of his master.[20] Significantly, the white mistress tries to arrange Zoraïde's love and marriage precisely because she treats the enslaved maid as her own daughter. And it is out of loving concern that the godmother gets angry at her wanting to marry a Negro working in the fields instead of the good-mannered body servant "M'sieur Ambroise," "with his shining whiskers like a white man's" (282). When Zoraïde confesses that she has sinned, her mistress is "so actually pained, so wounded" (285–86), as a mother would be. As for the purpose of taking away Zoraïde's baby, the old Negress narrates: "Madame had hoped, in thus depriving Zoraïde of her child, to have her young waiting-maid again at her side free, happy, and beautiful as of old. But there was a more powerful will than Madame's at work—the will of the good God, who had already designed that Zoraïde should grieve with a sorrow that was never more to be lifted in this world" (287). Through the old Negress as a mouthpiece of the implied author, the tragic suffering of the enslaved maid is attributed to the retributive design of "the good God" for her having "sinned" (285). When Zoraïde goes mad,

Madame [was] stung with sorrow and remorse at seeing this terrible affliction [from God] that had befallen her dear Zoraïde. Consulting with Doctor Langlé, they decided to bring back to the mother the real

Style, Surprise Ending, and Covert Mythologization   87

baby of flesh and blood that was now toddling about, and kicking its heels in the dust yonder upon the plantation.

It was Madame herself who led the pretty, tiny little "griffe" girl to her mother. . . . "Here," said Madame, approaching, "here, my poor dear Zoraïde, is your own little child. Keep her; she is yours. No one will ever take her from you again." (289)

The epithet "terrible" and the head noun "affliction" subtly indicate the white mistress's sympathy towards Zoraïde. The stylistic choices "was stung with sorrow and remorse" and "her dear Zoraïde" (also "my poor dear Zoraïde"), coupled with "consulting with Doctor Langlé," more explicitly present the white mistress as a loving mother of the enslaved girl. But Zoraïde, condemned by "the good God" to demented sorrow, cannot "be induced to let her own child approach her" (289). The story ends with a dialogue between the old Negress, as narrator, and her mistress; both of whom empathize with the enslaved girl—"the poor little one!"

Alice Petry (1996: 7) puts "La Belle Zoraïde" and "Désirée's Baby" on a par as narratives "in which Chopin explored such unsavory topics as miscegenation, suicide, illegitimacy, and madness." Regarding the former narrative, Lundie (1994: 138) asserts that there is "little question that [the Negress's] narrative contains an embedded social criticism and that Chopin herself therefore intends criticism of the system." She sees the white mistress as the sole victimizer of Zoraïde: "The double deprivation of lover and child changes Zoraïde from 'la belle' to 'la folle,' and the sanity of a black woman is forfeit to the selfish wishes of a white" (ibid.: 136). What such previous critics have overlooked is that, through a covert progression behind the plot development, the two narratives implicitly complement and reinforce each other in the mythologization of slavery under the cover of such unsavory topics. The white master and mistress in "Désirée's Baby" are very kind to field slaves, enabling them to live gaily, and the white master and mistress in "La Belle Zoraïde" treat house slaves (their "pet" slaves) as if they were their own children. To mythologize slavery, the implied author absolves the white victimizer, Zoraïde's mistress, of her responsibility for the enslaved maid's tragedy. If the suffering of (real or apparent) blacks in "Désirée's Baby" is ascribed to the black planter, in "La Belle Zoraïde" the suffering is attributed to God's inviolable "design," punishing Zoraïde not only for having "sinned" but also for the sexual love of her race (" 'But you know how the negroes are, Ma'zélle Titite,' added [the Negress as narrator], smiling a little sadly. 'There is no mistress, no master, no king nor priest who can hinder them from loving when they will' " [285]). Further, the white victimizer is even converted into an unsuccessful helper and protector of the black victim, in two ways. First, the mistress's cruel act of depriving Zoraïde of her baby is presented as a kind effort (only frustrated by "the good God") to help Zoraïde to return to her earlier state of being "free, happy, and beautiful." Second, the emphatic syntactic

88 *Style and Rhetoric of Short Narrative Fiction*

pattern "It was Madame herself who led the pretty, tiny little 'griffe' girl to her mother" combine with the promise "no one will ever take her from you again" to transform the white victimizer into a mother-like helper and would-be benefactor of the enslaved girl.[21]

Superficially, the implied author of "La Belle Zoraïde" uses the story as an indictment against a (white) tyrannical force that tries to determine a (black) woman's love and marriage. But if that were the case, God's punishment would fall on the tyrant rather than on the woman in love, and the former should have been depicted as the victimizer directly leading to the latter's tragedy: These are choices that the implied author most probably would make if the woman seeking her own love were also white. Since the narrative goes in the opposite direction, it seems likely that the implied author is using the feminist theme as a cover for the racist mythologization of slavery.

Compare another story by Kate Chopin, "The Bênitous' Slave" (1892). The protagonist, Oswald, is a freed slave who was owned by the Bênitous fifty years ago. This old black man is always trying to get back, despite all the dangers on the way, to serve as a slave again, and it is for his "own safety and happiness" that the Bênitous accept his "gratuitous services" (1894a: 146). The single-minded desire of the freed black man to return to his former happy life in slavery indicates the implied author's nostalgia for slavery.

DIFFERENT IMPLIED AUTHORS OF DIFFERENT CHOPIN NARRATIVES

In some of the narratives by "Kate Chopin," the implied authors' attitudes toward race are quite different due to different rhetorical purposes and thematic designs. As pointed out by Booth (1961: 71; see also Shen 2011, 2013), the implied author of a particular work "sets himself out with a different air depending on the needs of" that particular work. In "A Dresden Lady in Dixie" (written in March 1894), for instance, the implied author offers a quite positive picture of an old Negro, whose uprightness and honesty not only "have become proverbial on the plantation" but are comparable to those of St. Peter in the eyes of the white mistress (Chopin 1969: 345).[22] The narrative centers on the theft of a china relic from the planter's house. It is stolen by a poor Cajun girl of twelve, who, for the sake of her family honor and her mother's health, denies the theft of the relic found in her basket. To shield the white girl, who is very kind to him, the old black man invents a story of how he has taken the relic because of the victory of Satan over the good Spirit in him. Although the superiority of the white can still be seen in the black man's reasoning before the act: "She [is] w'ite [white], I is black. She young, I is ole [old]" (349), this narrative shows the black character's uprightness, kindness, and unselfishness, which form a stark contrast with Armand (and the yellow nurse depicted as "fanning herself") in "Désirée's Baby." Bearing the same author's name "Kate Chopin," the two fictional

Style, Surprise Ending, and Covert Mythologization 89

narratives present two different pictures of the black blood, implying two different authorial stances.

The reason underlying the difference is not far to seek. "A Dresden Lady in Dixie" is set in the postwar time, with a harmonious picture between whites and blacks, and the narrative focuses on an old black man's devotion to the whites, not only to the white girl but also to the white planter's family: He has served it "faithfully since boyhood and been all through the war" with the old master (345). It is therefore not surprising that the implied author presents the black character in a favorable light. "Désirée's Baby," by contrast, is set in the antebellum days with a very different thematic design. On the one hand, it displays severe sufferings, even tragic deaths in the racial system, and on the other, the implied author highlights the contrast between the superior white blood and the inferior black blood, so that the evils of the racial system can be attributed to the latter, and the happiness of blacks credited to the former.

In Chopin's narratives—even when they have a common subject—the implied author's racial stance varies greatly, in line with the text's thematic design. Such is the case with "The Bênitous' Slave," "A Dresden Lady in Dixie," and "For Marse Chouchoute," all depicting the devotion of the black protagonist to a white family or character. "The Bênitous' Slave" uses Uncle Oswald only as a tool to convey the nostalgia for slavery, and given this particular goal, there is no depiction of the black man's traits except for his single-minded desire to serve the Bênitous again and the fact that he can only live happily in that identity. This narrative is marked by a racist stance essentially in keeping with that of "Désirée's Baby" and "La Belle Zoraïde."

By contrast, "A Dresden Lady in Dixie" and "For Marse Chouchoute" (written in March 1891) present a harmonious relation between free(d) blacks and poor whites, and the implied authors treat the black protagonists more as individuals and depict certain good traits of theirs. If "A Dresden Lady in Dixie" shows the old black man's honesty, kindness, and unselfishness, "For Marse Chouchoute" depicts a black boy's responsibility and devotion. When the white youth, "born with an unlucky trick of forgetfulness" (Chopin 1894c: 213), fails to carry the mailbag to the train, the black boy helps fulfill the duty at the risk of his life and gets fatally injured. The implied authors (especially in "A Dresden Lady in Dixie") are relatively less racist in stance than that of "The Bênitous' Slave."

Another Chopin narrative about the devotion of the black protagonist is "Beyond the Bayou" (1894d). It aims to present a very affectionate, mother-and-son-like relationship between a black woman and the planter's son, focusing on how she overcomes her morbid fear of crossing the Bayou to save the life of the injured boy. The reader can sense the implied author's sincere appreciation of the black woman's courage, strength, and psychological growth in the process of saving the planter's son. She emerges as a full and developing human being. This narrative is hardly racist and differs greatly from those Southern nostalgic narratives that depict a flat or stereotyped

90   Style and Rhetoric of Short Narrative Fiction

"devoted black mammy" and as such "a trumped-up figure in the mytholo-gizing of slavery" (Clinton 1982: 202; see also Lundie 1994: 137–38). Because of the (possible) change in the implied author's stance along with the change in thematic design, we have to be very careful with intertextual associations. While the overt racist stance of "The Bênitous' Slave" and the covert parallel in "La Belle Zoraïde" may alert us to or help confirm the implicit racist stance of "Désirée's Baby," the implied authors' very different attitudes toward race in "A Dresden Lady in Dixie" and "Beyond the Bayou" may obscure that stance unless we open our minds to an alternative textual undercurrent and, equally importantly, unless we examine the stylistic choices in the text carefully and in an overall way.

TEXT AND CONTEXT

In narratives like Chopin's "Désirée's Baby," marked by a covert progression behind an overt plot, an overall close examination of the textual choices is very important for determining the large meaning-structure or the norms of the implied author. Acquiring information about the flesh-and-blood author in historical context is important to but not sufficient for this purpose. As indicated above, Per Seyersted has done much research on Chopin's family background and personal experiences, which enables him to explain why Chopin shows little resentment in the Negro against the whites (1969: 79). But having failed to examine the text in a careful and overall way, he has overlooked the implicit racist stance of "Désirée's Baby" as well as that of "La Belle Zoraïde." The former narrative, he writes, has "a suggestion of [George Washington] Cable's indignation over the fate of those of mixed blood, but in its taut compression and restrained intensity it is more like a story by Maupassant, and the surprise ending, though somewhat contrived, has a bitter, piercing quality that could not have been surpassed by the master himself" (1969: 94). Having missed the racist covert progression, Seyersted understates Armand's cruel treatment of Désirée: "when Armand, her Creole husband, blames her, she disappears with the child into the river" (ibid.). Nor does Seyersted refer to the opposition between the Satanic black Armand and the white Désirée as martyr.

Another culturally oriented scholar, Helen Taylor, also has ample knowledge of Chopin's background and the context of creation, which have led her to see "Chopin's racism" as "a central element in her writing" (1989: 156). But without examining "Désirée's Baby" in a careful and overall way, her understanding of the narrative—"a disgraced wife's suicide after bearing a black baby (which, as her husband discovers too late, comes from his own mixed blood)" (ibid.: 166)—goes no further than Seyersted's and her interpretation of Désirée's tragic death is very questionable. She takes it that Chopin makes the revelation of color drive Désirée to suicide for two reasons: a "racist" reason rooted in the social reality ("to avoid suggestions of mixed blood in

Style, Surprise Ending, and Covert Mythologization 91

the Louisiana community") and a feminist reason ("to emphasize the impossibility of transformation from social outcast to happy bride," given women's marginal social position) (ibid.: 50). If the first reason were true, it is the mulatto Armand who should die, instead of the white Désirée. The second reason makes sense only to a certain extent, since, as analyzed in detail above, the text implies that Désirée's tragedy could have been avoided if the black Armand had been human, a bit like the kind, nondiscriminating whites.

The emphasis on cultural context may even lead to severe distortions of textual facts. Based on historical materials, Margaret D. Bauer (1996: 161, 162) contends that "Désirée's Baby" is "one of the earliest examples of 'passing' literature" since Armand "has been aware all along of his own racial heritage." This misinterprets the ending of the narrative. There, as indicated above, the consistent use of simple past tense ("took," "read") rules out the possibility that Armand had read the letter earlier (see note 13). In quoting the relevant passage, Bauer (ibid.: 162) omits "He read it" and offers a countertextual argument: "That Armand had been passing is suggested by the fact that the narrator does not say this is the first time Armand has seen this letter, though many critics have made this assumption. The narrator merely says that '[t]here was the remnant of [a letter] back in the drawer from which he took [Désirée's letters]' (244)."

Bauer (ibid.: 161) not only denies that the ending of the story forms an ironic twist but also forces various textual details into the "passing" framework. She argues, for instance, that Armand himself has kept "this letter from his mother to his father" together with Désirée's letters, which "suggests that his courtship of Désirée is part of a plan to overcome the threat of his heritage to his position" (ibid.: 163).[23] But had Armand been "passing," surely he would have destroyed this incontrovertible evidence of his "heritage" rather than just keeping it "in the drawer." Bauer (ibid.: 174) presents the narrative in this way: "Because [he] grows up surrounded by the violent racism of his community, [Armand] develops into a cold, heartless man who will stop at nothing—neither brutal treatment of his slaves, nor cruel rejection of his wife and son—to hide what he perceives to be his shame." But the text's reference to Armand's "imperious and exacting nature" unequivocally signifies his innate qualities. On the other hand, there is simply no description or implication in the text of Armand's development into a cold, heartless man or of his having grown up "surrounded by the violent racism of his community"—the fictional world the implied author has created essentially goes in the opposite direction. In fact, the communal "violent racism" surrounding a free mulatto's growing-up process is what Bauer's admirably extensive and thorough historical research has found in the sociohistorical context of antebellum Louisiana or the antebellum South in general. She then takes Armand out of the fictional world, fits him into the historical reality, and interprets his behavior according to what happened to free mulattos there. When the social reality is imposed on or mixed up with the fiction, distortion becomes unavoidable.

92　Style and Rhetoric of Short Narrative Fiction

As significantly, the picture of the flesh-and-blood author tends to be unified, and this may conceal the differences among different implied authors. For example, Seyersted (1969: 93) generalizes that "Kate Chopin was not interested in society and issues, but in the individual and character, and whatever views she held on Southern problems she usually hid behind a serene objectivity." This general picture of Kate Chopin, however, surely does not apply to "Désirée's Baby" and "La Belle Zoraïde," whose implied authors aim at a defense or mythologization of the South's racial system dominated by whites. The picture of Chopin that Taylor (1989: xiii, 155–57) offers goes in the opposite direction, foregrounding the contrast between Chopin's progressive sexual stance and her reactionary racial stance. But Taylor's (ibid.: 156) conclusion that Chopin's racism is a central element in her writing does not apply to works like "A Dresden Lady in Dixie" or "Beyond the Bayou," whose implied authors are relatively less racist.

All in all, to gain a more accurate understanding of the rhetorical stance of the implied author of "Désirée's Baby," among other Chopin narratives, we need to pay attention to the following aspects. First, we need to make a conscious effort to find out whether there is a covert textual progression behind the overt plot development, otherwise we may map onto the plot development whatever textual details we find relevant and miss their significance in a parallel textual undercurrent. Second, it is crucial that we carry out a careful stylistic analysis, through which we can discover the implied author associating the symbolic house only with the black young master and old mistress, exclusive of the white old master and young mistress. It will also enable us to perceive that the implied author presents the black Armand himself as the (satanic) killer of the white Désirée as God's martyr and that, had Armand been human, the tragedy could have been avoided. Third, we need to take into consideration the interaction among the stylistic choices in different parts of the text, which enables us to discern that all the whites are free from racial discrimination and oppression, while the black characters are guilty of racial discrimination and only the black planter oppresses blacks. Fourth, since the implied author is the "second self" of the flesh-and-blood author and since the relevant works have intertextual connections, an extended consideration of the relation between the implied Chopin and the flesh-and-blood Chopin in historical context, as well as of the associations between the work under investigation and related works will help to put things in perspective and to test, supplement or reinforce the findings of the textual exploration.

In this part of the book, we have uncovered the covert progression behind the overt plot in three American narratives by three American authors, and now we proceed to Part Two to investigate three narratives by the (New Zealand-born) British writer Katherine Mansfield and try to reveal how dual dynamics function differently in these narratives.

Part II

Style and Different Forms of Covert Progression in Mansfield's Fiction

4 Style, Changing Distance, and Doubling Irony

Mansfield's "Revelations"

In contrast with her stories "The Singing Lesson" and "The Fly," both of which have given rise to opposed views or heated critical debates (see Chapters 5 and 6), Katherine Mansfield's "Revelations" (1920) has more or less received critical consensus. Sylvia Berkman regards "Revelations" as a case of "uncharitable studies of neurotic women" and holds that the female protagonist Monica Tyrell is "exposed as rapacious, selfish," being "of highly irritable nervous sensibility. One cannot help thinking that out of her own specialized knowledge of exacerbation Miss Mansfield, in part, was here turning her knife against herself" (1951: 121). In a like vein, Joanna Woods (2008) comments that in "Revelations" Mansfield "reveals her determination to write with greater honesty and integrity by ruthlessly exposing the weaknesses of the central, female figure, whose faults are very similar to her own." Critics who do not associate the characterization of the female protagonist with Mansfield's personal life have also come up with a similar thematic interpretation. Rhoda B. Nathan takes the theme of "Revelations" as "the selfish female of neurotic temperament in a merciless pursuit of shelter and comfort" (1988: 104–5). J. F. Kobler also says: "Probably most readers can take Monica no more seriously than her husband does; she really seems to have so little trouble accepting her own selfishness that she is not worth paying attention to" (1990: 88).

Making a comparison between this narrative and other narratives, Nathan observes that "there is a world of difference between the insecure Reginald coming courting in 'Mr. and Mrs. Dove' and the selfish spoiled Monica Tyrell in 'Revelations'. . . . the reader is aware of Mansfield's moral presence as surely as he is of Henry James's stern judgment of the egotistical John Marcher in 'The Beast in the Jungle' or of Chekhov's contempt for selfish Olga in 'The Grasshopper.' Monica Tyrell is a neurotic, and as such earns her creator's unmitigated scorn" (1988: 103). Also considering this narrative in relation to others, Joanne Trautmann Banks says that Mansfield "wrote about narcissism in both women and men, and how it causes people, particularly couples, to drift apart ('Prelude,' 'Marriage a la Mode,' . . . 'Revelations' . . . and 'A Cup of Tea')" (1993: 304).

However, if we open our minds to more than one textual progression and carry out a thorough stylistic analysis of the text, coupled with an intertextual

96 *Style and Rhetoric of Short Narrative Fiction*

comparison with some related texts, we may discover that behind the overt plot centering on the weaknesses of the female protagonist, there exists a covert progression directing irony against patriarchal discrimination and subjugation of woman. The ethical stance of the covert progression functions to subvert to a large extent that of the overt plot. In what follows, we will first take a more detailed look at the overt plot of "Revelations" and then proceed to the uncovering of the covert progression in this narrative.

OVERT PLOT OF "REVELATIONS"

The opening paragraph of "Revelations" reads:

> From eight o'clock in the morning until about half past eleven Monica Tyrell suffered from her nerves, and suffered so terribly that these hours were—agonizing, simply. It was not as though she could control them. "Perhaps if I were ten years younger. . . ." she would say. For now that she was thirty-three she had a queer little way of referring to her age on all occasions, of looking at her friends with grave, childish eyes and saying: "Yes, I remember how twenty years ago . . ." or of drawing Ralph's attention to the girls—real girls—with lovely youthful arms and throats and swift hesitating movements who sat near them in restaurants. "Perhaps if I were ten years younger. . . ." (Mansfield 1945a: 190) [1]

Here the mode of summary and the tone of irony work together to generate a considerable narrative distance between the female protagonist and the readers. In the first sentence, the thematized adverbial phrase "From eight o'clock in the morning until about half past eleven," which is not specified by a date, gives one the impression that the narrator-focalizer is ironically exaggerating the situation. Moreover, in this sentence, there is a subtle shift in point of view. If the repetitive and intensifying "suffered so terribly" are still the narrator's words, the following loose and colloquial clause, "these hours were—agonizing, simply," is apparently Monica's thought in free indirect discourse. The narrator's discourse and the character's discourse intertwine, making prominent the character's neurotic state and her tendency to grumble. Her inclination for dissatisfaction is further conveyed by the abrupt and thus prominent appearance of the conditional clause "Perhaps if I were ten years younger," the exaggerating adverbial "on all occasions," the ironic nominal phrase "a queer little way," as well as by the repetitive and circular textual movement from "Perhaps if I were ten years younger" to "how twenty years ago" to "Perhaps if I were ten years younger."

In the following narration, the narrator mainly adopts Monica's limited perspective. Although readers perceive the story primarily through Monica's consciousness, the apparent unreasonableness of Monica's thoughts and behavior functions to enlarge the narrative distance as created in the

Style, Changing Distance, and Doubling Irony 97

opening paragraph. Other characters also seem to serve as foils to foreground Monica's morbid mental state. The second paragraph consists of a question from Ralph: " 'Why don't you get Marie to sit outside your door and *absolutely forbid* anybody to come near your room until you ring your bell?' " (190, italics added). The italicized words seem to convey in an ironic way Monica's paranoia.

On this windy morning at half-past nine, Ralph makes a call to invite Monica to have lunch with him at Princes' at one-thirty. When the maid Marie comes to announce the call,

> Monica lay still [in bed] and half closed her eyes. "Tell Monsieur I cannot come," she said gently. But as the door shut, anger—anger suddenly gripped her close, close, violent, half strangling her. How dared he? How dared Ralph do such a thing when he knew how agonising her nerves were in the morning! Hadn't she explained and described and even—though lightly, of course; she couldn't say such a thing directly—given him to understand that this was the one unforgivable thing. And then to choose this frightful windy morning. Did he think it was just a fad of hers, a little feminine folly to be laughed at and tossed aside? (191)

The drastic contrast between the first two and the following sentences foregrounds Monica's unreasonableness. The free indirect discourse "How dared he? How dared Ralph do such a thing when he knew how agonising her nerves were in the morning! Hadn't she explained . . ." seems to be the narrator's ironic mimicking of Monica's thoughts, subtly criticizing Monica's unreasonable irritation, which enlarges the distance between Monica and the readers. The irritation goes on for over one page. A well-intentioned invitation to lunch meets in Monica such strong and endless resentment and exacerbation, bordering on hysteria.

After Monica gets up and goes to the hairdresser's, she feels upset at the hairdresser George's unusual absent-mindedness. Then George tells her that his daughter—a first child—died this morning. Monica rushes out to take a taxi to Princes' to meet Ralph. On the way she sees a flower shop and wants to buy flowers for the little girl. The narrative ends with the sentence "She tapped against the window [for the taxi driver to stop] but the driver fails to hear her tap at the window and she finds herself at Princes' already" (196).

As far as the plot development is concerned, the stylistic choices are seen as being used to represent the weaknesses of the female protagonist:

> The neurotic's inability to act, to think things through, to progress beyond narcissism to compassion, is manifest in the story's mode of narration. The breathless highly agitated style is formed by elliptical sentence structure, incomplete phrases punctuated by dashes to dramatize Monica's inability to sustain a thought, and irritated gestures

98   *Style and Rhetoric of Short Narrative Fiction*

of dismissal. Mansfield does not trouble to comment on the ludicrous aspects of Monica's resentment of being put upon by an inconsiderate spouse who requests her company for lunch. Her self-absorption juxtaposed against the real but contained grief of the bereaved hairdresser speaks for itself, as does her craven flight from the scene. (1988: 104)

UNCOVERING THE COVERT PROGRESSION

In focusing on the plot development, critics tend to overlook or misinterpret some key passages or stylistic choices that point to an implicit textual movement going in a different ethical direction. After getting up, Monica sits down before the mirror and

> she suddenly felt—oh, the strangest, most tremendous excitement filling her slowly, slowly, until she wanted to fling out her arms, to laugh, to scatter everything, to shock Marie, to cry: "[1] I'm free. [2] I'm free. [3] I'm free as the wind." [4] And now all this vibrating, trembling, exciting, flying world was hers. [5] It was her kingdom. [6] No, no, she belonged to nobody but Life. (192)

In the first sentence of this passage, the successive and progressive use of five infinitives ("she wanted to fling out her arms, to laugh, to scatter everything, to shock Marie, to cry"), which is stylistically foregrounded, emphatically conveys Monica's inner desire for freedom and liberation. The series of infinitives culminates in the verb "cry," functioning to make prominent Monica's desire to live her own life. The first three numbered sentences, expressing repeatedly the same cry for freedom in direct discourse, are reinforced by the following three sentences in free indirect discourse, which, with variation in form, also convey the same idea repeatedly.

In interpreting the plot development, critics tend to overlook this passage. Patrick Morrow is one critic who has not overlooked it, and his interpretation runs:

> *Monica is oppressed by wealth.* . . . When she gets her first revelation, her first glimpse of freedom, *the narrator says that she owns the world,* but then, perhaps by way of correction adds, "no, no, she belonged to no one but Life" (427). For Monica, to own is equivalent to being owned. She can't belong to Life while everything that makes up her life belongs to her. This illustrates a teaching older than Mansfield which says to "*be on guard against every form of greed* for not even when one has an abundance does his life consist of his possessions" (from the *New Testament*). (Morrow 1993: 68, italics added)

As just mentioned, the free indirect discourse (sentences numbered from 4 to 6) represents Monica's thoughts, rather than the narrator's comments

Style, Changing Distance, and Doubling Irony 99

on Monica. Without considering the stylistic function of the free indirect discourse, Morrow mistakes the positive representation of Monica's desire for the narrator's negative comment on Monica. Consequently, he comes to the wrong conclusion that the cause of Monica's suffering is her wealth and her greed. The following passage appearing later in the text reveals the real cause of Monica's suffering:

> How incredible men were! And she had loved him—how could she have loved a man who talked like that. What had she been doing ever since that dinner party months ago, when he had seen her home and asked if he might come and "see again that slow Arabian smile"? Oh, what non-sense—what utter nonsense. . . . Oh, to be free of Princes' at one-thirty, of being the tiny kitten in the swansdown basket, of being the Arabian, and the grave, delighted child and the little wild creature. . . . "Never again," she cried aloud, clenching her small fist. (192)

These words are crucial to perceiving the covert progression, which, how-ever, have eluded Patrick Morrow and other critics who concentrate on the personal weaknesses of Monica in the plot development. In this passage, the first exclamatory sentence representing Monica's thought in free indirect discourse directs attention to the relation between men and women in general. The following two sentences are Monica's self-interrogation in free indirect discourse, a mode that shifts at the end-focus position of the latter sentence to Ralph's words in direct speech "see again that slow Arabian smile." Ralph is an embodiment of patriarchy, treating Monica as a plaything and being interested merely in her "slow Arabian smile." The following free indirect discourse and Monica's determined loud cry "Never again" show Monica's awakening to her being oppressed by patriarchy. The series of prepositional phrases "to be free of Princes' at one-thirty, of being the tiny kitten in the swansdown basket, of being the Arabian, and the grave, delighted child and the little wild creature" indicates that the only role of Monica for Ralph is a doll and, moreover, that her neurosis may be ascribable, to a significant extent, to this humiliating and meaningless relationship.

When we open our minds to more than one textual movement and make a careful stylistic analysis of the interrelated passages in different parts of the text, we may come to perceive an undercurrent of social protest. Monica wants to be free, not from the so-called oppression of wealth as a result of her personal greed, but from the role of being merely a plaything of man in a patriarchal society—the real cause of her suffering. Feminist theory and criticism have shown how one "becomes" a woman under the cultural forces of gender, and in the covert progression of "Revelations" Mansfield is implicitly conveying how a woman becomes neurotic and hysteric very much as a result of gender subjugation.[2]

After getting her first revelation and driven by the desire for freedom, Monica asks her maid to call a taxi and she rushes out. At this stage, we get a depiction of Monica as she should be: "She got in [the taxi], and smiling

100 *Style and Rhetoric of Short Narrative Fiction*

radiantly at the cross, cold-looking driver, she told him to take her to her hairdresser's. . . . The cross, cold driver drove at a tremendous pace, and she let herself be hurled from side to side" (193). In striking contrast to the neurotic and hysteric Monica before the revelation, what we have here is a happy and tolerant woman. The words "smile" and "radiantly" used to depict Monica form a sharp contrast with the repeated epithets "cross" and "cold" employed to describe the driver. As the scene is narrated from Monica's limited perspective, readers are kept in the dark as to the reasons underlying the driver's anger, which therefore appears to be groundless and unreasonable. Against this background, Monica is seen as particularly normal and kind. Monica's tolerance is intensified by "she let herself be hurled from side to side."

Monica arrives at the hairdresser's. She "always had the feeling that they loved her in this shop and understood her—the real her—far better than many of her friends did. She was her real self here, and she and Madame had often talked—quite strangely—together" (193). The repeated epithet "real" in "the real her" and "her real self" further alerts us to the fact that Monica's weaknesses may be a result of patriarchal subjugation rather than her inherent characteristics.

At the hairdresser's, the atmosphere is unexpectedly cold and lifeless today. The hairdresser George keeps Monica waiting, and serves her in a mechanical way, without his usual warmth and without telling her the truth. Monica feels ill-treated and deceived, which makes her fall again into the state of neurosis and self-pity. After doing Monica's hair, George suddenly says, "'The truth is, Madame, since you are an old customer—my little daughter died this morning. A first child'" (196). This breaking of the truth comes to Monica as the second "revelation." She cries and rushes out into the taxi.

> The driver, looking furious, swung off the seat and slammed the door again. "Where to?" "Princes'," she sobbed. And all the way there she saw nothing but a tiny wax doll with a feather of gold hair, lying meek, its tiny hands and feet crossed. And then just before she came to Princes' she saw a flower shop full of white flowers. Oh, what a perfect thought. Lilies-of-the-valley, and white pansies, double white violets and white velvet ribbon. . . . From an unknown friend. . . . From one who understands. . . . For a Little Girl. . . . She tapped against the window, but the driver did not hear; and, anyway, they were at Princes' already. (196)

This is the very end of the narrative. Since it is mainly narrated from Monica's limited focalization, the readers are again kept in the dark as to the cause of the driver's anger, now even greater and accompanied by rude behavior ("looking furious," "slammed the door"). In this context, Monica is again seen as very reasonable and kind. Now the question arises: Why does the implied author dramatically create the contrast between Monica's

Style, Changing Distance, and Doubling Irony 101

neurosis before the revelations and her normality as an effect of the revelations?[3] To see things in perspective, it is necessary to examine a relevant passage in Mansfield's "Prelude":

> "Oh," she [Beryl] cried, "I am so miserable—so frightfully miserable. I know that I'm silly and spiteful and vain; I'm *always acting a part. I'm never my real self for a moment.*" And plainly, plainly, she saw her *false self* running up and down the stairs, laughing a special trilling laugh if they had visitors, standing under the lamp if a man came to dinner, so that he should see the light on her hair, pouting and pretending to be a little girl when she was asked to play the guitar. Why? She even kept it up for Stanley's benefit. Only last night when he was reading the paper her *false self* had stood beside him and leaned against his shoulder on purpose.... How despicable! Despicable! Her heart was cold with rage. "It's marvellous how you keep it up," said she to the *false self*. But then it was only because she was so miserable—so miserable. If she had been happy and *leading her own life, her false life would cease to be.* (Mansfield 1945b: 58–59, italics added)

Here we also see the interaction between direct discourse and free indirect discourse used to represent a woman's inner voice. The three juxtaposed adjectives "silly," "spiteful" and "vain" list Beryl's defects, but they are only indicators of her "false self," which reminds us of "the real her" and "her real self" in "Revelations." The thrice repeated "so miserable" emphatically brings out Beryl's suffering. The last sentence, "If she had been happy and leading her own life, her false life would cease to be," explicitly conveys the point that these weaknesses are not inherent in the character, but ascribable to her dependence on man for a living. Compared with Monica, Beryl is marked by a more conscious awareness of the opposition between her real self and her false self. Through Beryl, we can also see Mansfield's conscious awareness of how the patriarchal society reduces upper-middle-class women to morbid or faulty behavior. In Mansfield's time, upper-middle-class women had "no option in life but marriage" (Fullbrook 1986: 111) since their going out to work "would be considered undignified, unladylike, and therefore unspeakable" (Runkle 2002: 8). While waiting to get married, Beryl is living with her sister's family, financially dependent on Stanley, her brother-in-law. Beryl's only way to survive as offered by society is to please her brother-in-law (who provides for her present life), as well as male guests (one of whom may become her husband and future provider). Her various "feminine" weaknesses—vain, trivial, silly and flirtatious— indicate gender performativity "produced and compelled by the regulatory" cultural norms of the Western hegemonic society (Butler 1990: 24–25). They constitute a culturally-imposed false self, pointing to the patriarchal social conventions and the masculinist distortion of an upper-middle-class woman who depends on marriage for survival. A comparison of "Revelations" with

102   *Style and Rhetoric of Short Narrative Fiction*

"Prelude" helps us to see Monica's weaknesses in perspective, which may be regarded as aspects of her "false self" "produced and compelled by" gender discrimination and oppression.

It should be noted that both Monica and Beryl are marked by the lack of agency, unable to take any actions that might help them reconstitute themselves along different lines. After her impulsive cry for freedom, Monica still goes to Princes' to have lunch with Ralph; similarly, after criticizing her "despicable" "false self," Beryl still powders her nose to ingratiate herself with a male guest who might become her husband-provider. Their lack of agency and their fixed notions of gender identity are partly responsible for their own sufferings. Although in real life Mansfield herself was characterized by strong agency, having escaped from the restrictions of her well-to-do family and bourgeois social conventions to seek artistic development on her own, in writing "Revelations" or "Prelude," Mansfield seems to be less concerned with a critique of women's inability to act than with patriarchy's subjugation of women. As discussed above, Beryl strives "to be the object of desire" (Young-Eisendrath 1997: 62) primarily because of her economically dependent status ("If she had been happy and leading her own life, her false life would cease to be"). She is very much "trapped into complying with the demands and desires of men" (Young-Eisendrath 1997: 62) by the Western hegemonic economic structure. And, as will be discussed below, in "Revelations" Mansfield also puts emphasis on Monica's lack of other choices in society.

When we gradually discern the covert progression, we will come to see various textual details in a new light. Let us look at the opening passage again:

> From eight o'clock in the morning until about half past eleven Monica Tyrell suffered from her nerves, and suffered so terribly that these hours were—agonizing, simply. It was not as though she could control them. "Perhaps if I were ten years younger. . . ." she would say. For now that she was thirty-three she had a queer little way of referring to her age on all occasions, of looking at her friends with grave, childish eyes and saying: "Yes, I remember how twenty years ago. . . ." or of drawing Ralph's attention to the girls—real girls—with lovely youthful arms and throats and swift hesitating movements who sat near them in restaurants. "Perhaps if I were ten years younger. . . ."

While in the overt plot we only see in this opening passage the representation of Monica's personal weaknesses, in the covert progression we see how Monica, as a representative of Western upper-middle-class women, suffers from patriarchal subjugation. This class of women traditionally have social activities in the afternoon and evening, and the morning is a time when life is most idle, meaningless and lonely. It is, not surprisingly, a time when Monica suffers from her nerves. As a plaything of Ralph, Monica's value only lies

Style, Changing Distance, and Doubling Irony 103

in her youth and appearance. Consequently, her attention is exclusively focused on the age and appearance of herself and other women. What appears to be Monica's own shallow and trivial obsession with the passing of her youth, with real girls' "lovely youthful arms and throats," in effect, is the deplorable result of the gender discrimination and oppression in the patriarchal society, which reduces upper-middle-class women to "dolls" of men and values only their youth and beauty. Notice the abrupt textual movement from "It was not as though she could control them [her nerves]" to "Perhaps if I were ten years younger . . . ," which establishes a sort of cause-and-effect relationship between Monica's obsession with her age/appearance and her suffering from her nerves. Since the obsession is very much imposed on her by the male-dominated society, we now see Monica, to a great extent, as a victim of social injustice. That is to say, in the covert progression, our perspective is extended from the personal relationship between Monica and Ralph to the social relationship between women and men, and we come to see the narrative very much as a social protest.

A new interpretation may also emerge concerning Monica's not allowing Marie to sit outside her door. Monica explains the situation to Ralph:

> "Oh, if it were as simple as that!" She threw her little gloves down and pressed her eyelids with her fingers in the way he knew so well. "But in the first place I'd be so conscious of Marie sitting there, Marie shaking her finger at Rudd and Mrs. Moon, Marie as a kind of cross between a wardress and a nurse for mental cases! And then, there's the post. One can't get over the fact that the post comes, and once it has come, who—who—could wait until eleven for the letters?" (190)

In the overt plot, readers may see Monica's paranoia and triviality revealed in direct speech. In the covert progression, however, readers may see in the stylistic choices patriarchal discrimination and subjugation. Monica, a plaything of Ralph, is confined to the "prison ward" (as suggested by the term "wardress") of her home. It is out of a desire for a little freedom at home that she does not want Marie the half "wardress" to sit outside her door. Since Monica's life is empty, meaningless, and lonely, letters as a most important means of her communication with the outside world become highly significant for her ("who—who—could wait until eleven for the letters?"). Monica's explanation meets with Ralph's self-centered response: "*My* letters, darling?" (190, italics original) To Ralph, he himself constitutes the whole universe for Monica, even monopolizing her outside correspondence.

If we compare "Revelations" with Ibsen's *A Doll's House,* a feminist text that exerted strong influence on Mansfield (Murry 1954: 37), we may see that Mansfield is trying to highlight the "distorting" function of patriarchy through various textual choices. On the one hand, Mansfield's Monica and Ibsen's Nora assume a similar "doll"[4] role in front of their men: Monica

104 *Style and Rhetoric of Short Narrative Fiction*

acts a "tiny kitten in the swansdown basket," a "grave, delighted child," a "little wild creature" and an exotic "Arabian" girl, while Nora acts a "sweet little lark" (563), a "little songbird" (589), a "squirrel" (562), and "a Neapolitan peasant girl" (576) with exotic flavor. But, on the other hand, the two women differ drastically from each other in some other aspects. Nora is a woman who got married at the normal age, had three children and a strong ability to make a living by herself. In order to pay off the debt incurred to save her husband's life, Nora has to busy herself in "needlework, crocheting, embroidery" (565) and sometimes "writing every evening till late in the night" (567). Indeed, she is proud of "almost like being a man" (567). By contrast, Monica is from a rich class, living an idle life. As a 33-year old woman whose relationship with Ralph started just months ago, she is getting dangerously close to the age after which no one will marry her, and she has been taught that that is a fate worse than marriage to Ralph (see Chapter 5). The tension between Ralph's exclusive interest in her appearance and the fact that she has already passed her youth forms a most important reason underlying her obsession and neurosis, which is made worse by her idle way of living especially at the time of the day when she is most lonely.

Mansfield also conveys Monica's not daring to voice her opinion in front of Ralph: " 'Perhaps,' she drawled, softly, and she drew her hand over his reddish hair, smiling too, but thinking: 'Heavens! What a stupid thing to say!' " (190). The deplorable fact is that while secretly criticizing Ralph in her mind, Monica still has to perform her gender role and pretend to be pleased. A similar case is found in Monica's thoughts in free indirect discourse: "Hadn't she explained and described and even—though lightly, of course; she couldn't say such a thing directly—given him to understand that this was the one unforgivable thing" (191). The fact that Monica has to suppress her real thoughts and has to talk to Ralph in a roundabout or false way partly accounts for her neurosis. Through the dramatic choice of a 33-year old woman as the female protagonist, Mansfield seems to try to highlight how masculinist interest and oppression, coupled with idle upper-middle-class life (an idleness that has to do with the "doll" role), make a woman fall into morbidity.

We have seen that in the covert progression of "Revelations," Mansfield reveals how patriarchy imposes "a false self" on the female protagonist. The "false self" is firstly the gender role the upper-middle-class female character is asked to perform in a male-centered society (a doll, a mask), and secondly other weaknesses of the character, like paranoia and triviality, the second being a result of the first. As the female character is not satisfied with her lot in the patriarchal society and she also dares not display her dissatisfaction to the patriarch, her dissatisfaction is unconsciously vented out in a devious way, such as appearing nervous, sentimental, easy to provoke, hysteric, and hypercritical about some trifles. It is by exaggerating such aspects of female behavior that the implied author tries to illustrate the miserable conditions of females in that society.

Style, Changing Distance, and Doubling Irony 105

It should be mentioned that Ralph's hypocrisy forms another reason underlying Monica's neurosis. It is worth mentioning that, in Ibsen's *A Doll's House,* the male protagonist Helmer is also characterized by hypocrisy. He claims to be always ready to "stake [his] life and soul and everything" to save Nora from "some terrible danger" (589). But when the crisis comes, he immediately abandons Nora and is only concerned about himself. In "Revelations," Mansfield depicts Ralph's hypocrisy in a very subtle way:

> Why, only last night she had said: "Ah, but you must take me seriously, too." And he had replied: "My darling, you'll not believe me, but [1] I know you infinitely better than you know yourself. [2] Every delicate thought and feeling I bow to, I treasure. [3] Yes, laugh! I love the way your lip lifts"—and he had leaned across the table—"I don't care who sees that I adore all of you. I'd be with you on mountain-top and have all the searchlights of the world play upon us." "Heavens!" Monica almost clutched her head. Was it possible he had really said that? How incredible men were! (191–92)

Ralph's words "I know you infinitely better than you know yourself" remind us of Helmer's words to Nora: "just lean on me; I'll guide you and teach you" (591). Notice the contradiction in Ralph's speech between [1] and [2] (especially the tension between "infinitely better" and "bow to"), and that between [2] ("thought and feeling"; respecting Monica) and [3] (only outward appearance; ordering Monica to laugh as a father orders a little daughter). These self-contradictions bring out, subtly yet unequivocally, Ralph's hypocrisy. Ralph's self-contradiction is reinforced by various ironic contrasts between his words and Monica's words: (1) Ralph's "I bow to, I treasure" versus Monica's "to be laughed at and tossed aside;" (2) Ralph's "every delicate thought and feeling" versus Monica's "just a fad of hers, a little feminine folly;" (3) Ralph's "I adore all of you" versus Monica's "you must take me seriously." Monica's words and Ralph's words, that is to say, work together to lend support to Monica's conclusion in free indirect discourse "How incredible men were!"

In *A Doll's House,* Nora is not aware of Helmer's hypocrisy until the crisis comes. As soon as she sees through Helmer, she decides to leave him. By contrast, in "Revelations," Ralph's hypocrisy is immediately perceived by Monica and forms an important reason underlying her neurosis and hysteria. In the covert progression, we no longer see a reasonable Ralph and an unreasonable Monica, but a victimized Monica, who is treated as a silly doll and who has lost her real self, and a victimizing Ralph, who functions as an instrument of gender discrimination and oppression. The narrator's tone of irony is still poignant, but the object of irony has changed in the covert progression from the female protagonist's weaknesses to the Western hegemonic structure of masculine domination. In other words, the covert progression shows feminine triviality and neurosis in an upper-middle-class woman as

106 *Style and Rhetoric of Short Narrative Fiction*

produced and enforced by a patriarchal man who then uses them as a reason to despise the woman and circumscribe her autonomy.

Perceived as part of the covert progression, the following passage also takes on different meaning:

> Monica lay still and half closed her eyes. "Tell Monsieur I cannot come," she said gently. But as the door shut, anger—anger suddenly gripped her close, close, violent, half strangling her. How dared he? How dared Ralph do such a thing when he knew how agonising her nerves were in the morning! . . . And then to choose this frightful windy morning. Did he think it was just a fad of hers, a little feminine folly to be laughed at and tossed aside? (191)

Although "anger gripped somebody" is a dead personification, Mansfield's deviant and emphatic expression "But as the door shut, anger—anger suddenly gripped her close, close, violent, half strangling her" energizes it and transforms it into a live personification. The detailed description ". . . gripped her close, close, violent, half strangling her" arouses the association of a man's violating a woman after shutting the door. Mansfield seems to be purposefully utilizing the ambiguity in the two terms "violent" (an emotion's being very strong or using physical force as in violating a woman) and "strangle" (emotionally suffocating or physically constricting the neck) to create a double meaning: a surface meaning (Monica's unreasonable and hysteric anger) and a deeper meaning (Monica's being violated). In the overt plot, we only see the surface meaning: the conflict between Monica and Ralph, the former marked by self-centeredness, neurosis and hysteria. In the covert progression, however, we come to see the opposition between a man and a woman, and the former, as a tool or embodiment of masculinist domination, victimizing the latter physically, emotionally and mentally. As regards the last sentence, the overt plot lays more emphasis on the personal "fad of hers," while the covert progression sets more store by "feminine folly," which suggests gender discrimination. In the covert progression, the narrative tone in presenting Monica's free indirect discourse also changes from mocking mimicry to shared accusation against gender discrimination and oppression. In this light, the covert progression obliterates, to a great extent, the narrative distance in the overt plot between Monica and the implied author (also the narrator), and that between Monica and readers, who would become much more sympathetic towards her.

Reading the ending of the narrative in the covert progression, we may also arrive at a new understanding:

> And all the way there she saw nothing but a tiny wax doll with a feather of gold hair, lying meek, its tiny hands and feet crossed. And then just before she came to Princes' she saw a flower shop full of white flowers. Oh, what a perfect thought. Lilies-of-the-valley, and white pansies,

Style, Changing Distance, and Doubling Irony 107

double white violets and white velvet ribbon. . . . From an unknown friend. . . . From one who understands. . . . For a Little Girl. . . . She tapped against the window, but the driver did not hear; and, anyway, they were at Princes' already. (196)

In the overt plot, "Oh, what a perfect thought" only conveys Monica's vanity, but in the covert progression it seems to bear influence of Ibsen's *A Doll's House* since it echoes Nora's words when referring to her kind act: "I've got something to be proud and happy for" (appearing twice on page 566) and "my joy and pride" (571). The phrase "From an unknown friend" also seems to be linked with Nora's keeping herself unknown—"how painfully humiliating for him if he ever found out he was in debt to me" (567).

Despite these similarities, there is a striking contrast between the two female protagonists at the ending of the two narratives. While Nora frees herself from her "doll" roll by leaving Helmer, Monica still retains her "doll" role by going to Princes' to join Ralph. On her way, Monica sees "nothing but a tiny wax doll with a feather of gold hair, lying meek, its tiny hands and feet crossed." Significantly, what Monica sees is not only the corpse of the little girl. The words "lying meek" echo the earlier "she let herself be hurled from side to side [by the taxi driver]" and the words "a tiny . . . doll" echo "the tiny kitten in the swansdown basket," a "grave, delighted child," "the little wild creature." The echoing of the words points to the fact that Monica is seeing herself as the corpse in the form of a meek doll. The "small fist" Monica clenched while crying for freedom now becomes the lifeless tiny hand, and her loud cry now becomes the obedient silence of the corpse. Although the ending appears to be a conventionally happy one in the overt plot, in the covert progression, through metaphorically transforming Monica into a dead body, it actually forms an implicit indictment against patriarchal oppression of woman. But why does Mansfield end the story in this essentially tragic but non-rebellious and superficially conventional way?

As mentioned above, Monica differs greatly from Nora in terms of the ability to survive on one's own. When leaving her doll house, Nora has a definite destination in mind: "Tomorrow I'm going home—I mean, home where I came from. It'll be easier up there to find something to do." (592) By contrast, when Monica is rushing out of her doll house, such words appear in free indirect discourse: "Where was she going? Oh, anywhere. . . . She must be out; she must be driving quickly—anywhere, anywhere" (193). The thrice repeated "anywhere" emphatically conveys the point that Monica does not have any place to go to. After George has done her hair, the same question appears in free indirect discourse: "Where was she going now?" (196), but there is no answer, for the simple reason that she does not have any place to go to. Then George tells Monica about his daughter's death. George has stoically served her despite the great tragedy and breaks the truth to her because she is "an old customer." This, among other things, is an instance of a man taking her seriously. This second "revelation" helps

108 *Style and Rhetoric of Short Narrative Fiction*

Monica to get out of her morbid mental state, but the only choice facing her is to go to Princes' to meet Ralph for lunch.

It is important to note that Mansfield was writing to make a living. On New Year's Day of 1915, Mansfield put down the following words in her diary: "For this year I have two wishes: to write, to make money. Consider. With money we could go away as we liked, have a room in London, be as free as we liked, and be independent and proud with nobodies. It is only poverty that holds us so tightly" (Murry 1954: 64). In order to make money, Mansfield had to consider readers' reception, and at the beginning of the twentieth century, despite the influence of the New Women's Movement, a socially rebellious story would surely have met with resistance from conventional readers. This is perhaps a most important reason underlying Mansfield's giving "Revelations" a superficially conventional ending. However, by ingeniously transforming Monica into a meek doll and merging it with the dead body, the ending is in essence a tragic one, forming an implicit interrogation of and protest against patriarchal subjugation and oppression of woman.

When we trace the covert progression to the ending, we may also get a different interpretation of Monica's failing to buy the flowers. In the overt plot, this failure indicates her inability or insincerity to carry out the kind act (see the relevant criticism quoted above). In the covert progression, by contrast, the implied author directs attention to the fact that Monica's kind wish is thwarted by the driver, who consistently serves as Monica's foil and who seems to stand for male-power more broadly. If the driver had heard Monica's knocking and stopped the taxi, Monica would have bought the flowers. This thwarting of Monica's kind intention adds to the tragic tone of the ending in the covert progression: this is a society where a "doll" woman cannot fulfill her desires and can only accept the arrangements made by men whether wittingly or unwittingly. Indeed, the metaphorical identification of Monica with the corpse at the ending seems to close off the possibility for any change, implying that Monica's returning to her gender role is like returning to a tomb where she will again lose her "real self."

Contemporary feminist theory has penetratingly revealed the inescapable control of the political discourse of gender, among other kinds of political discourses. Judith Butler writes, "It would be wrong to think that the discussion of 'identity' ought to proceed prior to a discussion of gender identity for the simple reason that 'persons' only become intelligible through becoming gendered in conformity with recognizable standards of gender intelligibility" (1990: 16). From such a poststructuralist perspective, it is impossible to have one's "real self," since any identity is constructed by prior or ongoing political discourses. Applying the poststructuralist perspective to the analysis of Mansfield's "Prelude" and "The Daughters of the Late Colonel," Kim Runkle believes that the vagueness or elusiveness of the real selves of Beryl and Constantia (a female protagonist in "The Daughters") is to be attributed to the "impossible removal from a prior gender discourse" (2002: 14).

Style, Changing Distance, and Doubling Irony 109

And because of this impossibility, the uncovering of "the real self" can only remain "a fiction" (ibid.: 14). But writing at the beginning of the twentieth century, Mansfield seemed to have a much less sophisticated view of "the real self." As shown by her journal put down in February 1920, Mansfield, on the one hand, was conscious of the complexity of one's identity, and on the other, did believe in one's real self:

> Nevertheless, there are signs that we are intent as never before on trying to puzzle out, to live by, our own particular self. *Der Mensch muss frei sein*—free, disentangled, single. Is it not possible that the rage for confession, autobiography, especially for memories of earliest childhood, is explained by our persistent yet mysterious belief in a self which is continuous and permanent; which, untouched by all we acquire and all we shed, pushes a green spear through the dead leaves and through the mould, thrusts a scaled bud through years of darkness until, one day, the light discovers it and shakes the flower free and—we are alive—we are flowering for our moment upon the earth? (Murry 1954: 205)

Mansfield's "real self" is the self free from all cultural conventions—"untouched by all we acquire and all we shed." In "Prelude," Beryl's question, "And was there ever a time when I did not have a false self?" (Mansfield 1945b: 59), seems to convey not so much Mansfield's belief in the inescapable control of the political discourses as the inescapable control of the Western masculinist economy, which makes upper-middle-class women dependent on men for survival. Interestingly, in contrast to the vagueness of Beryl's "real self," the dramatic changes Monica undergoes after the two "revelations"—the parallel return to normality from neurosis—seem to indicate a kind of return to her "real self," a return that is regrettably and tragically transient because of her lack of other choices in society and because of her lack of agency.

Having uncovered the covert progression in "Revelations," we are now in a position to consider further previous interpretations of this narrative. There is a small body of feminist readings of Mansfield (Game 1998, Parkin-Gounelas 1991, Pratt 1992, Runkle 2002, Dunbar 1997, Fullbrook 1986), but they have not paid attention to "Revelations." However, in *Katherine Mansfield and the Origins of Modernist Fiction* (1991), Sydney Janet Kaplan, who takes a more or less feminist approach to Mansfield's fiction, has considered "Revelations." She interprets Monica in terms of "sexual restlessness" in relation to the city's "potential as a catalyst for sexual release" (1991: 69–70). In this light, Monica's rushing out of her confined home is regarded as "a female character rushing outside or desiring to be caught up in the rapid movement of life in the London streets" (1991: 69), which "displaces [women's] sexuality from the 'natural' to the 'artificial'" (70). Although focusing on female desire, this interpretation unwittingly neutralizes to a significant extent the gender politics involved. As analyzed above,

110   *Style and Rhetoric of Short Narrative Fiction*

Monica's desire for freedom arises not so much from sexual restlessness as from her awakening to patriarchal discrimination and oppression, and what she aims at is not to find sexual release in the city but to be free from being a plaything of man.

Adopting a more neutral stance, W. H. New sees in "Revelations," among other stories by Mansfield, "a contrast between a desire for freedom and a commitment to enclosure or safety" (1994: 93; cf. New 1999: 18–22). Although this reading focuses on the contrast between "freedom" and "enclosure," its neutral discussion of the contrast (especially putting "enclosure" on a par with "safety") also blocks from view the gender politics in the covert progression of "Revelations." Exploring Mansfield's "glimpses" in a similarly neutral way, Sarah Sandley says: "In stories such as 'Je ne parle pas francais,' 'Bliss,' 'Miss Brill,' and 'Revelations,' the narrative is directed either wholly or principally through the consciousness of a main character who is experienced at evading the present reality of a besetting situation to the degree that the narrative becomes *about* the very process of creating narrative fiction" (1994: 88).

Previous critics have investigated "Revelations" from various angles, but they have only paid attention to one textual movement—the plot development. Unless we open our minds to an undercurrent behind the plot, we may be hard put to discover the covert progression protesting against patriarchal discrimination and oppression of woman.[5] This covert progression belongs to the subversive category (see Introduction), and because of its subversiveness, our discernment of it radically changes our perception of various textual details. If we miss the covert progression, we may get a misleading picture of the ethical significance of the text, see a distorted image of the protagonist, and may only appreciate the narrative's aesthetic value in a limited way. This point applies to Mansfield's "The Singing Lesson," which also has a covert progression, functioning as a social protest against patriarchy, but which progresses in a different and an even more implicit way.

5 Style and Concealed Social Protest
Mansfield's "The Singing Lesson"

Katherine Mansfield's "The Singing Lesson" (originally published in 1920) centers on the marriage proposal of Basil to Miss Meadows, a thirty-year-old music teacher at a girls' school. At the beginning of the narrative, Miss Meadows is in a very bad mood on her way to teach a singing lesson, and when in the classroom, she treats her pupils very coldly and asks them to sing a mournful lament, all because her fiancé Basil has broken off their engagement. Then she is summoned to the school office where she receives from Basil a telegram to promise marriage again. This transforms Miss Meadows into a warm, happy, and kind woman. And when back in the classroom she asks her pupils to sing instead a joyful paean.

This plot development has received the following three kinds of interpretation. Some critics take the narrative optimistically as an illustration of Mansfield's effort to show "'that marvellous triumph' when beauty holds the balance over the ugliness in life" (O'Sullivan 1996: 137; Kobler 1990: 141). Some critics take the narrative as a satirical depiction of a shallow, stupid, and unkind spinster who blindly depends on a man, and the end of the narrative is seen as being not triumphant but "mournful," since Miss Meadows "would be better off to suffer the initial hurt than to be bound to Basil forever" (Morrow 1993: 85). Some other critics treat the narrative itself as being flawed by the author's morbid mentality or weak structural design. S. P. B. Mais (1993: 116) thinks that Mansfield "must have been ill" when writing "The Singing Lesson" and "Miss Brill," which are marked by a "low devitalized note." Mais exclaims, "Oh, these spinster schoolmistresses and their passionate aches! How we sigh for the full-blooded lusts of Somerset Maugham's heroes" (ibid.). Silvia Berkman (1951: 175) finds the parallel between Miss Meadows's grief at Basil's breaking their engagement and the melancholy lament she asks her pupils to sing as being "manipulated too obviously." The interaction between the two aspects functions undesirably to "sentimentalize the whole." Moreover, "the turnabout after Basil's telegram of recantation to a joyful paean is highly mechanical." All this leads her to conclude that "'The Singing Lesson' is one of Miss Mansfield's least successful stories" (ibid.).

As we will see below, the damning views on the female protagonist and the narrative as a whole are very much ascribable to the exclusive focus on

112 *Style and Rhetoric of Short Narrative Fiction*

the overt plot of the narrative. But in effect, behind the plot development, there exists an ethically oriented and artistically created covert progression. By way of perceiving the covert progression, we can come to not only a much better appreciation of the thematic significance and aesthetic value of the narrative, but also a much more sympathetic understanding of the female protagonist.

FROM INTERNAL DESPAIR TO SOCIETAL VICTIMIZATION

The beginning of the narrative reads,

> With despair—cold, sharp despair—buried deep in her heart like a wicked knife, Miss Meadows, in cap and gown and carrying a little baton, trod the cold corridors that led to the music hall. (343)

Here we have the perspective of the authorial narrator, who implicitly leads us to observe Miss Meadows from a specific angle. Although despair is Miss Meadows's own internal feeling, the implied author metaphorizes it into an external knife—a "cold, sharp" and "wicked" knife—piercing Miss Meadows's heart, starting to invite us to see her as a victim of external forces. From Mansfield's pen, the metaphorical adjunct "With . . . like a wicked knife" occupies the prominent position of the very beginning of the narrative, and its syntactic status as the marked theme of the sentence contributes to the foregrounding of the metaphor in the reading process. Then Miss Meadows encounters the Science Mistress:

> The Science Mistress stopped Miss Meadows. "Good mor-ning," she cried, in her sweet, affected drawl. "Isn't it cold? It might be win-ter."
> Miss Meadows, *hugging the knife*, stared *in hatred* at the Science Mistress. Everything about her was sweet, pale, like honey. You would not have been surprised to see a bee caught in the tangles of that yellow hair. "It is rather sharp," said Miss Meadows, grimly.
> The other smiled her sugary smile.
> "You look fro-zen," said she. Her blue eyes opened wide; *there came a mocking light in them. (Had she noticed anything?)*
> "Oh, not quite as bad as that," said Miss Meadows, and she gave the Science Mistress, in exchange for her smile, a quick grimace and passed on. (344, italics added)

Here the omniscient narrator's perspective interacts with Miss Meadows's limited perspective. As is revealed later in the narrative, Miss Meadows is in despair because she has received Basil's letter breaking off their engagement. Miss Meadows's hostility ("in hatred," "grimace") to the Science Mistress is ill-grounded since, without access to the personal letter, the Science Mistress is undoubtedly in the dark about the happening. What appears to be

Style and Concealed Social Protest 113

an objective narratorial description "there came a mocking light in them" can only be Miss Meadows's ungrounded suspicion, a point that gains support from the following free indirect thought "Had she noticed anything?" Through the free indirect thought, Mansfield signals to us that what Miss Meadows is afraid of is other people getting to know the breaking off of the engagement. The use of brackets surrounding Miss Meadows's speculative thought functions paradoxically to draw attention to it, subtly highlighting her worry about other people's opinion. This invites us to experience the social pressure Miss Meadows is in fear of. The authorial description "hugging the knife," coupled with Miss Meadows's own word "sharp," carries on the device of presenting internal despair as an external knife. The knife image appears again when Miss Meadows is teaching the music lesson:

> Miss Meadows, her hands thrust in her sleeves, the baton under her arm, strode down the centre aisle, mounted the steps, turned sharply, seized the brass music stand, planted it in front of her, and gave two sharp taps with her baton for silence. . . . She knew perfectly well what they were thinking. "Meady is in a wax." Well, let them think it! Her eyelids quivered; she tossed her head, defying them. *What could the thoughts of those creatures matter to someone who stood there bleeding to death, pierced to the heart, to the heart, by such a letter—*
> . . . "I feel more and more strongly that our marriage would be a mistake. Not that I do not love you. I love you as much as it is possible for me to love any woman, but, truth to tell, I have come to the conclusion that I am not a marrying man, and the idea of settling down fills me with nothing but—"and the word "disgust" was scratched out lightly and "regret" written over the top. (344–45, italics added)

The italicized words are Miss Meadows's thoughts in free indirect discourse. Her unconcern for her pupils' opinion of her contrasts sharply with her hypersensitivity to the Science Mistress' opinion. She does not care about how her pupils think of her because they are not yet in a position to know anything about her engagement. This points to the fact that whether other people know of Basil's retraction of the engagement is of paramount importance to Miss Meadows. From her own perspective, she is "pierced to the heart, to the heart" by Basil's letter. This joins hands with the narrator's earlier description of Miss Meadows's despair as an external "wicked knife" thrust deep into her heart, to highlight the victimization of her by external forces. The effect of shifting from the narrator's perspective to Miss Meadows's can be captured by an equation:

despair = cold, sharp, and wicked knife = Basil's letter

As quoted above, Basil's letter, or rather the part of Basil's letter that Miss Meadows remembers, centers on marriage. Similarly, Miss Meadows's own thoughts about the letter also concentrate on marriage:

114   *Style and Rhetoric of Short Narrative Fiction*

Good Heavens, what could be more tragic than that lament! Every note was a sigh, a sob, a groan of awful mournfulness. Miss Meadows lifted her arms in the wide gown and began conducting with both hands. "... <u>I feel more and more strongly that our marriage would be a mistake</u> ..." she beat. [. . .] The willow trees, outside the high, narrow windows, waved in the wind. They had lost half their leaves. The tiny ones that clung wriggled like fishes caught on a line. "... <u>I am not a marrying man</u>. ..." The voices were silent; the piano waited. [. . .] Again the two light taps; she lifted her arms again. *Fast! Ah, too Fast.* "... <u>and the idea of settling down fills me with nothing but disgust</u>—" <u>Disgust was what he had written. That was as good as to say their engagement was definitely broken off. Broken off! Their engagement!</u> (346–47, underlining added, original italics indicating words from the lament)

Most of the space of the narrative is devoted to the singing lesson, the title event of the narrative. Amidst the narration of Miss Meadows's teaching, setting, and words of the song, there now and then abruptly appear Miss Meadows's thoughts about Basil's letter, indicating that she is haunted by the letter. Through various subtle devices, Mansfield implicitly leads us to see that Miss Meadows does not really care whether Basil loves her or not—what she cares about is whether Basil will marry her. Almost all the words of the letter that figure in Miss Meadows's mind only concern marriage or engagement. Surrounded by the narration of Miss Meadows's teaching activity and marked off by inverted commas coupled with ellipses, Basil's words "I feel more and more strongly that our marriage would be a mistake" and "I am not a marrying man" appear psychologically very prominent in our reading process. Indeed, through the use of ellipses within the inverted commas, Mansfield subtly signals to us that Miss Meadows is only concerned with marriage/engagement itself. The word "disgust" in Basil's letter hurts Miss Meadows most, but in Mansfield's thematic design, the hurting is only due to the word's signifying the breaking off of the engagement (*"That was as good as to say their engagement was definitely broken off"*), instead of due to the word's indicating the man's not loving the woman, as is usually expected in such a situation. The short curt inner exclamation "Broken off!" emphatically repeats the last two words of the previous sentence "broken off." This interacts with the following short curt exclamation "Their engagement!" to underline Miss Meadows's preoccupation with engagement or marriage itself. The question arises: Why is Miss Meadows so much preoccupied with marriage? When we reach the following words, we may get some idea:

"But, my darling, if you love me," thought Miss Meadows, "I don't mind how much it is. Love me as little as you like." But she knew he didn't love her. Not to have cared enough to scratch out that word "disgust," so that she couldn't read it! *Soon Autumn yields unto Winter Drear.* She would have to leave the school, too. She could never face

Style and Concealed Social Protest 115

the Science Mistress or the girls after it got known. She would have to disappear somewhere. *Passes away.* The voices began to die, to fade, to whisper . . . to vanish. . . . (348)

In the earlier part of this passage, the mode of thought presentation shifts from direct discourse to indirect discourse, which quickly slips into free indirect discourse. The beginning of the direct thought "But, my darling, if you love me" is abruptly interrupted by "I don't mind how much it is. Love me as little as you like," with the interruption emphatically indicating Miss Meadows's not caring about whether Basil loves her or not. What Miss Meadows cares about is other people's opinion of her after they get to know the breaking off of the engagement. If it is got known, the consequences would be very grave, as conveyed by Miss Meadows's free indirect thought: "She would have to leave the school, too. She could never face the Science Mistress or the girls. . . . She would have to disappear somewhere." Interestingly, the words of the lament "*Soon Autumn yields unto Winter Drear*" are subtly integrated by Mansfield into Miss Meadows's apprehension through the use of the adverb "too" in the immediately following free indirect thought "She would have to leave the school, too." Moreover, from Mansfield's ingenious pen, the words "*Passes away*" echo both the preceding "disappear" and the following "to die" and "to vanish," to form a series of death images. In this passage, which is narrated from Miss Meadows's perspective, Mansfield makes the italicized words from the lament and the voices of the pupils flow with and appear integrated into Miss Meadows's consciousness, emphatically yet unobtrusively convey the severe consequences after the breaking off of the engagement is "got known" by other people.

Why, then, does other people's opinion concerning the engagement or marriage matter so much to the female protagonist? To answer this question, we need to look into the Victorian social context. Victorian England was marked by "the universal obsession with marriage," which "the entire weight of nineteenth-century ideology put forward as being the culminating point of a woman's life" (Basch 1974: 16). Victorian society believed that a woman who failed to bag herself a husband was unattractive, unintelligent, and useless, often making herself an outcast (Auerbach 1982: 111; Napolitano). The Victorian spinster, "as commonly perceived," was "grotesque, out of nature," "unwanted even by the devil" (Auerbach 1982: 109).

In "The Singing Lesson," although there is no reference to any historical period, the most severe consequences the discarded Miss Meadows faces indicate that Mansfield has in mind a phallocentric society like that of the Victorian age where marriage is of paramount importance to a woman and where a man's desertion of a woman can deprive the woman of all her value. But of course, even in Victorian society, a woman unwanted by men would not have to "disappear" from society, even without room for survival. In "The Singing Lesson," the implied author is using the fictive covert progression to satirize and indict, in a highly dramatized yet implicit manner, the

116 *Style and Rhetoric of Short Narrative Fiction*

phallocentric discrimination against a woman discarded by a man, threatening her job, and even her very existence.

In the overt plot, when we read Miss Meadows's free indirect thought, "Good Heavens, what could be more tragic than that lament! Every note was a sigh, a sob, a groan of awful mournfulness," we may feel that Miss Meadows is too sentimental since Basil's love does not really mean much to her ("I don't mind how much it is. Love me as little as you like"). But when we reach this point of the covert progression, we are guided by Mansfield to see that the breaking off of the engagement is socially destructive to Miss Meadows, and her despair becomes perfectly understandable. Further, we are guided by Mansfield to perceive that the knife that is thrust deep into Miss Meadows's heart, in the final analysis, is phallocentric discrimination or subjugation, and the earlier equation can be extended as follows:

despair = cold, sharp, and wicked knife = Basil's letter = phallocentric discrimination

It should have become clear that, behind the overt plot development centering on Miss Meadows's personal relationship with Basil, we have a covert textual progression centering on the relationship between Miss Meadows as a (thirty-year-old) woman unwanted by men and a patriarchal society discriminating against such a woman, threatening to deprive her of her job, even her room for survival. In the overt plot, Miss Meadows is very much her own victim figuring as an object of authorial irony, since she is "drunk from the naivete of her love for Basil" and she "suffocates herself internally at the thought of terminating the relationship" (Morrow 1993: 85). In the covert progression, by contrast, Mansfield implicitly presents Miss Meadows as a victim of phallocentric discrimination, inviting our negative ethical judgment on the social injustice and our sympathy towards the victimized female protagonist.

As regards the protagonist's relation with other characters, in the overt plot, her hostility towards the Science Mistress is only a matter of her own bad temper, and we see her unreasonably venting her frustration on her colleague. In the covert progression, however, Mansfield leads us gradually to understand Miss Meadows' hostility since the Science Mistress will unwittingly form part of the social force functioning to drive Miss Meadows away, even driving her into death. Similarly, in the overt plot, we form a negative ethical judgment of "the wicked" Miss Meadows' treatment of her innocent pupils, inflicting suffering on them (Morrow 1993: 84). By contrast, in the covert progression, Mansfield invites us to form a negative judgment of patriarchal discrimination which, as a "wicked knife," reduces a kind woman to behaving in a wicked way (see below).

In the textual movement, Miss Meadows' thought about the unbearable social pressure is interrupted by a little girl, who suddenly enters the classroom and asks Miss Meadows to go to the head mistress' office, where Miss

Style and Concealed Social Protest   117

Meadows receives a telegram from Basil: "Pay no attention to letter must have been mad bought hat-stand [for a family of three] today Basil" (349). Saved by the telegram from the formidable prospect of having to leave the school and "disappear" from society, Miss Meadows is overjoyed.

> On the wings of hope, of love, of joy, Miss Meadows sped back to the music hall, up the aisle, up the steps, over to the piano.
> "Page thirty-two, Mary," she said, "page thirty-two," and, picking up the yellow chrysanthemum, she held it to her lips to hide her smile. Then she turned to the girls, rapped with her baton: "Page thirty-two, girls. Page thirty-two."
> "We come here To-day with Flowers o'erladen,
> With Baskets of Fruit and Ribbons to boot,
> To-oo Congratulate . . ."
> "Stop! Stop!" cried Miss Meadows. "This is awful. This is dreadful." And she beamed at her girls. "What's the matter with you all? Think, girls, think of what you're singing. Use your imaginations. With Flowers o'erladen. Baskets of Fruit and Ribbons to boot. And Congratulate." Miss Meadows broke off. "Don't look so doleful, girls. It ought to sound warm, joyful, eager Congratulate. Once more. Quickly. All together. Now then!"
> And this time Miss Meadows' voice sounded over all the other voices—full, deep, glowing with expression. (349–50)

This is the last part of the narrative. In the overt plot, we have Miss Meadows' personal relationship with Basil whose love she does not really care, and the drastic change in her mood and behavior after receiving Basil's telegram appears somewhat ridiculous and laughable. In the covert progression, however, the implied author invites us to discern that whether Miss Meadows can have the engagement/marriage determines whether she can go on teaching in the school, even whether she can survive in society, and the drastic change the telegram brings about becomes quite understandable.

In the quoted passage, the word "congratulate" appears three times. The first appearance "To-oo Congratulate . . ." forms the last line of the cited sentence of the paean. In semantic meaning, this line is the purpose of the sentence, which occupies the end focus position. As for the second appearance, "*Congratulate*" is the sole concern of the two-word sentence ("And *Congratulate*"). In its third appearance, "*Congratulate*" is the only word of the paean that figures in Miss Meadows' direct speech. Although the word "love" appears in the narrator's description "On the wings of hope, of love, of joy," readers already know that Miss Meadows does not really love Basil. It is marriage that Miss Meadows is concerned with and it is her regaining the chance of getting married that she wants the pupils to "congratulate" with their song.

Although Miss Meadows has regained Basil's promise of marriage, the fact that a woman unwanted by men is under formidable social pressure

118 *Style and Rhetoric of Short Narrative Fiction*

remains unchanged, and if the capricious Basil discards her again, the spinster would be reduced to a similar desperate and tragic state. Having traced the whole movement of the covert progression as a social protest, I will investigate some aspects of it more carefully.

TWO FACETS FURTHER EXAMINED

Now let us examine in more detail the following two facets of the covert progression.

Kind Woman versus Wicked Woman

In the covert progression, the implied author invites us to see how phallocentric discrimination reduces a kind woman to behaving in a cold and harsh manner:

> What could the thoughts of those creatures matter to someone who stood there bleeding to death, pierced to the heart, to the heart, by such a letter [. . .]
> Miss Meadows stalked over to the piano. And Mary Beazley, who was waiting for this moment, bent forward; her curls fell over her cheeks while she breathed, "Good morning, Miss Meadows," and she motioned towards rather than handed to her mistress a beautiful yellow chrysanthemum. This little ritual of the flower had been gone through *for ages and ages, quite a term and a half*. It was *as much part of the lesson as opening the piano. But this morning, instead of* taking it up, *instead of* tucking it into her belt while she leant over Mary and said, "Thank you, Mary. How very nice! Turn to page thirty-two," what was Mary's horror when Miss Meadows totally ignored the chrysanthemum, made no reply to her greeting, but said in a voice of ice, "Page fourteen, please, and mark the accents well." (345, italics added)

Through elaborate stylistic choices, Mansfield emphatically creates the contrast between Miss Meadows' usual kindness and her abnormal unkindness this morning. The exaggerating adjunct "for ages and ages" and the appositional "quite a term and a half" interact with the adversative "but" and the repeated "instead of" to show that Miss Meadows is habitually or characteristically very kind to her pupils. This point is reinforced both by the comparison "as much part of the lesson as opening the piano" and by the noun "horror" which points to the unexpectedness of Miss Meadows' temporary unkindness. Preceding this, Mansfield presents Miss Meadows' reaction to Basil's letter: "someone who stood there bleeding to death, pierced to the heart, to the heart, by such a letter," which invites the reader's understanding of Miss Meadows' uncharacteristic harshness. In the overt plot, we only see Miss Meadows as a victimizer of the innocent pupils:

Style and Concealed Social Protest 119

Staggering moment! Mary blushed until the tears stood in her eyes, but Miss Meadows was gone back to the music-stand; her voice rang through the music-hall. [. . .] "Quite good," said Miss Meadows, but still in <u>such a strange,</u> stony tone that the younger girls began to feel positively frightened. [. . .] "That ought to break out—a loud, strong *forte*—a lament. And then in the second line, *Winter Drear,* make that *Drear* sound as if a cold wind were blowing through it. *Dre-ear!*" said she so awfully that Mary Beazley, on the music stool, wriggled her spine. [. . .] "Repeat! Repeat!" said Miss Meadows. "More expression, girls! Once more!" *Fast! Ah, too Fast.* The older girls were crimson; some of the younger ones began to cry. (345–48, italics original and underlining added)

Behind the relationship between Miss Meadows as the victimizer and the innocent girls as the victimized in the overt plot, in the covert progression, the implied author invites us to see patriarchal discrimination as the victimizer and Miss Meadows as a victim, who, facing the fearful prospect of losing her job and even her room in society, behaves in a "strangely" cold way to the girls. In fact, in the covert progression the girls are not as innocent as they appear. Miss Meadows "could never face the Science Mistress or the girls after it [the breaking off of the engagement] is got known. . . ." That is to say, like the Science Mistress, the girls would unwittingly form part of the social force driving Miss Meadows away from the school, even from society.

At the beginning of the narrative, the implied author sets the resentful Miss Meadows in contrast with the joyful pupils, but after receiving Basil's telegram, Miss Meadows is presented as behaving in a way quite similar to the pupils. Compare:

Girls of all ages, rosy from the air, and bubbling over with that gleeful excitement that comes from running to school on a fine autumn morning, hurried, skipped, fluttered by. (343–44)
On the wings of hope, of love, of joy, Miss Meadows sped back to the music hall, up the aisle, up the steps, over to the piano. (349)

Compared with adult women seeking marriage or already married, the young pupils are relatively free from patriarchal discrimination, and Miss Meadows, temporarily free from the social pressure against a woman unwanted by men, appears not very different from the girls. This functions to bring into relief how patriarchal social pressure can reduce a woman to morbid behavior, which echoes a similar thematic concern of the covert progression in Mansfield's "Revelations" as analyzed in the preceding chapter.

Interactive Point of View

The covert textual progression in "The Singing Lesson" is marked by the subtle interaction of two perspectives: the narrator's omniscient perspective

120 *Style and Rhetoric of Short Narrative Fiction*

and Miss Meadows's limited focalization. The interaction occurs both locally and across passages. For instance,

> The Science Mistress stopped Miss Meadows.
> "Good mor-ning," she cried, in her sweet, affected drawl. "Isn't it cold? It might be win-ter."
> Miss Meadows, hugging the knife, stared in hatred at the Science Mistress. <u>Everything about her was sweet, pale, like honey. You would not have been surprised to see a bee caught in the tangles of that yellow hair.</u>
> "It is rather sharp," said Miss Meadows, grimly.
> The other smiled her sugary smile.
> "You look fro-zen," said she. Her blue eyes opened wide; *there came a mocking light in them. (Had she noticed anything?)*
> "Oh, not quite as bad as that," said Miss Meadows, and she gave the Science Mistress, in exchange for her smile, a quick grimace and passed on . . . (344, italics and underlining added)

Locally, the italicized words mark an unobtrusive shift from the omniscient narrator's perspective ("hugging the knife," "stared in hatred at," "grimly") to Meadows's, who is hypersensitive to other people's view on the breaking off of her engagement ("a mocking light," "Had she noticed anything?").

On a wider scale, the underlined words from Miss Meadows' viewpoint "Everything about her was sweet, pale, like honey. You would not have been surprised to see a bee caught in the tangles of that yellow hair" seem to interact covertly with the following underlined expression from the narrator's perspective at a later stage of the textual movement:

> "The headmaster's wife keeps on asking me [Basil] to dinner. It's a perfect nuisance. I never get an evening to myself in that place."
> "But can't you refuse?"
> "Oh, well, it doesn't do for a man in my position to be unpopular."
> *Music's Gay Measure,* wailed the voices. The willow trees, outside the high, narrow windows, waved in the wind. They had lost half their leaves. <u>The tiny ones that clung wriggled like fishes caught on a line.</u> ". . . I am not a marrying man. . . ." (346–47, original italics indicating words of the song, underlining added)

In this passage, the opening dialogue, as part of Miss Meadows' reminiscence, appears in Miss Meadows' mind while she is teaching. Similarly, the last sentence " '. . . I am not a marrying man . . .' " are Basil's words emerging in Miss Meadows' mind during the teaching process. They join hands to indicate that Miss Meadows is absorbed in the reminiscence of her relationship with Basil, and she is not in a state to notice the scene outside the window. The simile from the narrator's point of view "fishes caught on a

Style and Concealed Social Protest 121

line" bears similarity to Miss Meadows' earlier perception "a bee caught in the tangles of that yellow hair." Both suggest two related points: one, the entity itself goes into the trap, and the other, it is "caught" there, unable to get free. This reminds us of some words in Mansfield's journal put down in May 1908:

> I feel that I do now realize, dimly, what women in the future will be capable of. They truly as yet have never had their chance. Talk of our enlightened days and our emancipated country—pure nonsense! We are firmly held with the self-fashioned chains of slavery. Yes, now I see that they *are* self-fashioned, and must be self-removed. . . . Here then is a little summary of what I need—power, wealth and freedom. It is the hopelessly insipid doctrine that love is the only thing in the world, taught, hammered into women, from generation to generation, which hampers us so cruelly. We must get rid of that bogey—and then, then comes the opportunity of happiness and freedom. (Murry 1954: 36–37, italics original and underlining added)

In "The Singing Lesson," the "chains of slavery" take the shape of phallocentric discrimination against a woman unwanted by men, and the women characters subject themselves to the bondage. Miss Meadows and the Science Mistress, among other women in the school, are caught or on the hook, being victimized by it or unwittingly functioning as a tool to enforce it. From this angle, we may gain a better understanding of the authorial description of Miss Meadows "hugging the knife," with the verb "hug" subtly hinting her embracing the "self-fashioned chain of slavery."

DEVICES OF CAMOUFLAGE AND CLUES TO THE COVERT PROGRESSION

Although "The Singing Lesson" was published in 1920, its covert progression as social protest has not yet received critical attention. Apart from the traditional concentration on the plot development, this critical neglect is ascribable, to a certain extent, to various devices of camouflage Mansfield has used to keep the social protest implicit.

First, the overt plot development vividly presents a spinster who behaves in a cold, harsh, naïve, and shallow manner. Readers' attention tends to focus on the weaknesses of the female protagonist, which partly accounts for the overlooking of the social factors underlying the female protagonist's behavior. Morrow (1993: 84), for instance, calls the female protagonist "wicked Miss Meadows" and criticizes her "dagger-like stare and cold remarks." He ascribes Miss Meadows' sudden change of mood after receiving Basil's telegram to her being "drunk from the naivete of her love for Basil" (84–85).

122 Style and Rhetoric of Short Narrative Fiction

Second, the overt plot development centers on the personal relationship between Miss Meadows and Basil, and in the whole text there is no explicit mentioning of phallocentric discrimination against a woman unwanted by men, which is only indirectly and unobtrusively suggested by Miss Meadows's own inner thoughts.

Third, the plot development is marked by a highly dramatic change from despair to happiness. Some readers focus on this dramatic change, taking the narrative as a comedy, marked by " 'that marvellous triumph' when beauty holds the balance over the ugliness in life" (see above), which also leads to the overlooking of the covert progression as an implicit social protest.

Fourth, the setting of the narrative is a girls' school, where only female characters appear. The formidable patriarchal social pressure Miss Meadows would face, if the breaking off of the engagement is got known, would be embodied primarily by other women in the school. What Miss Meadows is in fear of ("She would have to leave the school, too. She could never face the Science Mistress or the girls after it got known. She would have to disappear somewhere") appears having to do only with the conflict among females.

Why, then, did Mansfield use such devices of camouflage to keep the social protest implicit? One reason might be economical. As we know, Mansfield left her well-off parents in New Zealand and went to London to seek self-development. As a professional writer, she had to earn a living through publishing her stories. As mentioned in the preceding chapter, on January 1, 1915, Mansfield expressed in her journal her wish to make money and explained the necessity of making money. After she was diagnosed with tuberculosis a couple of years later, she was under more economic pressure to cover medical costs, and she had to try to publish stories that could appeal to a wide audience. At the beginning of the twentieth century, England was still very conservative despite the influence of the New Women movement of the 1890s. As just quoted, Mansfield wrote in her journal: "Talk of our enlightened days and our emancipated country—pure nonsense! We are firmly held with the self-fashioned chains of slavery." In that sociohistorical context, to make money, it would be much safer to produce a story depicting the personal relationship between a woman and a man than to present a social satire against patriarchal discrimination and subjugation, since the personal drama would be much more appealing to readers in general. But as we have seen in "The Singing Lesson," as well as in "Revelations" (see the preceding chapter), Mansfield does implicitly direct social satire against patriarchal discrimination and subjugation in a covert progression behind the overt plot development. While in "Revelations," the female protagonist functions as a doll or plaything of the male protagonist, in "The Singing Lesson," the female protagonist is a music teacher earning her own living, which also functions as a camouflage.

However, Mansfield does give readers subtle clues to the implicit social protest in the covert progression. As analyzed above, the stylistic choices at the very beginning of the text deviantly present Miss Meadows's despair as

Style and Concealed Social Protest 123

a wicked external knife piercing her heart. This is followed by the subtle indication of Miss Meadows's fear of social pressure in her first interpersonal encounter, that with the Science Mistress. Through adopting Miss Meadows's focalization and the ingenious use of free indirect thought in brackets, Mansfield unobtrusively yet emphatically shows Miss Meadows's worry about other people's opinion concerning the breaking off of the engagement. In the reading process, when we get to know Miss Meadows's ungrounded worry as such and the reason underlying her hostility towards the Science Mistress, we will be in a position to start perceiving the covert progression. Miss Meadows's fear of other people's discrimination against her as a woman unwanted by men appears again in a most intense form at the turning point: "She would have to leave the school, too. She could never face the Science Mistress or the girls after it got known. She would have to disappear somewhere. *Passes away.* The voices began to die, to fade, to whisper . . . to vanish. . . . Suddenly the door opened. A little girl in blue walked fussily up the aisle" (348, italics original). The words crucial to the perceiving of the covert progression are positioned right before the sudden reversal of the textual progression, and are therefore structurally significant. Moreover, in describing Miss Meadows's being haunted by Basil's letter, Mansfield uses many ellipses to highlight the point that Miss Meadows is obsessed with the engagement or marriage, while strangely not caring much about Basil's love for her. This obsession with engagement/marriage is closely linked with the fear of social discrimination against a woman unwanted by men.

In existing criticism, the overlooking of the covert progression in Mansfield's "The Singing Lesson" may have to do with traditional interpretive frames. In a letter to Mansfield's husband J. Middleton Murry on October 25, 1923, D. H. Lawrence wrote, "I got *Dove's Nest* here. Thank you very much. Poor Katherine, she is delicate and touching. —But not Great!" (Lawrence 1979: 520) Lawrence's words remind us of Mais's exclamation, "Oh, these spinster schoolmistresses and their passionate aches! How we sigh for the full-blooded lusts of Somerset Maugham's heroes." In *Some Studies in the Modern Novel,* Dorothy M. Hoare comments that Mansfield, like Chekhov, tries

> to arrest within the limits of the short-story, an emotion, an evanescent moment that lights up the play of character, an atmosphere, rather than to narrate an event or record a crisis. From both [Mansfield and Chekhov] one obtains a sense of adjustment, of harmony. This harmony results partly from the fact that Katherine Mansfield does not shrink from the ugly aspects of life but accepts them as part of it. The story in *Bliss, Je ne parle pas francais,* shows a deliberate attempt to grapple with not only the ugly but the abnormal, and though it is not a complete success, it shows a power of dealing with other people's emotions from the inside and of making an unfamiliar character live. (1938: 148–49)

124 *Style and Rhetoric of Short Narrative Fiction*

Hoare's view is quite representative of existing criticism on Mansfield's fiction, which concentrates on her sensitive and perceptive characterization and atmosphere-building. It is a critical consensus that Mansfield is not concerned with social problems, and that her work is marked by "harmony." This view holds for many of Mansfield's short stories, but as we have seen in "The Singing Lesson" and "Revelations," in some of Mansfield's fiction, behind an overt plot concerned with individual characterization and personal relationships, there is a covert progression functioning as an ethical protest against social injustice. In a letter of 1918 to her husband Murry, Mansfield writes,

> I've two "kick offs" in the writing game. *One* is joy—real joy. . . . The other "kick off" is my old original one, and, had I not known love, it would have been my all. Not hate or destruction (both are beneath contempt as real motives) but an *extremely* deep sense of hopelessness, of everything doomed to disaster, almost willfully, stupidly, like the almond tree and 'pas de nougat pour le noel.' There! as I took out a cigarette paper I got it exactly—*a cry against corruption*—that is *absolutely* the nail on the head. Not a protest—a cry. And I mean corruption in the widest sense of the word, of course. I am at present fully launched, right out in the deep sea, with this second state. (Murry 1929: 106, italics original)

In "The Singing Lesson," the covert progression presents an implicit "cry against" phallocentric discrimination as one kind of corruption. If we overlook the covert progression, we would be hard put to appreciate adequately the ethical significance of the narrative and, moreover, may miss a substantial part of its aesthetic value. As mentioned at the beginning of this chapter, this text by Mansfield has been regarded as an emotionally too sentimental and artistically deficient narrative, but when the covert progression gradually comes into view, the sentimentality would become quite understandable and the narrative would become increasingly artistic with various textual details newly taking on aesthetic value, and, moreover, the female protagonist would invite much more understanding and sympathy.

6 Style and Secretly Unifying the Digressive

Mansfield's "The Fly"

Katherine Mansfield's "The Fly" (originally published in 1922) is "the subject of considerable, often heated, critical debate" (Barnard 2000: 199). Indeed, "none of her stories have come in for so much commentary as 'The Fly' " (O'Sullivan 2011: 21). As mentioned in the introduction, the narrative has a simple plot: Mr. Woodifield, who retired after having a stroke, makes his weekly visit to his old boss in the office. He tells the boss about the graves of his son and the boss's son, who were both killed in the war. After Woodifield leaves, the boss recalls his son in pain but finds himself unable to shed tears. Then he notices that a fly has fallen into his inkpot and is struggling to get free. The boss first draws the fly out of the inkpot, then he changes his mind and keeps dropping blots of ink on the fly until it is killed, which leaves the boss wretched, frightened, and forgetful. As F. W. Bateson and B. Shahevitch (1962) observe, this plot development may be divided into three Acts. Act 1 is the Woodifield episode, Act 2 is the re-enactment of the son's death, and Act 3 is the killing of the fly, with "a mounting intensity, a transition from the near-comic to the near-tragic" (52).[1]

As various critics have indicated, this plot development has rich symbolic and biographical associations. The title "The Fly" and the way the fly suffers death at the boss's hand remind us of the well-known lines in Act 4, Scene 1 of William Shakespeare's King Lear, "As flies to wanton boys are we to th' gods, / They kill us for their sport" (2007a: 131). That is to say, the narrative may be taken as "a chilling commentary on divine indifference" (Woods 2008). The narrative also recalls Mansfield's journal on December 31, 1918, entitled "The Fly":

> Oh, the times when she had walked upside down on the ceiling, run up glittering panes, floated on a lake of light, flashed through a shining beam!
> And God looked upon the fly fallen into the jug of milk and saw that it was good. And the smallest Cherubim and Seraphim of all, who delight in misfortune, struck their silver harps and shrilled: 'How is the fly fallen, fallen!' (Murry 1954: 153)

126 *Style and Rhetoric of Short Narrative Fiction*

On January 11, 1918, Mansfield sent a letter to her husband, John Middleton Murry. There she writes, after an exhausting wartime train trip, "I feel like a fly who has been dropped into the milk-jug and fished out again, but is still too milky and drowned to start cleaning up yet" (Murry 1929: 86). Since the narrative was created just a few months before Mansfield died of tuberculosis, many critics treat the fly as a symbol of the dying and helpless Mansfield herself, who struggled against the tuberculosis "which was beating her, blow by blow, into the grave" (Jacobs 1947; see also Bledsoe 1947, Coroneos 1997). In a recent essay, Vincent O'Sullivan (2011: 22) says: "It is difficult not to read 'The Fly' biographically, regardless of how earnestly Theory advises against such old humanist practice; hard not to see the Boss as God, as Harold Beauchamp [Mansfield's father], as Fate, as the stopping and starting of disease. . . . Whatever, it is a story of unrelenting grimness, a story that supposes, 'What if nothing can be done?' While somewhere in the background frolic the 'wanton boys' from King Lear, and Hardy's President of the Immortals."

Although critics tend to agree that "The Fly" is a symbolic story, they differ as to how well Mansfield uses her symbol. Robert Wooster Stallman (1945) finds that Mansfield very "cleverly" "inverts her symbol": the boss is the boss of the other human characters in "his little world" ("all are as flies to him") and "of the little life of the Fly who has fallen into his inkpot," but "at the first stage of the experiment [on the fly] the Boss is to be equated with the Fly. He is, ironically then, at once both boss and fly." Sylvia Berkman (1951: 195) however, finds the symbolism in "The Fly" confused,

> Obviously the boss stands for a superior controlling power—God, destiny, or fate—which in capricious and impersonal cruelty tortures the little creature struggling under this hand until it lies still in death. At the same time the boss is presented as one who has himself received the blows of this superior power through the death of his only son in the war. Thus the functional role which the boss plays in the story does not fuse with the symbolic role.

Mary Rohrberger (1966: 69) challenges this view and argues that Berkman "fails to perceive the symbolic relationship between microcosm and macrocosm which makes the boss part in relation to whole and shows him acting both as father figure and God figure." Rohrberger (71) asserts that the fly "must be recognized as a symbol for all the characters in the story. The boss, the boss's son, and old Woodifield are all flies in relation to a controlling force," since the boss has lost his son, who is killed in the war, and Woodifield "has suffered a stroke which has brought him to premature senility" (see also Bledsoe 1947). As for the boss, "who had lived for his son," in "finally recognizing the boy's death" he is "at the moment of his own symbolic death" (72).

Moreover, although critics tend to agree on the symbolic nature of the narrative, they have come up with conflicting interpretations of the thematic

Style and Secretly Unifying the Digressive 127

meaning of the plot development. Stallman (1945) takes the plot development as being marked by "the conflict between time and grief" and its theme as "time conquer[ing] grief." To Thomas Bledsoe (1947), however, "the whole movement of the story" centers on the cruelty and indifference of the boss (mankind) and fate (the gods), and the boss's cruel treatment of the fly is to divert his own grief. J. D. Thomas (1961: 261) sees the theme of the plot development as "the recovery or escape of the protagonist *from* his grief; if the death of the fly stands for the death of the grief, then the ink is the agency of that very recovery." In contrast, Clinton W. Oleson (1961: 585) argues that the narrative "should be read as the depiction of the boss's escape from facing the reality of death and the sterility of his own existence." Paulette Michel-Michot (1974) divides the narrative into three parts (similar to the division made by Bateson and Shahevitch) and carefully analyzes them one by one in an attempt to "capture" the characteristics of the boss. She says in conclusion, "Here, as in many of her stories, Katherine Mansfield opposes the hard, the cruel, the possessive, the egotistical and the life-killers to the sensitive in a tightly-structured story rendering a critical hour in the life of the boss" (91).

Further, challenging previous critics who regard the narrative as Mansfield's best creation, Clare Hanson and Andrew Gurr (1981: 95–135) argue that the story's crucial symbolist patterning is flawed because it is too inflexible. To Sydney Janet Kaplan, this narrative "demonstrates how power corrupts, how patriarchal dominance victimizes" the fly as a small and powerless "other" (1991: 189). Even though the boss's "sadistic behavior" results from what he has suffered, Mansfield "does not condone it" (ibid.). Viewing the plot development more in narratological terms, Patrick Morrow (1993: 15) observes that the sequence of events "constitutes a process, and a process to [Mieke] Bal may be either one of improvement or deterioration," but he finds that "Mansfield's story confounds easy classification" along such lines. "If we see the boss's inability to call up his son's memory as proof that time heals all wounds, the process seems one of improvement; but if we interpret the events as evidence that the boss has forgotten his son rather quickly and thus, in spite of his protests, never really cared for the boy, the process shows deterioration." And he concludes that since "the boss's torturing and killing of the fly leads readers to an unsympathetic reading of his character, the process is most likely one of deterioration" (ibid.).

Again, Con Coroneos (1997), calling into question the earlier assumption that "the story is a complex rendering of grief, memory and loss," argues that part of the ambiguity of the text "arises from its ideological containment of actions which sit uneasily between sadism and sentimentality" and that its element of sadism "excuses itself through the idea of a 'truth to psychology,' " which enables the reader "to participate in the spectacle of suffering without the anxiety of guilt" (quoted in Barnard 2000: 230–32). By contrast, Kathleen Jones (2010: 441) finds the plot development not ambiguous or ambivalent but entirely "cruel and cynical, without sentiment or romance." In a concentrated attempt to apply Sigmund Freud's psychoanalytic theory to this narrative, Clare Hanson (2011: 125–26) finds "The

128 *Style and Rhetoric of Short Narrative Fiction*

Fly" "perhaps the most uncanny of Mansfield's stories," and the plot development "dramatizes the incursion of death into the private sphere." In the process of killing the fly, "the boss plays with death, keeps coming up to its frontier, re-enacting his son's death in ways which reflect his ambivalent feelings about it" (126). To Hanson, the end of the plot development where the boss cannot remember what he was thinking earlier marks the completion of repression and disavowal (ibid.).

A fuller picture of existing criticism may be gained by taking a look at the summary of the major themes of the plot development of "The Fly" offered by Anja Barnard (2000: 200). The story

> is frequently seen as an indictment of the brutal horror of World War I, along with the hopelessness and despair left in its wake. Many scholars have remarked that the timetable that the story sets for the death of the two sons coincides with the 1915 death of Mansfield's brother, a victim of wartime fighting. The war dead, it is claimed are likened to flies innocently slaughtered by cruel forces over which they have no control. Some critics have pointed to references Mansfield made in her journals and letters about flies to show that the fly represents herself, struggling to fight the ravages of her tuberculosis, only to be crushed in the end by a selfish and cruel father much like the boss in her story. Other critics have resisted such autobiographical interpretations, insisting they detract from a more universally compelling existential message concerning the inevitability of death and man's unwillingness to accept its truth. These scholars see the story as essentially about the boss's brief realization of his own pitiful ambitions and mortality before he subconsciously tries to suppress this horrible knowledge.

As all this shows, generations of critics have tried to offer interpretations of the plot development of "The Fly," often probing into the depths of its thematic import from diverse angles. I will not offer judgments on which interpretations are better than others, since the aim of this essay is not to try to come up with a more valid interpretation of the plot, but to reveal a covert progression behind the plot development which has eluded existing critical attention. While the plot development centers on war, death, existence, grief, memory, helplessness, suffering, loss, control, cruelty, indifference, victimization, and so forth, the covert progression has a different thematic concern, namely, to direct a silent and continuous irony against the boss's own vanity. Given the two parallel movements with their different—yet not conflicting—thematic concerns, overlooking the covert progression may result in the failure to understand certain textual elements when mapping them unto the plot development. In what follows, I will first concentrate on revealing the covert progression itself, and then I will discuss some misunderstandings that arise from missing it.

Style and Secretly Unifying the Digressive   129

IRONIC COVERT PROGRESSION

Since the covert progression is an undercurrent that runs throughout the narrative, the analysis will trace it step by step, and we now begin with the first paragraph of the text:

"Y'are very snug in here," piped old Mr. Woodifield, and he peered out of the great, green-leather armchair by his friend the boss's desk as a baby peers out of its pram. His talk was over; it was time for him to be off. But he did not want to go. Since he had retired, since his . . . stroke, the wife and the girls kept him boxed up in the house every day of the week except Tuesday. On Tuesday he was dressed and brushed and allowed to cut back to the City for the day. Though what he did there the wife and girls couldn't imagine. Made a nuisance of himself to his friends, they supposed. . . . Well, perhaps so. All the same, we cling to our last pleasures as the tree clings to its last leaves. So there sat old Woodifield, smoking a cigar and staring almost greedily at the boss, who rolled in his office chair, stout, rosy, five years older than he, and still going strong, still at the helm. It did one good to see him.

Wistfully, admiringly, the old voice added, "It's snug in here, upon my word!"

"Yes, it's comfortable enough," agreed the boss, and he flipped the Financial Times with a paper-knife. As a matter of fact he was proud of his room; he liked to have it admired, especially by old Woodifield. It gave him a feeling of deep, solid satisfaction to be planted there in the midst of it in full view of that frail old figure in the muffler. (422–23)

The narrative begins abruptly in the middle with the direct quotation of old Mr. Woodifield's words "Y'are very snug in here." Semantically, this foregrounded direct speech somewhat clashes, at least in surface meaning, with old Woodifield's later exclamation "It's snug in here, upon my word!" in that the former only has to do with the snugness of "you," but the latter is concerned with that of both "you" and Woodifield himself. Given the fact that old Woodifield feels snug himself, the opening direct speech exclusively concerned with the snugness of the boss appears to be odd. The oddity helps foreground old Woodifield's admiration for the boss, an admiration that is reinforced by the adjunct "almost greedily" and then "Wistfully, admiringly," the latter even markedly occupying the initial thematic position in the clause. These stylistic choices interact to change implicitly the sense of the exclamation "It's snug in here," making it newly convey Woodifield's admiration for the boss rather than his own snugness.

The boss's agreement, "Yes, it's comfortable enough," likewise conveys more than the boss's feeling of comfort: the following narratorial comment, "As a matter of fact he was proud of his room; he liked to have it admired, especially by old Woodifield," exposes the boss's self-satisfaction and vanity.

130 *Style and Rhetoric of Short Narrative Fiction*

The next sentence regarding his "feeling of deep, solid satisfaction to be planted there in the midst of it in full view of that frail old figure in the muffler" further indicates that the vanity goes with selfishness. In what precedes, Woodifield's frailty is emphatically conveyed through the contrast between his age ("old") and his state ("as a baby peers out of its pram"). Readers will surely feel sympathetic towards the pitiable "frail old figure in the muffler," forming a contrast with the boss's selfish feeling. The narratorial commentary led by "as a matter of fact," in particular the adjunct "especially" and the epithets "deep, solid," convey the implied author's implicit irony against the boss's selfish vanity, inviting the authorial audience to make negative ethical judgment on the boss in this aspect.

Given old Woodifield's deplorably frail state, his wife and daughters believe that he "ma[kes] a nuisance of himself" when visiting his friends. Actually, Woodifield's weekly visit to the boss's office is most welcome, for his very frailty intensifies the self-satisfaction of the boss. The clash between the supposition of Woodifield's family and the real fact gives rise to irony, but it is not so much dramatic irony at the family's supposition (which is normal and sensible) as ethical irony against the boss's selfish vanity.

From the viewpoint of the plot development centering on war, death, existence, grief, and so forth, the various textual details in the opening passage as analyzed above appear unimportant and even somewhat irrelevant. But in terms of the ironic covert progression directed against the boss's moral nature, starting from the abrupt direct speech at the very opening sentence, the trivial details interact to form the first stage of the implicit textual movement. Even at this initial stage, the perception of the covert irony starts to establish a secret communication between the implied author and us at the expense of the central character. We start to take pleasure in perceiving the ethical significance and aesthetic value of what appears to be trivial and digressive to the thematic concerns of the plot development, pleasure that will gradually increase with the progression of the undercurrent. The following passage reads:

> "I've had it done up lately," he explained, as he had explained for the past—how many?—weeks. "New carpet," and he pointed to the bright red carpet with a pattern of large white rings. "New furniture," and he nodded towards the massive bookcase and the table with legs like twisted treacle. "Electric heating!" He waved almost exultantly towards the five transparent, pearly sausages glowing so softly in the tilted copper pan.
>
> But he did not draw old Woodifield's attention to the photograph over the table of a grave-looking boy in uniform standing in one of those spectral photographers' parks with photographers' storm-clouds behind him. It was not new. It had been there for over six years. (423)

The first paragraph of this passage continues to direct implicit irony at the boss's vanity. He keeps showing off his newly furnished office to old

Style and Secretly Unifying the Digressive 131

Woodifield, flaunting one by one the new furnishings in the room. The detailed and somewhat mocking description of "the bright red carpet with a pattern of large white rings [. . .] the table with legs like twisted treacle [. . .] the five transparent, pearly sausages glowing so softly in the tilted copper pan" brings out the ludicrous pettiness of the boss's attention, which is incongruous with his social identity as a "boss" conventionally expected to concentrate on bigger things. But the very incongruity of the petty perception effectively highlights and ironizes the boss's vanity. The description here also echoes the preceding one, where old Woodifield "peered out of the great, green-leather armchair by his friend the boss's desk as a baby peers out of its pram." The boss offers his guest a "great" armchair to reflect his own importance and somehow to "belittle" the other, at least in his own perception.

Interestingly, although the narrator is omniscient, a question mark appears in the parenthesis "as he had explained for the past—how many?—weeks." The feigned narratorial uncertainty (suggesting the unusual length of time), coupled with the adjunct "almost exultantly," foregrounds the boss's repetitively and enthusiastically showing off his office to his visitors. It is true that the death of the boss's son six years ago is a crucial event in the plot development, and this requires dramatic contrast between the newly equipped office and the old "photograph over the table"; but for that contrastive purpose it is only necessary to mention the new appearance of the office. The boss's repetitive, enthusiastic parading and petty perception of the new things therefore appear to be unimportant or even redundant in terms of the plot development. But these redundant details are significant constituents of the undercurrent Mansfield has artistically produced. Through such artful stylistic and structural choices, Mansfield guides the reader's interpretive effort in an ethical direction different from that of the plot development, as well as inviting the reader to appreciate a different layer of the subtle artistry of the text. This ethical-aesthetic undercurrent, as we will see, runs throughout the text.

In what follows, Woodifield tries to tell the boss something but cannot remember what. After drinking the whisky offered by the boss, he remembers that when his daughters went to Belgium to visit the tomb of his son, they came across that of the boss's son. After seeing Woodifield off, the boss says he does not want to be disturbed for half an hour. He shuts the door and sits down in his spring chair:

> leaning forward, the boss covered his face with his hands. *He wanted, he intended, he had arranged to weep. . . .*
> It had been a terrible shock to him when old Woodifield sprang that remark upon him about the boy's grave. It was exactly as though the earth had opened and he had seen the boy lying there with Woodifield's girls staring down at him. For it was strange. Although over six years had passed away, the boss never thought of the boy except as lying

132 *Style and Rhetoric of Short Narrative Fiction*

unchanged, unblemished in his uniform, asleep for ever. "My son!" groaned the boss. But no tears came yet. In the past, in the first few months and even years after the boy's death, he had only to say those words to be overcome by such grief that nothing short of a violent fit of weeping could relieve him. Time, he had declared then, he had told everybody, could make no difference. Other men perhaps might recover, might live their loss down, but not he. How was it possible? His boy was an only son. Ever since his birth the boss had worked at building up this business for him; it had no other meaning if it was not for the boy. Life itself had come to have no other meaning. How on earth could he have slaved, denied himself, kept going all those years without the promise for ever before him of the boy's stepping into his shoes and carrying on where he left off?

And that promise had been so near being fulfilled. The boy had been in the office learning the ropes for a year before the war. Every morning they had started off together; they had come back by the same train. And what congratulations he had received as the boy's father! No wonder; he had taken to it marvellously. As to his popularity with the staff, every man jack of them down to old Macey couldn't make enough of the boy. And he wasn't the least spoilt. No, he was just his bright natural self, with the right word for everybody, with that boyish look and his habit of saying, "Simply splendid!"

But all that was over and done with as though it never had been. The day had come when Macey had handed him the telegram that brought the whole place crashing about his head. "Deeply regret to inform you . . ." And he had left the office a broken man, with his life in ruins.

Six years ago, six years. . . . How quickly time passed! It might have happened yesterday. The boss took his hands from his face; he was puzzled. Something seemed to be wrong with him. He wasn't feeling as he wanted to feel. He decided to get up and have a look at the boy's photograph. But it wasn't a favourite photograph of his; the expression was unnatural. It was cold, even stern-looking. The boy had never looked like that. (425–26; italics added)

If the only son falls in battle, the father cannot as a rule help shedding tears in a situation like this. But from Mansfield's ironic pen, shedding tears for his dead son becomes for the boss a task impossible to carry out at present. Mansfield uses three parallel clauses—"He wanted, he intended, he had arranged to weep"—to convey the abnormality of the boss's feeling. Normally, "wanting to weep" in such a situation means having the spontaneous urge to weep out of grief, but the reader's conventional expectation is somewhat defeated by the second clause, "he intended to weep"—instead of being spontaneous, weeping becomes something the boss plans to do. The oddity is reinforced and the reader's expectation further defeated by the third clause, "he had arranged to weep," which further highlights the lack of

Style and Secretly Unifying the Digressive 133

spontaneous grief. The adjunct "yet" in the sentence below ("But no tears came yet.") leads the reader to expect the boss's tears at a later point in time, but this expectation is again frustrated. And in the last paragraph of the above quote, the boss's own reflection, "he was puzzled. Something seemed to be wrong with him. He wasn't feeling as he wanted to feel," demonstrates even further and more explicitly that the boss no longer has real grief.

In the passage quoted, moreover, we see not only the contrast between the boss's "violent fit of weeping" in the past and the vain effort to weep at present but also the contrast between his past prediction that time "could make no difference" to him and the fact that time has actually made a big difference to him. These contrasts also explain another one between the narratorial comment "he had left the office a broken man, with his life in ruins" and the boss's pride and self-satisfaction as shown at the beginning of the narrative. Besides, his son's present expression on the photo appears to the boss, as never in the past, "cold, even stern-looking," against his expectation.

What, then, are the reasons underlying these contrasts between present and past? The heart of the contrasts lies in the relationship between the boss and his son, one that is only depicted in the quoted passage. In the interpretive process, the boss at first appears to be selflessly working for his son, but when we reach the sentence, "How on earth could he have slaved, denied himself, kept going all those years without the promise for ever before him of the boy's stepping into his shoes and carrying on where he left off?," it turns out that he is only working for the succession of his own business. The boss's reminiscence centers on his hope that his son will step into his shoes and the smashing of that hope by war, as clearly indicated by the two topic sentences of the two paragraphs that follow ("And that promise had been so near being fulfilled." "But all that was over and done with as though it never had been"). Significantly, there is no mention of their family life and family affection in the whole narrative. This helps to show that to the boss his son is only a means to carry on his business and to bring him honor and glory in his lifetime and after his death. The boss's brief reminiscence puts emphasis on the inseparability or even the identity of the father and son in business ("Every morning they had started off [for the office] together; they had come back by the same train") and on the glory his son has brought him ("And what congratulations he had received as the boy's father!"). The boss's deep grief at his son's death is in essence a matter of his business continuity and his personal vanity.

At this point, let us recall the beginning of the narrative, where, we have seen, the boss has already found other means to regain his sense of self-importance, such as doing up and showing off his office, a self-flattering comparison between his own health and the frailty of Woodifield, and the flattery of his friends. These means have replaced his son's role in satisfying his vanity, enabling him to live a proud life instead of one "in ruins." This is a fundamental reason underlying his present inability to shed tears for his

134 *Style and Rhetoric of Short Narrative Fiction*

son. We can now understand why "the boss never thought of the boy except as lying unchanged, unblemished in his uniform, asleep for ever": unable to accept his son's death because of his vanity, he always self-deceivingly thinks of his dead son in that peculiar way. The narratorial comment that introduces the boss's peculiar mental attitude, "For it was strange," takes on an ironic ring which becomes more intense in the words: "the [boy's] expression was unnatural. It was cold, even stern-looking. The boy had never looked like that." As we all know, a person's expression on a photo never changes. Rather, the change observed in the boy's look indicates the change of the boss's own state of mind—he has found other means to satisfy his vanity and no longer feels grief for the loss of his son. Arguably, the term "cold" is used by Mansfield to convey implicit irony against the boss's treating his son only as a means of carrying on his business and the term "stern" seems to go further in conveying implicit authorial criticism against the boss's selfish vanity, which subtly invites readers' negative ethical judgment on the boss.

Now we come to the last passage of the text—the title scene of the boss killing the fly, which, as the crucial ending of the narrative, is of much importance to the covert progression centering on the boss's vanity as well as to the plot development centering on death, control, victimization, and so forth. I will discuss the thematic implications of the passage for these two contexts in turn.

> At that moment the boss noticed that a fly had fallen into his broad inkpot, and was trying feebly but desperately to clamber out again. Help! help! said those struggling legs. But the sides of the inkpot were wet and slippery; it fell back again and began to swim. The boss took up a pen, picked the fly out of the ink, and shook it on to a piece of blotting-paper. For a fraction of a second it lay still on the dark patch that oozed round it. Then the front legs waved, took hold, and, pulling its small, sodden body up, it began the immense task of cleaning the ink from its wings. [. . .] The horrible danger was over; it had escaped; it was ready for life again.
>
> But just then the boss had an idea. He plunged his pen back into the ink, leaned his thick wrist on the blotting-paper, and as the fly tried its wings down came a great heavy blot. What would it make of that? What indeed! The little beggar seemed absolutely cowed, stunned, and afraid to move because of what would happen next. But then, as if painfully, it dragged itself forward. The front legs waved, caught hold, and, more slowly this time, the task began from the beginning.
>
> He's a plucky little devil, thought the boss, and he felt a real admiration for the fly's courage. That was the way to tackle things; that was the right spirit. Never say die; it was only a question of . . . But the fly had again finished its laborious task, and the boss had just time to refill his pen, to shake fair and square on the new-cleaned body yet another

Style and Secretly Unifying the Digressive   135

dark drop. What about it this time? A painful moment of suspense followed. But behold, the front legs were again waving; the boss felt a rush of relief. He leaned over the fly and said to it tenderly, "You artful little b . . ." And he actually had the brilliant notion of breathing on it to help the drying process. All the same, there was something timid and weak about its efforts now, and the boss decided that this time should be the last, as he dipped the pen deep into the inkpot.

It was. The last blot fell on the soaked blotting-paper, and the draggled fly lay in it and did not stir. The back legs were stuck to the body; the front legs were not to be seen.

"Come on," said the boss. "Look sharp!" And he stirred it with his pen—in vain. Nothing happened or was likely to happen. The fly was dead.

The boss lifted the corpse on the end of the paper-knife and flung it into the waste-paper basket. But such a grinding feeling of wretchedness seized him that he felt positively frightened. He started forward and pressed the bell for Macey.

"Bring me some fresh blotting-paper," he said sternly, "and look sharp about it." And while the old dog padded away he fell to wondering what it was he had been thinking about before. What was it? It was. . . . He took out his handkerchief and passed it inside his collar. For the life of him he could not remember. (426–28; italics added)

Critics tend to take this final scene as showing the boss's sadistic cruelty (see, for instance, Berkman 1951: 195; Jones 2010: 441), but in terms of narrative progression, the boss at first actually takes action to save the fly's life out of pity. The personifying expression "Help! help! said those struggling legs" conveys the boss's empathetic point of view. Only when the fly is ready to fly away does the boss suddenly have an "idea" which leads to the death of the fly. The text never explicitly mentions what the "idea" is. But a careful examination of the stylistic choices made here will enable us to discover that the boss is trying to test through the fly his own ability to survive under pressure, and that the boss increasingly identifies with the fly. After dropping the first blot of ink on the fly, there is presented the inner thought of the boss in free indirect discourse "What would it make of that? What indeed!" When the boss sees that the fly is making a strenuous effort to clear its wings from the ink, he feels "a real admiration for the fly's courage." We are again given direct access to his inner thoughts in free indirect discourse: "That was the way [for us] to tackle things; that was the right spirit [for us]. Never say die; it was only a question of . . ." The inclusive referring expression "things," the absence of qualification of "right spirit," and the categorical adverb "never" interact to suggest that the boss is conducting an experiment to test the ability to survive in difficult circumstances in general and his own ability in particular. If the fly fails to survive, it will be a heavy blow to his own confidence, pride, and vanity.

136 *Style and Rhetoric of Short Narrative Fiction*

Then the boss further tests the fly's representative ability to survive by dropping another blot of ink on it. "A painful moment of suspense follow[s]," and when the front legs of the fly are again waving, the boss "[feels] a rush of relief." We have good reason to infer that because of his identification with the fly, the boss feels "painful suspense" and "a rush of relief": he is feeling anxious not so much about the fly as about himself—about his own ability to survive. Precisely because of his anxiety about his own chances of survival, he wants to breathe on the fly "to help the drying process." Having then noticed that "there [is] something timid and weak about [the fly's] efforts" at this stage, he decides to try the fly for the last time, thinking that the fly may still survive it (after all, there is only "something" timid and week about the fly's efforts). But contrary to the boss's expectation, after the "last blot [falls] on the soaked blotting-paper," the fly does not stir. "'Come on,' [says] the boss. 'Look sharp!' And he stir[s] it with his pen—in vain": the dash highlights "in vain," implicitly casting irony on the boss's overestimating the ability of the fly's (and his own) power of survival. The curt two-word sentence "It was [the last time]" is the narrator's comment, referring to the fly's inability to survive. This forms a contrast with the boss's wish when dropping the last blot of ink, a contrast that implicitly generates irony at the boss's overconfidence and his urging and stirring the fly "in vain." This ironic dissonance between the viewpoint of the narrator and that of the boss has eluded critical attention.

In the past the boss identified himself with his son, on whom he placed his own confidence and pride; and when his son was killed, he was totally "broken." Similarly, at this moment, the boss identifies himself with the fly, on which he places his confidence and his hope to survive under pressure; so when the fly dies instead, his confidence and hope are destroyed and he is seized by "such a grinding feeling of wretchedness," feeling "positively frightened." It is meaningful that Mansfield chooses the epithet "grinding" to modify the boss's feeling. Apart from referring to the state of being oppressive or tedious, this word also has the sense "seemingly without end" (Pearsall 1998: 808). When his son died, the boss thought he would remain wretched all his life, but he soon regained his pride and self-importance through other means. Similarly, after the fly's death the boss may overcome the "grinding feeling of wretchedness" and regain his pride and self-importance through other means, as soon emerges from his "stern" command to old Macey and his treating the old clerk as an "old dog" (a referring expression that indicates the narrator's ironic mimicking of the boss's contemptuous point of view).

In terms of the boss's attitude towards the old clerk, let us take a look at a relevant preceding description: When old Woodifield had left, "for a long moment the boss stayed, staring at nothing, while the grey-haired office messenger, watching him, dodged in and out of his cubby-hole like a dog that expects to be taken for a run. Then: 'I'll see nobody for half an hour, Macey,' said the boss. 'Understand? Nobody at all.' 'Very good, sir' " (425). Macey's dog-like obsequiousness and servility in the boss's presence ("watching

Style and Secretly Unifying the Digressive 137

him") indicate the kind of behavior the boss expects from his "grey-haired" clerk as a means to satisfy his vanity and sense of self-importance.

Now we come to the last paragraph of the narrative, which focuses on the boss's forgetfulness. This ending seems quite irrelevant to the title "The Fly" and to the plot's themes of war, death, and victimization. But it has a key role to play in the ironic covert progression since it implicitly conveys most powerful and penetrating irony against the boss's vanity. Compare:

(a) "There was something I wanted to tell you," said old Woodifield, and his eyes grew dim remembering. "Now what was it? I had it in my mind when I started out this morning." His hands began to tremble, and patches of red showed above his beard. Poor old chap, he's on his last pins, thought the boss. (423)

(b) And while the old dog padded away he fell to wondering what it was he had been thinking about before. What was it? It was. . . . He took out his handkerchief and passed it inside his collar. For the life of him he could not remember. (428)

As the page numbers indicate, the two passages are widely apart, but they are near-symmetrical. In passage (a), Woodifield wants to tell the boss about their sons' graves, but he temporarily forgets his intention. At the beginning of the narrative, the boss gains "a feeling of deep, solid satisfaction" at the frailty of Woodifield, and at this moment, viewing the deplorable state of Woodifield in his forgetfulness, the boss's sense of superiority reaches its climax as shown by his condescending thought, vividly presented in free indirect discourse: "Poor old chap, he's on his last pins."

However, in passage (b), the boss himself ironically turns out to be as forgetful as Woodifield. Notice the striking points of similarity between the two characters in their forgetfulness: The boss's "What was it?" directly echoes Woodifield's "Now what was it?" Moreover, in their respective anxious efforts to remember, Woodifield's "hands beg[in] to tremble, and patches of red [show] above his beard," while the boss perspires and he has to take out his handkerchief and pass it "inside his collar" to wipe off his sweat. Without any explicit comment, just by such unobtrusive similarities between different parts of the textual sequence, Mansfield ironically reveals that there is in fact no "deep, solid" ground for the boss to feel self-complacent and condescending at the forgetfulness of Woodifield. Mansfield uses "for the life of him" to put emphasis on the boss's own forgetfulness. The narrative ends very abruptly with the sentence, "For the life of him he could not remember," which occupies the end-focus position of the whole text and which in the reading process is psychologically very prominent, thus ironically highlighting the boss's own forgetfulness. It is at once the climax and the denouement of the narrative's covert progression.

As we have seen, starting from the very beginning of the narrative, behind the plot development centering on war, death, existence, victimization,

138 *Style and Rhetoric of Short Narrative Fiction*

helplessness, and so forth, Mansfield has created another covert textual movement going in a contrastive, yet not conflicting, thematic direction—continuously directing subtle irony against the boss's own vanity and implicitly inviting the reader's negative judgment on this ethical defect of the boss. In the covert progression, various existents are used as vehicles to convey the ethical irony: Woodifield, the boss's snug office, the new furnishings, the office messenger, the boss's son (including the son's photo and dead body), and the fly. It should be noted that female characters, though very minor, also play the role of vehicle in this ironic covert progression. This fictional world focuses on men, but there is one place that touches on the boss's relation to women. In order to help Woodifield recall what he wants to tell, the boss offers him whisky, and Woodifield accepts, observing that his wife and daughters do not allow him to drink whisky at home. The boss then makes a contemptuous comment on them: "'Ah, that's where we know a bit more than the ladies,' cried the boss, swooping across for two tumblers that stood on the table with the water-bottle, and pouring a generous finger into each" (424). In fact, it is common knowledge shared by men and women that a person who has had a stroke should not drink spirits (and "a generous finger" in this context takes on irony—the more generous, the worse). That is to say, the boss actually knows less than the ladies, not "more," and certainly cares less. The boss is sitting very near Woodifield (whose armchair is just by the boss's desk) and there is therefore no need for the boss to "cry" out his response. By making the boss negate the commonsensical knowledge and cry out his negation in a self-complacent and self-glorifying way, Mansfield subtly directs irony against the boss.

As mentioned earlier, irony in the covert progression differs from more local kinds of irony, since it characteristically relies on the interaction among elements in different parts of the textual sequence. In the last paragraph of "The Fly," the description that "[the boss] took out his handkerchief and passed it inside his collar" is by no means ironic in itself, but when considered in relation to the preceding "[Woodifield's] hands began to tremble, and patches of red showed above his beard," it implicitly takes on irony against the boss's sense of superiority at Woodifield's forgetfulness and his condescending generally.[2] Similarly, the last sentence, "For the life of him he could not remember," does not convey irony when viewed locally by itself, but it assumes an ironic ring against the boss's complacence in relation to the boss's earlier sense of superiority to Woodifield's forgetfulness. Moreover, it reinforces in retrospect the irony aimed at the beginning of the narrative against the boss's "deep, solid satisfaction" at the sight of Woodifield's frailty. In this final paragraph, the referring expression "old dog" also becomes ironic, or at least more ironic, when interacting with the earlier detailed description of the aged clerk's obsequiousness in the boss's presence.

To say that in the covert progression later textual elements take on, or intensify, ironic effects in relation to earlier textual elements and vice versa is to say that the uncovering of the ironic undercurrent calls for reading the

Style and Secretly Unifying the Digressive 139

text forward and backward and that careful attention is required to see the complicated interaction among subtle stylistic and structural choices in different parts of the textual sequence.

As to the ethical weakness ironized, it is worth mentioning that in daily life, Mansfield—the "real author" (see Shen 2011a, 2013)—was strongly against vanity as an ethical defect. In a letter in 1920 to her husband Murry, Mansfield writes: "How I do scorn all that horrible old twisted existence I mean really the weekends at Garsington—the paralysis of everybody the vanity and ugliness of so much" (O'Sullivan and Scott 1993, 3: 240). Here Mansfield couples "vanity" with "ugliness" and places both in apposition to "paralysis," making the former explain and illustrate the latter. "Paralysis" in turn is used to explain "that horrible old twisted existence." Clearly, then, "vanity" (like "ugliness," or the more general "paralysis" and "horrible old twisted existence") is an object of Mansfield's "scorn." In a letter of 1921 to her friend Richard Murry describing how she wrote "Miss Brill," Mansfield hastens to add: "Don't think I'm vain about the little sketch. It's only the method I wanted to explain" (O'Sullivan and Scott 1993, 4:165). It would thus appear that she was on her guard against the ethical weakness of being vain, which she despised and condemned.

Not surprisingly, in "The Fly," Mansfield creates a covert textual progression to wage a continuous, subtle, yet scathing attack on this specific weakness. And once alerted to this covert progression, we also gain a fuller, rounder picture of the boss as protagonist and a more comprehensive view of the textual dynamics: It consists not of the plot development alone but of two parallel textual movements which together drive and shape the thematic concerns of the whole narrative.

COVERT PROGRESSION AND PLOT DEVELOPMENT

Although the covert progression and the plot development are two parallel textual movements with distinct concerns, unraveling the former may enable us to understand better various textual elements in relation to the latter sequence. With the interaction in mind, let us examine some previous readings of the story. Since the covert progression centers on the boss, we start with a summary of previous interpretations on him as offered by Anja Barnard:

Much attention has been paid to the central character of the boss. He has been seen as [1] a symbol of malignant forces that are base and motiveless, a representative of the generation that sent its sons to their slaughter in a cruel war, and [2] a god-like figure who, in the words of King Lear, toys with the lives of human beings for sport. Most critics agree that the reader's early good impression of the boss is continuously undermined as the story unfolds. In the end, some have claimed, [3] he can be viewed as a sadomasochist who likely cowed

140 *Style and Rhetoric of Short Narrative Fiction*

his son as he does Woodifield and his clerk. [4] He is a bully who torments the fly for boyish pleasure, and his sense of loss is no more than self-pity. However, some commentators claim that [5] the boss should not be viewed as an unsympathetic character, but simply as a man whose experiments on a common housefly are manifestations of an unconscious metaphysical questioning about the meaning of life. The answer comes to him briefly, but he becomes frightened and quickly pushes it out of his mind. [6] Other critics have seen the boss as a man coming to terms with his own selfishness and heartlessness, who recognizes briefly that his grief for his son has been based on a kind of self-deception. As a result, when the fly dies the boss suffers a spiritual death. (2000: 200; brackets added)

Against interpretation [1], the covert progression helps us see and explain that the boss is not "a representative of the generation that sent its sons to their slaughter in a cruel war": instead, the boss would like his son to step into his shoes in the family business as a way to satisfy his vanity. Interpretation [2] is at once sensible and problematic. On the one hand, the title "The Fly" and the way the fly suffers death at the boss's hand do remind us of the well-known lines in *King Lear* about the fate of the flies, but the picture is more complicated than it appears. We have noticed that the boss first empathizes with the fly and rescues it, and he starts to drop ink on it only when he wants to test through the fly his own ability to survive; and moreover, he wants the fly (with which he identifies) to survive even the last drop of ink. The killing, that is to say, is not as "motiveless," "sadistic," or "capricious and impersonal" as many critics have believed. Rather, through depicting the boss's increasing identification with the fly and his "grinding feeling of wretchedness" and, moreover, his feeling "positively frightened" at the death of the fly, Mansfield seems to suggest that the boss is like a fly himself—unable to control his own fate, liable to destruction by external forces, like his son and Woodifield's son who are killed in the war as flies killed by wanton boys (cf. Bell 1960).

As already indicated, some previous critics have pointed out that the fly symbolizes the boss himself, but the reasons they give for it tend to be partial or somewhat far-fetched. Stallman (1945) maps the climactic scene to the theme of "time conquering grief" and offers this interpretation of how the boss relates to the fly: "At the first stage of the experiment the Boss is to be equated with the Fly" in that "like the Fly, [the boss] conquers the first drop of ink—the grief he suffers"; but when the boss drops the second drop of ink, "the Fly and the Boss can no longer be equated," since "the Fly survives his grief," while the boss "no longer has any grief to conquer." This interpretation goes counter to the textual fact that the boss increasingly identifies with the fly when dropping ink on it. Bledsoe (1947) takes the boss as a fly because "an inexorable fate has already broken his own life and his son's," likewise missing the increasing identification of the

Style and Secretly Unifying the Digressive 141

boss with the fly in the climactic final scene (see a similar interpretation in Rohrberger 1966: 71).

Significantly, the boss's increasing identification with the fly in the climactic scene has different thematic implications for the plot development and the covert progression. Within the former, Mansfield depicts the boss's increasing identification with the fly, which fails to survive the test of ink (thus representing the victims of war and humankind at large in echoing the "flies" of *King Lear*). She thereby intensifies our sense of the boss as a helpless fly-like entity subject to external uncontrollable forces (his losing his son in the war is an earlier manifestation). This interpretation may find support in the testimony of Mansfield's husband Murry: "The profound and ineradicable impression made upon her [Mansfield] by the War . . . found perfect utterance in the last year of her life in the story 'The Fly' " (1954: 107; cf. Bell 1960). But this thematic association with the war is quite irrelevant to the covert progression, where, as we have seen, the climactic final scene plays a very different thematic role: the death of the fly (with which the boss identifies) ironically deals a heavy blow to the boss's own vanity and confidence. In the preceding analysis I emphasized that textual elements that appear peripheral or irrelevant to the thematic concerns of the plot may be central to the covert progression. Here we see another basic possibility: the same textual elements are important to both the plot development and the covert progression but in different ways and to different thematic effects.

When it comes to interpretation [3], tracing the covert progression helps show that it is ill grounded. To satisfy his vanity, the boss wants his son to be as capable and confident as himself, and by contrast he wants "Woodifield and his clerk" to be as frail and humble as possible. This difference in the boss's attitude has eluded existing critical attention, so much so that interpretation [3] finds a similarity, instead. An important reason for the neglect is that this difference in attitude (associated with the boss's vanity) mainly pertains to the thematic concern of the covert progression. And unless we trace the covert progression, we will be hard put to see its thematic significance and, what is worse, we are liable to misinterpret the textual facts in question when mapping them onto the themes of the plot development.

Interpretation [4] is quite similar to interpretation [2], and we have found that the boss drops ink on the fly in order to test his own ability to survive rather than "for boyish pleasure."

In terms of interpretation [5], we cannot view the boss "simply" as a sympathetic character experimenting on a fly. He is indeed sympathetic as a fly-like victim of external forces, such as the war, but otherwise ironized and so a more complicated personality. Concerning the "unconscious metaphysical questioning," notice that the experiment on the fly is actually the result of a conscious "idea" and that to say that the boss "quickly pushes [the answer] out of his mind" contradicts the textual fact that the boss tries very hard to remember. This obvious misreading is quite understandable, since the boss's pitiable state of endeavoring to remember can only gain a

142 *Style and Rhetoric of Short Narrative Fiction*

satisfactory thematic explanation in the covert progression (its ironic similarity to Woodifield's earlier pitiable lapse of memory). Critics who overlook this progression tend either to leave unmentioned the boss's effort to remember or, as in interpretation [5], to misinterpret it when mapping it onto the plot development. The latter is also the case for Bledsoe (1947), who takes the boss's killing the fly as a way to divert his "sorrow Woodifield has unwittingly aroused." In the end, Bledsoe claims, the boss's "Sport" having proved good, the boss forgets "his grief" (ibid.). But, in fact, there is no need for the boss to divert his grief; rather, he wants to feel grieved without success ("He wanted, he intended, he had arranged to weep . . . But no tears came yet . . . He wasn't feeling as he wanted to feel").

As regards interpretation [6], there is no evidence in the text that the boss comes to terms with his selfishness and heartlessness. Being unaware of them, he simply cannot understand why his son's expression becomes cold and stern and why he is no longer able to weep for his son. At the ending, moreover, he still regards the "grey-haired" clerk contemptuously as a "dog," which indicates that he remains selfish and conceited. Most of the details here are more relevant to the boss's ethical defects as ironized in the covert progression, than to the themes of the plot development. Tracing the covert progression, therefore, enables us to provide a much more convincing explanation for Mansfield's stylistic and structural choices in depicting the boss in this aspect.

Now let us turn from the boss to the whole narrative. As outlined at the beginning of this chapter, generations of critics have challenged previous interpretations in an effort to come up with a more convincing reading of "The Fly." As a rule, attention is only paid to one textual movement—that of the plot, and critics tend to map onto it whatever textual elements they find relevant in order to establish the thematic unity of the text. Bledsoe (1947) thus sees the "whole movement of the story" as "explicat[ing] a central theme: 'As flies to wanton boys, so are we to the gods; they kill us for their sport.'" He takes the boss's treatment of Woodifield as "sadistic." Bledsoe notices that the boss derives pleasure from Woodifield's feebleness, but if we open our minds to an alternative undercurrent, we will see that the pleasure is not so much sadistic as conceited. To Bledsoe (ibid.), the boss also gains sadistic pleasure from displaying his newly furnished office "to this broken down hack." But the text runs, "[the boss] was proud of his room; he liked to have it admired, especially by old Woodifield," implying that the boss displays his office to all his visitors and that, in all cases, it is a matter associated with his pride and vanity rather than sadistic cruelty. In terms of the boss's treatment of the fly, Bledsoe (ibid.) notices the boss's being "amicable," but he only sees the boss "murder[ing] the fly with wanton and amicable cruelty" (see a similar view in Coroneos 1997), failing to perceive the boss's identification with the fly.

Stanley B. Greenfield (1958) instead associates the only movement he perceives in the narrative with a different theme: "Time and Life Conquer

Style and Secretly Unifying the Digressive   143

Grief." Greenfield discerns what has been overlooked by many other critics, namely, the boss having to arrange to weep casts doubt on his "real love for his son." But in trying to assimilate everything to the theme of the plot development, Greenfield distorts various textual facts and even contradicts himself. He argues that the boss "has tried to keep his grief alive" so as to be different from other people:

> He cannot weep, and his distraction from his effort to do so by the fly is the final blow to his attempt to be different from other men. The fly's successive weakening struggles to free itself from the ink parallel the boss' past efforts to keep his grief alive. Each time is more difficult than the last for the fly, and has been more difficult for the boss [to keep his grief alive]. . . . Appropriately enough, with the death of the fly comes the death of the boss' grief. (Greenfield 1958)

This contradicts Greenfield's earlier interpretation that the boss lacks real grief (born of real love) for his son. Nor is there any textual evidence that the boss has endeavored "to keep his grief alive." On the contrary, the narrative begins with the boss showing off his newly furnished office and drawing old Woodifield's attention to the things in the room but not "to the photograph" of his dead son. Moreover, when Woodifield mentions the grave of the boss's son in connection with that of his own, would the reference come as such a shock to a father who has been trying "to keep his grief alive"? As analyzed above, by the time the boss starts dropping ink on the fly, his grief has clearly died.

The specific readings and points offered by Bledsoe and Greenfield are not representative, but their essays are quite typical of critical efforts to discover the thematic meaning of "a single, seamless whole" (Hagopian 1963–64: 387) or of the narrative's "whole movement" reduced to that of the plot. This narrow focus, apart from distorting certain textual facts, is likely to lead to the underrating or overlooking of certain textual elements that play an important thematic role in the covert progression. As early as the opening part of "The Fly," for instance, Woodifield's foregrounded direct speech and the wrong supposition of his family, among other details, appear unimportant or digressive from the viewpoint of the plot development as such: They have indeed usually escaped critical notice.[3] But they are found to be important elements in the first stage of the covert progression, shaped to direct ethical irony against the boss's vanity. When these elements gradually fall into place in the covert progression, they will take on new relevance and gain their due thematic significance. Moreover, they will be recognized as being artful behind their trivial and digressive appearance.

As we have seen, numerous existing interpretations of "The Fly" have shed much light on the narrative from various angles and have greatly helped reveal the rich thematic significance and complicated dynamics of the plot development. But no matter how cogent, ingenious, thorough, and

144 *Style and Rhetoric of Short Narrative Fiction*

deep-going the analysis is, the picture that emerges is bound to be a partial one unless we perceive at the same time the ironic covert progression behind the symbolic plot development. The two progressions—the plot centering on war, death, grief, time, existence, victimization/being victimized etc. and the covert progression concentrating on the boss's vanity and self-importance—constitute two interacting dimensions of the whole textual dynamics. They complement each other in characterizing the boss and in generating thematic or ethical significance of the narrative.

Coda

Although *Style and Rhetoric of Short Narrative Fiction* has focused primarily on six short fictional narratives, the findings can be extended to many others: in addition to the overt plot development, there is frequently a covert textual progression which develops important countervailing or supplementary themes that are crucial to the proper understanding of the implied author's rhetorical design. It is true that what is covert for one reader might be overt for others. But as indicated by the present analysis, the covert progression may remain covert. Indeed, despite the rich variety of reading strategies over the past century or so, the covert progressions in the six narratives under discussion, which were published at least ninety years ago, have eluded previous critics. This is not surprising. Starting from Aristotle, critical attention to narrative movement has focused on the sequence of actions, on, that is, the development of the plot. Modern narratology, since the Russian Formalists, operates with two sequences: one, the story events in their original causal, chronological order (the *fabula*); and the other, the textual sequence of these events (the *sjuzhet*). As regards the *sjuzhet*, narratologists have fruitfully investigated various authorial/narratorial formal operations on the *fabula*, but they have not typically paid attention to another textual movement behind or underneath the plot development. To descry the covert progression, it is a prerequisite that we free ourselves from the bondage of the critical tradition and open our minds to the possible existence of a parallel or alternative textual movement behind the plot development.

The previous chapters have shown from various angles that stylistic analysis is indispensable for uncovering the covert progression. For the past half-century or so, many literary critics have remained resistant to stylistics because they tend to believe that the "stylistic insight ultimately proves no more far-reaching than an insight reached by simply intuiting from the text" (Simpson 2004: 3). Answering the challenge, this book tries to demonstrate how stylistic analysis can help advance literary interpretation. Stylistics, which was quite popular in the United States in the 1960s and 1970s, was almost "dead" there in the late 1980s and 1990s because of the attacks from deconstructive and reader-response critics, coupled with the shift in

146 *Style and Rhetoric of Short Narrative Fiction*

attention from the text to sociohistorical contexts, but in the new century it has been enjoying a gradual revival in the United States. In Britain and many other countries, although stylistics has retained its momentum and has played an important role in college education and academic research, it has not been very successful in appealing to literary critics because efforts are not often made to show the usefulness of stylistics in helping produce new literary interpretations. This project hopes to contribute to the revival of stylistics in the United States and in attracting the attention and participation from literary critics over the world. With the wide audience in mind, I have tried to avoid linguistic technicalities to make the stylistic analysis more accessible to literary critics.

Before bringing the book to an end, I would like to offer the following eight theses for uncovering the covert progression:

Thesis one: In many fictional narratives, there are dual narrative dynamics—a covert progression behind the overt plot development, but the covert is not immediately noticeable and we need therefore make a conscious effort to search for it.

Thesis two: Different implied authors of different narratives may hold divergent stances. To uncover a hidden progression in a narrative conveying a particular stance, we often need to break free of the received understanding of the author's ethical and ideological positions.

Mansfield, for instance, is widely regarded as a non-feminist writer and this general image can easily lead to the neglect of a feminist covert progression in some of her narratives like "Revelations" and "A Singing Lesson."

Thesis three: To discover the covert progression, we need to pay attention to both stylistic and structural techniques.

As we have seen in the previous chapters, style often functions to shape character and event in very subtle and significant ways, thus more or less changing on a deeper level the nature of the communication among authors, narrators, and readers. However, contemporary narratology and rhetorical narrative studies have often focused on structure and very much neglected or consciously precluded the linguistic details of the text, with, of course, the exception of linguistically-conveyed structural features such as voice and perspective. I have called for careful consideration of style in those fields in the Introduction and elsewhere (see Shen 2005, 2011b). This is particularly important in the case of narratives marked by a covert progression behind the plot development, since the covert progression is characteristically wrought by the implied author with subtle stylistic choices, and we need to trace carefully the stylistic patterning from the beginning to the end of the text to discover the implicit textual dynamics.

Coda 147

Thesis four: Attention to the covert progression often reveals covert motives or other not immediately apparent causes of characters' behavior.

In Mansfield's "The Singing Lesson," for instance, Miss Meadows's bad mood and wicked behavior in the earlier part of the narrative and her later transformation into a happy woman is indeed caused by Basil's breaking off their engagement and his later promise of marriage. But stylistic analysis leads us to recognize a covert progression and find the deeper social causes underlying her behavior. The covert progression dramatically indicates and implicitly protests against the phallocentric social prejudice against a woman unwanted by men, social prejudice which drives the woman into despair and reduces her to behaving in a wicked way. In the covert progression hinging on this deeper social cause, Miss Meadows's "wicked" behavior becomes quite understandable and as a result readers' ethical judgments and affective responses to her change. In "Désirée's Baby," things go in a different direction: Armand's cruelty towards the slaves and his "colored" wife and son appears to be a result of the influence of the Southern racist system, but on a deeper level, it is attributed to his black blood by the covert progression.

Thesis five: Textual elements which are peripheral or redundant to the overt plot development may take on much importance in the covert progression.

In "An Episode of War," for instance, the lieutenant's dividing coffee and a brigade's "making coffee and buzzing with talk like a girl's boarding school" have little or no role to play in the main line of action, but they are important constituents of the covert textual progression that emasculates the soldiers throughout. On the other hand, although the lieutenant's injury and amputation are key events in the plot development, they are not that important to the covert progression which does not rest on instabilities of the story events, but on the clash between what is conventionally expected of heroic soldiers and how the soldiers are made to appear in the narrative.

This thesis may even be applicable to different aspects of the same event or utterance. In "The Tell-Tale Heart," the last paragraph goes, "'Villains!' I shrieked, 'dissemble no more! I admit the deed!—tear up the planks! here, here!—It is the beating of his hideous heart!'" As regards this single utterance, in the plot development where the resolution lies in the old man's beating heart leading to the exposure of the protagonist's crime, the emphasis falls on the last sentence, "It is the beating of his hideous heart!" But in the covert progression building up the overall dramatic irony, the emphasis falls instead on "Villains! dissemble no more!"—the unconscious self-condemnation of the speaker as the only dissembling villain in the narrative.

Thesis six: To bring to light the covert textual progression, we need examine carefully the implicit interaction among textual details—both

148 *Style and Rhetoric of Short Narrative Fiction*

story facts and discourse (stylistic as well as structural) devices—in different parts of the text.

We need to explore, behind the plot development, whether textual details—no matter how minor or redundant to the main line of action—in the beginning, middle and end *implicitly* play a similar thematic function. If we find such a pattern, we may see a continuous textual undercurrent that conveys a hidden thematic import. In "The Fly," for instance, the discernment of the hidden similarity among the textual elements at different stages of the narrative enables us to descry a covert progression directing irony against the Boss's vanity and self-importance. The discovery not only enriches our understanding of the narrative but also makes it possible to account for various story facts and discourse devices which appear redundant or digressive to the plot development.

Moreover, we need to find out whether there is any *hidden* contrast between or among similar situations. As discussed in Chapter 1, in "The Tell-Tale Heart," the protagonist-narrator's contrastive attitude towards his own dissemblance (during the whole textual movement) and towards that of the policemen (at the dénouement) is of vital importance for the covert progression towards self-condemnation, a contrast that has been previously overlooked. In "Désirée's Baby," when Désirée's white foster father asks Armand to consider Désirée's obscure origin, it seems to indicate the racial discrimination on his part, but he himself does not hesitate to adopt Désirée with the obscure origin, and when Désirée is mistaken for being colored, he and his wife not only offer her their home but also claim her to be their "own." This forms a contrast with the (really) black Armand's racist behavior. Careful attention to the implicit and consistent contrast between the whites and the (really) blacks in similar racial situations in this narrative enables us not only to find out that Mr. Valmondé's words merely form an artistic device of foreshadowing but also to discern the overall covert mythologization of slavery.

Thesis seven: The covert progression may have to do with the life of the author and the historical context of creation, and attention needs to be paid to the relation between text and context.

As we have seen in the previous chapters (especially Chapters 2 and 3), paying attention to the experiences of the "flesh-and-blood person" outside the writing process may help much in discovering a covert textual progression that is associated in various ways with the author's life.

It is of course also important to consider the relevant sociocultural circumstances (see especially Chapters 1 and 5). In Poe's "The Tell-Tale Heart," the protagonist-narrator continuously insists on his sanity, a textual phenomenon that has received various interpretations but none appears convincing. By going beyond the text into the historical context, we can find that the narrator's insistence on his sanity actually embodies Poe's response to the contemporary

Coda 149

controversy over the "insanity defense." The murderous narrator's sustained assertion in that cultural context that he is sane amounts to an unconscious self-conviction, adding a dimension to the overall dramatic irony and enriching the covert ethical progression. This case points to the fact that contextual information not only can test or back up the findings of the intratextual analysis but also may shed new light on certain textual phenomena.

However, we need to keep in mind that the text is always primary in exploring the covert progression. Some critics today tend to pay too much attention to the historical context while more or less neglecting the text. If one fails to respect the text, the emphasis on cultural context may lead to severe distortions of textual facts (see Chapter 3 for a critique of Margaret Bauer's imposition of context on text). What we should do is to carry out a very careful stylistic-structural examination of the text while also paying sufficient attention to context.

Thesis eight: Attention often needs to be paid to the contrast or similarity between the text under investigation and other related texts.

In order to uncover the covert progression, we also need to pay attention to relevant intertextual matters. What is particularly important to the descrying of the covert progression is the detailed comparison of stylistic choices between the text under investigation and other related texts (see in particular Chapters 2, 3, and 4).

Of the eight theses, the last two usually cannot be used directly to uncover the covert progression, but they can be employed to test or back up the findings of the intratextual analysis, hence adding to the "shareability" of the investigation. As for the preceding six theses, in bringing to light the covert progression in a given narrative, some of them may be more important than others, and some may even be irrelevant; but they may also all come into play and lend support to each other.

The covert progression forms a significant part of the implied author's rhetorical design, inviting the authorial audience to uncover and integrate a distinct line of textual dynamics, a line that complicates the audience's response to the narrative in various ways. In the Introduction, I mentioned that the thematic or ethical import of the covert progression either supplements or subverts that of the plot development. The covert progressions in "The Tell-Tale Heart" and "The Fly" belong to the supplementary category, while the covert progressions in the other narratives under discussion are more or less subversive. In both cases, the covert progression plays a significant thematic and aesthetic role. If we miss it, we may only get a partial (in the supplementary case) or distorted (in the subversive case) picture of the thematics, the characters, and the aesthetic values of the narrative. In short, in those narratives marked by dual dynamics as such, it is necessary and desirable to go beyond the plot development and try to uncover the covert progression.

Notes

NOTES TO THE INTRODUCTION

1. Apart from ethical import, the covert progression can, of course, generate other kinds of thematic significance, but this book would like to focus on the ethical. With the thriving development of ethical criticism after its revival by J. Hillis Miller (1987), Wayne C. Booth (1988), and Martha Nussbaum (1990), among others, over two decades ago, there is nowadays little resistance to the connection between art and ethics in the investigation of narrative fiction. For surveys of the ethical turn, see Altes 2005 and Buell 1999.
2. When investigating a more local aspect of a narrative, such as the function of a minor character, attention is often paid to textual elements that appear to be digressive or peripheral to the main line of action, but in investigating the narrative progression of a whole text, attention is usually focused on the main line of action.
3. As pointed out by Booth, a serious ethical criticism cannot be divorced from political criticism since when "we talk about changing persons we are also talking about changing societies" (1988: 12; see also Diamond 1983: 163–64). Indeed, concepts of moral philosophy such as "right" and "wrong," "good" and "evil," "justice" and "injustice" are applicable both to individuals and to societies.
4. Although summaries of the plot of this narrative usually take for granted Désirée's committing suicide, Ellen Peel (1990: 233–34), from a poststructuralist perspective, casts doubt on the certainty of Désirée's death, but the interaction of the relevant textual details do strongly imply that Désirée has committed suicide (see Chapter 3 for a detailed discussion).
5. See Shen 2005b for a comparison between *Narrative Discourse* by Genette and *Style in Fiction* by Leech and Short, which also shows that narratology's "discourse" and stylistics' "style" respectively cover part of the techniques on the level of presentation.
6. In contrast with Chatman, some narratologists like Monika Fludernik (1996, 2003) and David Herman (2002) brought with them into the narratological camp their remarkable expertise in stylistics or linguistics, which is still evident in their narratological works.
7. This point is highlighted by being printed on the front and back flaps of the book. However, Phelan offers a critique in this book of Elder Olson's attack on William Empson, and in part two of the book, Phelan shows that works like *Lolita* depend primarily on the authors' stylistic virtuosity for success. As editors, Phelan and Rabinowitz fully endorsed my essay published in *A Companion to Narrative Theory* (2005), an essay that calls for paying attention

152 Notes

to both "style" (verbal/language techniques) and "discourse" (structural techniques) in investigating the formal aspect of narrative. In *Living to Tell about It* (2005) and *Experiencing Fiction* (2007), Phelan at least theoretically pays more attention to style/language since he mentions "style" (or words, language) together with "narrative discourse," which forms a contrast with his earlier works such as *Narrative as Rhetoric* (1996) where he mentions "narrative discourse" alone (see, for instance, p.19). But in the two more recent books, Phelan still has not made style or language a central element in practical analysis.

8. Cognitive criticism is often concerned with what I call "generic audience" (see Shen 2005c: 155–57). In terms of the large genre of narrative, the "generic audience" share interpretation through sharing the same narrative conventions as typically embodied by stereotypic assumptions, expectations, frames, scripts, plans, schemata, or mental models in narrative comprehension.

9. In "*Tom Jones*: The Form in History," Rader criticizes R. S. Crane and Sheldon Sacks for neglecting the historical context of *Tom Jones,* which leads to a partial understanding of the form of the text (see also Phelan and Richter 2011). Apart from drawing attention to cultural history, Rader has directed much attention to the relation between character's experiences and the historical author's experiences, focusing on various autobiographical elements in the text (see Rader 1978/79, 1984). It should also be mentioned that, in recent years, James Phelan has become increasingly receptive to the consideration of context and real-author influences (see, for instance, Phelan 2011).

10. The term "real author" is potentially misleading, since the person in daily life outside the writing process is referred to as "author." To avoid ambiguity or misconception, it is better to use "the historical person" or "the flesh-and-flood person" (meaning without role-playing). In his recent essay "The Resurrection of the Implied Author" (2005), Booth consistently uses "the flesh-and-flood person" ("the FBP"), instead of "the real author."

11. Rader (1978/79, 1984) has paid much attention to how characters' experiences resemble those of the real author's. But as indicated by "Désirée's Baby" analyzed in Chapter 3, the autobiographical influences may function in a contrastive way. For instance, while in real life Kate Chopin's father-in-law was a harsh slave owner, Désirée's is described as very benevolent towards his slaves. Underlying this contrast are the historical Chopin's racist experiences which constitute a motivating factor in her mythologization of the Southern slave system (see Chapter 3).

12. In contrast with reader-response, constructivist, and deconstructive approaches to fictional narrative, underlying the rhetorical critics' efforts to arrive at authorial reading is the belief that different readers are willing or eager to accept the implied author's invitation and will more or less succeed in entering the authorial audience, thus be able to share readings (see, for instance, Phelan 2007).

13. It is worth noting that linguistic meaning is not as indeterminable as many critics hold. Saussure's theory of the sign has been widely taken as lending to the indeterminacy of meaning. But in effect Saussure puts emphasis on the conventional "union of meanings and sound-images" that is "the only essential thing" in "a system of signs" (Saussure 1960: 15), where "although both the signified and the signifier are purely differential and negative when considered *separately,* their *combination* is a *positive* fact" (ibid.: 120–21; italics added). In discussing linguistic value, Saussure stresses the conventional nature of the link between the signifier and the signified: "The arbitrary nature of the sign explains in turn why the social fact alone can create a linguistic system. The community is necessary if values that owe their existence solely to usage and

Notes 153

general acceptance are to be set up; by himself the individual is incapable of fixing a single value" (ibid.: 113). In the English language "community" (needless to say, any linguistic convention only obtains in relation to a given language community), "sun" (/sʌn/) can function as a sign not only because of its difference from other signs in sound or "sound-image," but also because of the *conventional* union between the sound-image "sun" and the signified concept. Given, for instance, the following sound-images "lun"(/lʌn/), "sul" (/sʌl/) and "qun" (/kwʌn/), although each can be identified by its difference from the others, none of them can function as a sign, because there is *no conventional link* between the signifier and the signified.

NOTES TO CHAPTER 1

1. In "The Poetic Principle" Poe makes it clear that he cherishes "as deep a reverence for the True as ever inspired the bosom of man," but he would exclude it from the realm of poetry because Truth is incompatible with the "efflorescence" of the poetic language: "The demands of Truth are severe. She has no sympathy with the myrtles. All *that* which is so indispensable in Song, is precisely all *that* with which *she* has nothing whatever to do. It is but making her a flaunting paradox to wreathe her in gems and flowers. In enforcing a truth, we need severity rather than efflorescence of language. We must be simple, precise, terse. We must be cool, calm, unimpassioned. In a word, we must be in that mood which, as nearly as possible, is the exact converse of the poetical. *He* must be blind, indeed, who does not perceive the radical and chasmal difference between the truthful and the poetical modes of inculcation. He must be theory-mad beyond redemption who, in spite of these differences, shall still persist in attempting to reconcile the obstinate oils and waters of Poetry and Truth" (1984c: 76).
2. Another more obvious reason for this oversight is that critics soon associated Poe with the label "Art for Art's sake" and have formed a permanent posthumous association of Poe with the late-nineteenth-century movement of "aestheticism" (see Polonsky 2002).
3. Cleman quotes from Poe's "Poetic Principle" and 1842 review of *Twice-Told Tales*.
4. The tale is in first-person narration and there is no explicit mentioning of the narrator's sex, but the narrator consistently refers to himself as a "madman." Gita Rajan argues that Poe's narrator may be female (1988: 295), but the argument is far from persuasive. Poe describes the murdering act as follows: "With a loud yell, I threw open the lantern and leaped into the room. [The old man] shrieked once—once only. In an instant I dragged him to the floor, and pulled the heavy bed over him" (558). Rajan unconvincingly interprets the scene in this way: "In that one moment of possession, she becomes the aggressor; she even assumes a male sexual posture, forcing the old man to receive her, almost raping him" (1988: 295).
5. Edgar Allan Poe, "The Tell-Tale Heart," in *Edgar Allan Poe: Poetry and Tales*, ed. Patrick F. Quinn (New York: Literary Classics of the United States, 1984), 555–59. All subsequent references are to this edition and only page numbers are given parenthetically in the text.
6. For the emphasis of the consistency in question, see in particular Poe, "Philosophy of Composition," p.13, and Poe, 1842 review of *Twice-Told Tales*, p. 573.
7. At the dénouement of Poe's "The Black Cat" (first published in 1843, the same year as "The Tell-Tale Heart"), the murderer, in a triumphant mood in front of

154 Notes

the policemen for having walled up the corpse in a projection without leaving any trace, raps upon the very spot; there comes unexpectedly the informing cry of the black cat from within the wall, which leads to the murderer's arrest and hanging (see Poe 1984e). This event is fantastic in the following ways: first, the murderer displaces the bricks in the projection in order to insert the corpse, and he very carefully walls the whole up again without being in the least aware of the cat's being walled up together with the corpse; second, after having been walled up for three days by a plaster made of mortar, sand, and hair, the cat is not suffocated to death; and third, the cat keeps silent for three days and only cries out to inform the policemen of the murder. Equally fantastically, in "The Fall of the House of Usher" (first published in 1839), after having been buried for "seven or eight" days in a vault "at a great depth" underground with thin air and a metal door of "immense weight," the female protagonist Madeline, who had been much weakened by malady and was almost laid up in bed before she was thought dead, rends the screwed coffin, breaks through the locked heavy metal door, and returns to the house, shocking her twin brother Roderick to death. Moreover, Roderick, whose senses are over-acute, can hear in the house his sister's "feeble movements" in the coffin deep underground, and, more dramatically, Madeline in the vault deep underground can enact simultaneously what her brother's friend is reading from the "Mad Trist" in the house (see Poe 1984f).

8. But he is not beyond self-pity: "I knew the sound well. Many a night, just at midnight, when all the world slept, it has welled up from my own bosom, deepening, with its dreadful echo, the terrors that distracted me. I say I knew it well. I knew what the old man felt, and pitied him, although I chuckled at heart" (556). The expression "[I] pitied him" only shows the protagonist's self-pity, since he is not really pitying the old man—"although I chuckled at heart."

9. His nervousness greatly contributes to the horror effect at the killing scene: "It [the living old man's heart beating] grew louder, I say, louder every moment!—do you mark me well I have told you that I am nervous: so I am. And now at the dead hour of the night, amid the dreadful silence of that old house, so strange a noise as this excited me to uncontrollable terror" (557).

10. Poe takes a drastically different stance towards the protagonists' dissemblance in "The Cask of Amontillado" (1846) and "Hop-Frog" (1849), in which the protagonists take revenge for unbearable insults by murdering without being punished. In these tales the murderers' dissemblance seems to be regarded by Poe as a laudable device. This change in stance has to do with Poe's personal life—his desire for revenge upon his two literary enemies. See Demond 1954; Bonaparte 1949: 505–9; Quinn 1969: 501–6; Poe 1948: 318–20.

11. Bynum notes that, according to Rush, "the insane were 'for the most part easily terrified, or composed, by the eye of a man who possessed his reason' " (1989: 146; Bynum quotes from Rush 1830: 173). But of course, Poe is very likely making use of the popular superstition of the "Evil Eye" to enhance the dramatic effect (see Bourguignon 1993). Mabbott argues that Poe may even be suggesting that it is the old man's eye which drives the narrator-protagonist mad (1978: 789). Some analytical critics take the eye as the Symbolic Gaze of the Father, the sign of paternal surveillance or domination (see, for instance, Hoffman 1972: 222–26; Davis 1983; Rajan 1988). When the protagonist's murder is perceived as a justifiable act of resistance or rebellion against paternal domination, the covert progression directing irony against the protagonist would naturally remain unseen.

12. Judge Tracy, Rex v. Arnold, 16 How. St. Tr. 695 (1724), quoted in Maeder 1985: 10–11.

13. Bynum quotes from "Baron Rolfe's Charge to the Jury, in the case of the Boy Allnutt, who was tried at the Central Criminal Court, for the Murder of his

Notes 155

Grandfather, on the 15th Dec., 1847," *Journal of Psychological Medicine and Mental Pathology* 1 (1848): 214.

NOTES TO CHAPTER 2

1. See, for instance, Johnson 1963: 251; Gibson 1968: 94–96; Wolford 1989: 68–69; Schaefer 1996: 118–22; Wertheim 1997: 96–97. Some critics, however, take it as an impressionistic story (see, for instance, McCartney 1988; Nagel 1980: 101–2).
2. Crane, "An Episode of War," *Great Short Works of Stephen Crane* (New York: Harper and Row, 1965) p. 268. All subsequent references to this story are to this edition and are cited parenthetically in the text.
3. To reach a wider audience including literary critics, I try to avoid linguistic technicalities, but I sometimes use the more or less self-explanatory terms and models in functional grammar, such as "transitivity" (Halliday 2004).
4. The unpublished title appeared two years earlier in Crane's 1897 inventory (Schaefer 1996: 114; Wertheim 1997: 96).
5. See, for instance, Berryman 1950: 256; Gibson 1968: 95–96; Holton 1972: 144; Swann 1981: 100; Beaver 1982: 192; Delbanco 1982: 49.
6. Shaw acknowledges here the influence of Gibson (1968: 9), who locates the point of view in the lieutenant's comrades.
7. Mary Shaw puts the lieutenant on a par with the surgeon, taking it that both persons "dramatize the attitudes of traditional heroism" (1991: 26). But as analyzed above, the surgeon, acting as a dominating parent, actually functions to emasculate (even criminalize) the protagonist.
8. The following description goes, "Sitting with his back against a tree a man with a face as gray as a new army blanket was serenely smoking a corncob pipe. The lieutenant wished to rush forward and inform him that he was dying." While the adverb "serenely" seems to be commending the army man's calmness, the following sentence, especially the verb "inform," ironically indicates that the serenity arises out of ignorance rather than courage.
9. This is Poem 76 in Crane's collection of poems *War is Kind and Other Lines* (p. 81) first published in 1899, accessed June 7, 2011, at http://theotherpages. org/poems/crane01.html (italics added).
10. See the copyright page of Crane, *Great Short Works of Stephen Crane;* also Stallman, 2002: 217; Solomon 1966: 124.

NOTES TO CHAPTER 3

1. Summaries of the plot of the narrative usually take for granted Désirée's suicide (see, for instance, the summaries given by Taylor and Seyersted below; see also Arner 1996: 140; Lundie 1994: 130–31; Erickson 1990: 61). Peel (1990: 233–34), from a poststructuralist perspective, casts doubt on the certainty of Désirée's death and suggests that perhaps Désirée, instead of committing suicide, has escaped and "freed herself from those who once projected their desires on her." But the relevant stylistic choices do strongly imply that Désirée committed suicide. When suspected of being colored, Désirée writes to her foster mother, "My mother, they tell me I am not white. Armand has told me I am not white. For God's sake tell them it is not true. You must know it is not true. I shall die. I must die. I cannot be so unhappy, and live" (Chopin 1976: 176; all subsequent references to "Désirée's Baby" are to the 1976 edition and are cited parenthetically in the text). When spurned by her husband for being colored, Désirée, without changing "the thin white garment nor the slippers

156 *Notes*

which she wore . . . walked across a deserted field, where the stubble bruised her tender feet, so delicately shod, and tore her thin gown to shreds," and she then "disappeared among the reeds and willows that grew thick along the banks of the deep, sluggish bayou; and she did not come back again" (177).

2. Such shift in critical focus may also have to do with historical changes. Lundie (1994: 130) observes that although "readers of the 1990s may see the tale's primary theme as woman's subordination to man, readers of the 1890s would have been concerned with the issue of miscegenation."

3. Some critics pay more attention to the form and structure of the narrative. Erickson (1990), for instance, focuses on the fairytale features and the tension created by the use of these formal features in this realistic story.

4. To show the true racial picture of "Désirée's Baby" produced at the end of the nineteenth century, I have kept some terms used in Chopin's time such as "Negro (negro)," "Negress (negress)," "black blood," and "slave" (as a noun), which are nowadays considered offensive.

5. For a discussion of the term "L'Abri" and the gothic imagery "the black cowl," see Fitz 2000: 84–85.

6. Arner has offered a loveless Freudian reading of the transforming power: "Désirée is the superego, to put the case in Freudian terms, to Armand's id. For a brief while she acts as the civilizing and humanizing consciousness for his primitive and animalistic unconscious. . . . During this brief period of marital felicity, significantly, Armand stops mistreating his slaves. But when he discovers, or thinks he discovers, that Désirée is tainted with *the blackness* that confirms in his mind her *essential similarity to his inner sensual and aggressive self*, she loses her efficacy for him as a means to grace. Marriage to her was not salvation but, in both racial and psychological terms, surrender to the self within and therefore damnation. Predictably, Armand reverts to his old ways; if anything, he is more cruel to his slaves than formerly, linking them to his "betrayal" by a woman but unaware that *they are projections*, literally and symbolically, *of the darkness that lurks within him*" (1996: 145, italics added). This reading not only blocks the racial issue from view but also unjustifiably puts the racial "blackness" on a par with the inner "darkness" of human beings. In commenting on the narrative, Cynthia Wolff (1978) also unwittingly submerges the racial issue with the psychological and the personal, as can be seen in her claims like "Chopin is clearly not primarily interested in dissecting the *social problem* of slavery (as Cable might be); rather, she limits herself <u>almost entirely</u> to the personal and the interior" (ibid.: 127, italics original and underlining added).

7. With a firm belief in the implied author's antiracist stance, Peel (1990: 228) says, "An outsider observing Armand's general harsh treatment of slaves might, however, see his baby's darkness as another instance of poetic justice, the return of the oppressed."

8. In the New Testament, Satan is closely associated with darkness as opposed to light (see, for instance, Acts 26:18 and Ephesians 6:12). Toth (1981: 206) observes that "Armand's Satanic conduct associates him, as do his funereal surroundings, with the powers of darkness, in contrast with the whiteness of Désirée," but her conclusion is that "white and black are thus signs of morality, not of race" (ibid.: 206). Wolff (1978: 129) refers to Armand's being possessed by Satan as "by the only absolute darkness in the tale" but she likewise loses sight of the racial issue in treating Satan as representing the inner darkness of human beings. She concludes that the "lesser existence into which Armand sinks stems not from his Negroid parentage, but from a potential for personal evil that he shares with all fellow creatures" (ibid.). There is, however, little doubt that Armand's Satanic inner darkness and outward conduct are not shared by the white characters in the narrative.

Notes 157

9. In *Women on the Color Line*, Elfenbein (1989: 129) has pointed out that the "imagery that surrounds [Désirée] as she takes the last walk to the bayou is reminiscent of depictions of saints and martyrs, for Désirée is enveloped in a nimbus of light playing golden gleams on her hair. Her tender feet and diaphanous white gown are torn by the stubble."

10. Black blood may become invisible on the skin, as in the case of La Blanche, but it is unequivocally indicated by "dark" skin.

11. One may argue that, since Louisiana's racial system forbad inter-racial marriage by law, Armand's mother could not possibly return to Louisiana (Bauer 1996: 163–64). But we should also be aware that the rhetorical structure of this narrative in itself requires that the identity of Armand's mother be kept in the dark for the sake of the surprise ending.

12. Arner (1996: 140) has a similar view: "[Armand] comes upon the fragment of a letter lodged in a drawer that ironically used to contain Désirée's love letters to him. This letter, however, was written by his mother . . . and its final words are also the last words in the story." Ziff (1966: 297) shares this view: "Armand, who is clearing the old bureau of all of Désirée's belongings, happens upon an old letter in his mother's handwriting." In Erickson's words (1990: 62), Armand during that moment "accidentally stumble[s] across a letter from his mother to his father indicating that she was of mixed race."

13. Although Arner, Ziff, and Erickson (see note 12) have not mentioned Armand reading the letter, their argument invariably implies that upon accidentally discovering the letter in the drawer, Armand knows its content—a result of reading it of course. Wolff (1978: 129) thinks that Armand reads the remnant by the light of the bonfire. But notice that the narrator uses "took them" rather than "had taken them" to indicate that the action of "taking" and "reading" happened in the same spatiotemporal frame. Compare: "There was the remnant of one back in the drawer from which he had taken them [earlier in the room]. . . . He read it [later in the back yard]." On the other hand, it is not surprising that the narrator does not use the past perfect tense for "read." Compare "There was the remnant of one back in the drawer from which he *took* them. . . . He *had read* it." The inconsistency in tense would indicate that Armand had read that remnant before collecting the letters, which would alter the dynamics of the story and destroy to a significant extent the effect of the surprise ending. Besides, it is not surprising that the narrator does not use the past perfect both for "take" and "read" ("There was the remnant of one back in the drawer from which he *had taken* them . . . He *had read* it") since it may involve an undesirable consequence—namely, indicating the anteriority of "read" over "take," as in "from which he *took* them . . . He *had read* it." Moreover, the original "he took them . . . He read it" is more economical and stylistically sounds better than "he *had taken* them . . . He *had read* it."

14. As for the relation between Armand and his black mother, it is true that the text depicts the loving words of Armand's mother in the letter rather than her satanic spirit. But since Armand's "imperious and exacting nature" is "softened greatly" and his satanic spirit suppressed when he is in love with and close to the white Désirée, it is not surprising that Armand's black mother bears no grudge against God for her black blood when she is in love with and close to her white husband. The letter shows her love for her son, but it is only a matter of a black mother's loving her own black son—in the same case as the 'white' Armand's loving his 'white' son. In the only other place where the mother is mentioned—the depiction of the house as analyzed above, the text implicitly establishes an essential similarity between the black mother and the black son: The mother is held responsible for the depressing condition of the house and the son's bad "nature" is compared to that condition of the house.

158 Notes

15. As for the association between Satan and fire in the Bible, see, for instance, Matthew 25:41, where Jesus mentions the eternal fire prepared for Satan and his angels. As regards literature, see, for instance, John Milton's *Paradise Lost,* which depicts Satan falling into the lake of fire and what happens afterwards.

16. Toth (1981: 207–8) sees Armand as a typical "Tragic Octoroon male": "In the end Armand, not Désirée, is the tragic octoroon. The signs of Désirée's whiteness that Armand rejects are the conventional ones . . . Désirée has the physical qualities of a Tragic Octoroon, but Armand has the more important psychological traits."

17. As for the former narrative, see Stowe, *The Key to Uncle Tom's Cabin* (1854), which presents the original facts and documents upon which the story is based.

18. It may be worth noting that St. Louis, the city where Kate Chopin grew up and returned in 1883, was racially very conservative, insisting on segregated schools and colleges even during Reconstruction despite various progressive measures relating to women (Taylor 1989: 143).

19. All subsequent references to "La Belle Zoraïde" are to the 1894 edition and are cited parenthetically in the text.

20. They are apparently "pet Negroes," see Lundie 1994: 134.

21. To make the mistress's kindness appear realistic, the implied author has used three devices: First, the story is narrated as a "true" one since the mistress "would hear none but those which were true" (281); second, frame narration is used to tell the reader how the old Negress is reminded of the "true" story by a lover's lament sung by a man in a boat (281); and third, using the old Negress as the narrator adds much to the superficial credibility or objectivity of the narration.

22. All subsequent references to "A Dresden Lady in Dixie" are to the 1969 edition and are cited parenthetically in the text.

23. Actually "this letter from his mother to his father" is only a "remnant . . . back in the drawer," apparently unintentionally left there by Armand's father.

NOTES TO CHAPTER 4

1. All the narratives by Mansfield analyzed in the second part of this book are from *Collected Stories of Katherine Mansfield* (London: Constable, 1945). All subsequent references are to this edition, and only page numbers are given parenthetically in the text.

2. Beauvoir's *The Second Sex* was a pioneering feminist attempt, and it formed the basis for numerous later feminist discussions about "One is not born but rather becomes a woman" (see, for instance, Moi 2001).

3. The "revelations" seem to be both secular and religious. The title of the story "Revelations" echoes the title of the last book of the Bible and reminds one of the divine revelations of God. In the body of the narrative, just before George breaks the truth of his daughter's death, Monica "saw herself looking at him in the white kimono like a nun" (195). In real life, Mansfield did not conform to Christianity, but just a few months before the publication of "Revelations," Mansfield put down the following words in her journal: "I don't want a God to praise or to entreat, but to share my vision with" (Murry 1954: 192; see also Alpers 1982: 312; Arvidson 1996: 211–12). Perhaps Mansfield was trying to borrow from religion to make the revelations more powerful.

4. Henrik Ibsen, *A Doll House,* translated by Rolf Fjelde, in *The Bedford Introduction to Drama,* edited by Lee A. Jacobus, 2nd ed. (Boston: Bedford Books of St. Martin's Press, 1993), p. 593. All subsequent references are to this edition and are cited parenthetically in the text.

Notes 159

5. It should have become clear that Mansfield's "Revelations," "Prelude," and "The Singing Lesson" (see the next chapter), which polarize gender relations and which are based on the belief in the woman's initial "real self" prior to patriarchal distortion, are more susceptible to a feminist than a postfeminist reading (for a discussion of the difference between feminism and postfeminism, see Looser and Kaplan 1997). However, it should be stressed that Mansfield's conception of a woman's "false self," as discussed above, points to gender performativity "produced and compelled by the regulatory" cultural norms of the Western hegemonic society.

NOTES TO CHAPTER 6

1. Bateson and Shahevitch (1962) point out that the episodes combine similitude with dissimilitude in a kind of extended metaphor, and they offer a detailed analysis of the parallelism among the three episodes.
2. This is a case of what I designate "context-determined irony": Words that mean what they say or actions that are non-ironic become ironic in a given context (see Shen 2009).
3. If such details receive critical attention, they tend to be misread when assimilated to the theme of the plot development. For instance, Robert Wooster Stallman, who takes Woodifield to be a fly in the plot development, says: "his wife keeps him 'boxed up in the house [like a fly] every day of the week except Tuesday.' On Tuesday he is brushed off (like a fly) 'and allowed to cut back to the City for the day' " (1945, original brackets). This interpretation of the textual details involved seems to be ill-grounded (do we ever "brush off" a fly?).

Works Cited

Abrams, M. H., and Geoffrey Galt Harpham. *A Glossary of Literary Terms*. Florence, KY: Wadsworth Cengage Learning, 2009.

Alber, Jan, Stefan Iversen, Henrik Skov Nielsen, and Brian Richardson. "Unnatural Narratives, Unnatural Narratology: Beyond Mimetic Models." *Narrative* 18, no. 2 (2010): 113–36.

Alpers, Anthony. *The Life of Katherine Mansfield*. Oxford: Oxford University Press, 1982.

Altes, Liesbeth Korthals. "Ethical Turn." In *Routledge Encyclopedia of Narrative Theory*, edited by David Herman, Manfred Jahn, and Marie-Laure Ryan, 142–46. New York: Routledge, 2005.

Arner, Robert D. "Pride and Prejudice: Kate Chopin's 'Désirée's Baby.' " In *Critical Essays on Kate Chopin*, edited by Alice Hall Petry, 139–46. London: Prentice Hall, 1996.

Arvidson, Ken. "Dancing on the Hand of God: Katherine Mansfield's Religious Sensibility." In *The Critical Responses to Katherine Mansfield*, edited by Jan Pilditch, 211–18. Westport, CT: Greenwood, 1996.

Auerbach, Nina. *Woman and the Demon: The Life of a Victorian Myth*. London: Harvard University Press, 1982.

Bais, H. S. S. *Stephen Crane: Pioneer in Technique*. New Delhi: Crown, 1988.

Baker, Joseph E. "Aesthetic Surface in the Novel." *The Trollopian* 2, no. 2 (1947): 91–106.

Banks, Joanne Trautmann. "Virginia Woolf and Katherine Mansfield." *Twentieth-Century Literary Criticism*, Vol. 39, 300–5. Detroit: Gale. (1993). Originally published in *The English Short Story, 1880–1945: A Critical History*, edited by Joseph M. Flora, 57–82. New York: Twayne, 1985.

Bardot, Jean. "French Creole Portraits: The Chopin Family from Natchitoches Parish." In *Kate Chopin Reconsidered*, edited by Lynda S. Boren and Sara Desaussure Davis, 26–35. Baton Rouge: Louisiana State Univ. Press, 1992.

Barnard, Anja. "The Fly." In *Short Story Criticism*, Vol. 38, edited by Anja Barnard, 199–232. Detroit: Gale, 2000.

Basch, Francoise. *Relative Creatures: Victorian Women in Society and the Novel*. New York: Schocken, 1974.

Bateson, F. W., and B. Shahevitch. "Katherine Mansfield's 'The Fly': A Critical Exercise." In *Essays in Criticism* 12, no. 1 (1962): 39–53.

Bauer, Margaret D. "Armand Aubigny, Still Passing After All These Years." In *Critical Essays on Kate Chopin*, edited by Alice Hall Petry, 161–83. London: Prentice Hall, 1996.

Beauvoir, Simon de. *The Second Sex*, trans. E. M. Parshley. New York: Vintage, 1973.

Beaver, Harold. "Stephen Crane: The Hero as Victim." *Yearbook of English Studies* 12 (1982): 186–93.

162   Works Cited

Bell, Pauline P. "Mansfield's 'The Fly.' " *The Explicator* 19, no. 3 (1960), item 20.

Benfey, Christopher. *The Double Life of Stephen Crane*. New York: Knopf, 1992.

Berkman, Sylvia. *Katherine Mansfield: A Critical Study*. New Haven, CT: Yale University Press, 1951.

Berryman, John. *Stephen Crane*. New York: Sloane, 1950.

Bledsoe, Thomas. "Mansfield's 'The Fly.'" *The Explicator* 5, no. 7 (1947), item 53.

Bonaparte, Marie. *The Life and Works of Edgar Allan Poe: A Psychoanalytical Interpretation*. London: Imago Publishing, 1949.

——. "Psychoanalytic Interpretations of Stories of Edgar Allan Poe." In *Psychoanalysis and Literature*, edited by Hendrik M. Ruitenbeek, 19–101. New York: E. P. Dutton, 1964.

Booth, Wayne C. *The Rhetoric of Fiction*. 2nd ed. Chicago: University of Chicago Press, 1983 [1961].

——. *A Rhetoric of Irony*. Chicago: University of Chicago Press, 1974.

——. *The Company We Keep: An Ethics of Fiction*. Berkeley: University of California Press, 1988.

——. "Resurrection of the Implied Author: Why Bother?" In *A Companion to Narrative Theory*, edited by James Phelan and Peter Rabinowitz, 75–88. Oxford: Blackwell, 2005.

Bourguignon, Erika. "Evil Eye." In *Encyclopedia Americana*, edited by Mark Cummings. Danbury, CT: Grolier, 1993.

Brooks, Cleanth. "Irony and 'Ironic' Poetry." *College English* 9, no. 5 (1948): 231–37.

——. *The Well Wrought Urn: Studies in the Structure of Poetry*. London: Methuen, 1968.

——. "Irony as a Principle of Structure." 1971. In *Critical Theory since Plato*, edited by Hazard Adams and Leroy Searle, 1043–50. 3rd ed. Belmont, CA: Thomson Wadsworth, 2005.

Brooks, Cleanth, and Robert Penn Warren. *Understanding Fiction*. New Jersey: Prentice-Hall, 1979.

Brooks, Peter. *Reading for the Plot: Design and Intention in Narrative*. New York: Knopf, 1984.

Buell, Lawrence. "Introduction: In Pursuit of Ethics." *PMLA* 144 (1999): 7–19.

Buranelli, Vincent. *Edgar Allan Poe*. New York: Twayne, 1961.

Butler, Judith. *Gender Trouble: Feminism and the Subversion of Identity*. New York: Routledge, 1990.

Bynum, Paige Matthey. " 'Observe How Healthily—How Calmly I Can Tell You the Whole Story': Moral Insanity and Edgar Allan Poe's 'The Tell-Tale Heart.' " In *Literature and Science as Modes of Expression*, edited by Frederick Amrine, 141–52. Boston: Kluwer Academic, 1989.

Canario, John W. "The Dream in 'The Tell-Tale Heart.' " *English Language Notes* 7, no. 3 (1970): 194–97.

Carlson, Eric T. "Introduction." *Two Essays on the Mind*. Benjamin Rush. New York: Brunner/Mazel, 1972.

Chatman, Seymour. *Story and Discourse: Narrative Structure in Fiction and Film*. Ithaca, NY: Cornell University Press, 1978.

——. *Coming to Terms: The Rhetoric of Narrative in Fiction and Film*. Ithaca, NY: Cornell University Press, 1990.

Chopin, Kate. "Désirée's Baby." In *The Awakening and Selected Stories of Kate Chopin*, edited by Barbara H. Solomon, 173–78. New York: New American Library, 1976.

——. "The Bênitous' Slave." In *Bayou Folk* by Kate Chopin, 143–46. Boston: Houghton, Mifflin, 1894a.

——. "La Belle Zoraïde." In *Bayou Folk* by Kate Chopin, 280–90. Boston: Houghton, Mifflin, 1894b.

Works Cited 163

———. "For Marse Chouchoute." In *Bayou Folk* by Kate Chopin, 210–22. Boston: Houghton, Mifflin, 1894c.

———. "Beyond the Bayou." In *Bayou Folk* by Kate Chopin, 99–110. Boston: Houghton, Mifflin, 1894d.

———. "A Dresden Lady in Dixie." *The Complete Works of Kate Chopin,* edited by Per Seyersted, 345–51. Baton Rouge: Louisiana State University Press, 1969.

Cleman, John. "Irresistible Impulses: Edgar Allan Poe and the Insanity Defense." *American Literature* 63, no. 4 (1991): 623–40.

Clinton, Catherine. *The Plantation Mistress.* New York: Pantheon, 1982.

Colebrook, Claire. *Irony.* London: Routledge, 2004.

Collier, John. "De Mortuis." In *The Touch of Nutmeg, and more Unlikely Stories by John Collier,* 11–18. New York: The Press of the Readers Club, 1943.

Coroneos, Con. "Flies and Violets in Katherine Mansfield." In *Women's Fiction and the Great War,* edited by Suzanne Raitt and Trudo Tate, 197–218. Oxford: Clarendon Press, 1997.

Crane, R. S. "The Concept of Plot and the Plot of *Tom Jones.*" In *Critics and Criticism Ancient and Modern,* edited by R. S. Crane, 614–47. Chicago: University of Chicago Press, 1952a.

———. "Introduction." In *Critics and Criticism Ancient and Modern,* edited by R. S. Crane, 1–24. Chicago: University of Chicago Press, 1952b.

———. "History versus Criticism in the Study of Literature." 1935. In *Idea of the Humanities and Other Essays: Critical and Historical,* edited by R. S. Crane, 3–24. Chicago: University of Chicago Press, 1967.

Crane, Stephen. "An Episode of War." In *Great Short Works of Stephen Crane,* 268–72. New York: Harper and Row, 1965.

———. "The Upturned Face." In *Great Short Works of Stephen Crane,* 272–76. New York: Harper and Row, 1965.

———. "A Mystery of Heroism." In *Great Short Works of Stephen Crane,* 259–68. New York: Harper and Row, 1965.

———. *Reports of War,* edited by Fredson Bowers. *The Works of Stephen Crane,* Vol. 9. Charlottesville: University Press of Virginia, 1971.

———. *The Complete Poems of Stephen Crane,* edited by Joseph Katz. Ithaca, NY: Cornell University Press, 1972.

———. "The Open Boat." In *Stephen Crane: Prose and Poetry,* 885–909. New York: Literary Classics of the United States, 1984.

———. "The Kicking Twelfth." Electronic version. Electronic Text Centre, University of Virginia Library. http://etext.virginia.edu/toc/modeng/public/CraKick .html, accessed Feb. 12, 2011.

Cuddon, J. A. *A Dictionary of Literary Terms.* Rev. ed. London: Andre Deutsch, 1979.

Dannenberg, Hilary P. "Plot." In Routledge Encyclopedia of Narrative Theory, edited by David Herman, Manfred Jahn, and Marie-Laure Ryan. 435–39. London: Routledge, 2005.

Davidson, Edward H. *Poe: A Critical Study.* Cambridge, MA: Harvard University Press, 1966.

Davis, Robert Con. "Lacan, Poe, and Narrative Repression." *MLN* 98, no. 5 (1983): 983–1005.

Davis, Todd F., and Kenneth Womack, eds. *Mapping the Ethical Turn.* Charlottesville: University Press of Virginia, 2001.

Dayan, Joan. *Fables of Mind.* New York: Oxford University Press, 1987.

Delbanco, Nicholas. *Group Portrait: A Biographical Study of Writers in Community.* New York: William Morrow, 1982.

Demond, Francis P. " 'The Cask of Amontillado' and the War of the Literati." *Modern Language Quarterly* 15, no. 2 (1954): 137–46.

164 Works Cited

Diamond, Cora. "Having a Rough Story about What Moral Philosophy Is." *New Literary History* 15 (1983): 155–69.

Dickens, Charles. *Great Expectations,* edited by Angus Calder. Harmondsworth, UK: Penguin, 1985.

Dominguez, Virginia R. *White by Definition.* New Brunswick, NJ: Rutgers University Press, 1986.

Dunbar, Pamela. *Radical Mansfield: Double Discourse in Katherine Mansfield's Short Stories.* Basingstoke, UK: Macmillan, 1997.

Elfenbein, Anna Shannon. *Women on the Color Line.* Charlottesville: University of Virginia Press, 1989.

Erickson, Jon. "Fairytale Features in Kate Chopin's 'Désirée's Baby.' " In *Modes of Narrative,* presented to Helmut Bonheim, edited by Reingard M. Nischik and Barbara Korte, 57–67. Wurzburg, Germany: Konig, Shausen & Neumann, 1990.

Fludernik, Monika. *Towards a 'Natural' Narratology.* London: Routledge, 1996.

———. "Chronology, Time, Tense and Experientiality in Narrative." *Language and Literature* 12 (2003): 117–34.

Fogle, Richard H. *Hawthorne's Fiction: The Light and the Dark.* Norman: University of Oklahoma Press, 1952.

Foster, Derek W., and Kris Lejeune. " 'Stand By Your Man . . .': Désirée Valmondé and Feminist Standpoint Theory in Kate Chopin's 'Désirée's Baby.' " *Southern Studies* 8, nos. 1–2 (1997): 91–97.

Foucault, Michel. *Madness and Civilization: A History of Insanity in the Age of Reason,* translated by Richard Howard. New York: Vintage-Random, 1988 [1961].

Fowler, Roger, ed. *A Dictionary of Modern Critical Terms.* London: Routledge and Kegan Paul, 1973.

Foy, Roslyn Reso. "Chopin's Désirée's Baby." *The Explicator* 49, no. 4 (1991): 222–23.

Freeman, William. *The Porous Sanctuary: Art and Anxiety in Poe's Short Fiction.* New York: Peter Lang, 2002.

Frye, Northrop. *Words with Power.* New York: Harcourt Brace Jovanovich, 1990.

Fullbrook, Kate. *Katherine Mansfield.* Brighton, UK: Harvester, 1986.

Game, Emily Paige. *The Anxiety of Gender in Katherine Mansfield's Fiction.* Dissertation, University of Alabama, 1998.

Geismar, Maxwell. *Rebels and Ancestors.* Boston: Houghton Mifflin, 1953.

Gibson, Donald B. *The Fiction of Stephen Crane.* Carbondale: Southern Illinois University Press, 1968.

Greenfield, Stanley B. "Mansfield's 'The Fly.' " *The Explicator* 17, no. 1, item 2 (1958).

Gullason, Thomas A. "Stephen Crane: Anti-Imperialist." *American Literature* 30, no. 2 (1958): 237–41.

Hagopian, John T. "Capturing Mansfield's 'Fly.' " *Modern Fiction Studies* 9, no. 4 (1963–64): 385–90.

Halliday, M. A. K. *An Introduction to Functional Grammar.* Revised by Christian Matthiessen. London: Routledge, 2004.

Hanson, Clare. *Short Stories and Short Fictions, 1880–1980.* London: Macmillan, 1985.

———. "Katherine Mansfield's Uncanniness." In *Celebrating Katherine Mansfield: A Centenary Volume of Essays,* edited by Gerri Kimber and Janet Wilson, 115–30. New York: Palgrave Macmillan, 2011.

Hanson, Clare, and Andrew Gurr. *Katherine Mansfield.* New York: St. Martin's Press, 1981.

Hart, James D. *The Oxford Companion to American Literature.* 6th ed. New York: Oxford University Press, 1983.

Hawthorne, Nathaniel. *Twice-Told Tales,* edited by William Charvat and Fredson Bowers. *The Centenary Edition of the Works of Nathaniel Hawthorne 9.* Columbus: Ohio State University Press, 1974.

Works Cited 165

———. "Young Goodman Brown." In *Young Goodman Brown, and Other Short Stories*, 24–34. New York: Dover, 1992.

Herman, David. *Story Logic: Problems and Possibilities of Narrative*. Lincoln: University of Nebraska Press, 2002.

Hoare, Dorothy M. *Some Studies in the Modern Novel*. London: Chatto and Windus, 1938.

Hoffman, Daniel. "Grotesques and Arabesques." *Poe Poe Poe Poe Poe Poe Poe*. Garden City: Doubleday, 1972. 201–28.

———. "Stephen Crane." In *Novelists and Prose Writers*, edited by James Vinson, 287–90. London: Macmillan, 1979.

Holton, Milne. *Cylinder of Vision: The Fiction and Journalistic Writing of Stephen Crane*. Baton Rouge: Louisiana State University Press, 1972.

Hopkins, Gerard Manley. *Poems and Prose*. New York: Everyman's, 1995.

Ibsen, Henrik. *A Doll House*, translated by Rolf Fjelde. In *The Bedford Introduction to Drama*, edited by Lee A. Jacobus, 559–94. 2nd ed. Boston: Bedford Books of St. Martin's Press, 1993.

Jacobs, Wills D. "Mansfield's 'The Fly.'" *The Explicator 5*, no. 4 (1947), item 32.

Johnson, George W. "Stephen Crane's Metaphor of Decorum." *PMLA* 78, no. 3 (1963): 250–56.

Jones, Kathleen. *Katherine Mansfield*. Edinburgh, UK: Edinburgh University Press, 2010.

Kaplan, Sydney Janet. *Katherine Mansfield and the Origins of Modernist Fiction*, Ithaca, NY: Cornell University Press, 1991.

Kennedy, J. Gerald. *Poe, Death, and the Life of Writing*. New Haven, CT: Yale University Press, 1987.

Kobler, J. F. *Katherine Mansfield: A Study of the Short Fiction*. Boston: Hall, 1990.

Knapp, Bettina L. *Stephen Crane*. New York: Ungar, 1987.

LaFrance, Marston. *A Reading of Stephen Crane*. Oxford, UK: Clarendon, 1971.

Lawrence, D. H. *The Letters of D. H. Lawrence*, Vol. 4, edited by James T. Boulton. Cambridge: Cambridge University Press, 1979.

Looser, Devoney, and E. Ann Kaplan, eds. *Generations: Academic Feminists in Dialogue*. Minneapolis: University of Minnesota Press, 1997.

Lundie, Catherine. "Doubly Dispossessed: Kate Chopin's Women of Color." *Louisiana Literature* 11, no. 1 (1994): 126–44.

Mabbott, Thomas-Ollive, ed. *The Collected Works of Edgar Allan Poe*. Vol. 3. Cambridge, MA: Harvard University Press, 1978.

Maeder, Thomas. *Crime and Madness: The Origins and Evolution of the Insanity Defense*. New York: Harper and Row, 1985.

Mais, S. P. B. "Katherine Mansfield." In *Critical Essays on Katherine Mansfield*, edited by Rhoda B. Nathan, 113–16. New York: Hall, 1993.

Mansfield, Katherine. "Revelations." In *Collected Stories of Katherine Mansfield*, 190–96. London: Constable, 1945a.

———. "Prelude." In *Collected Stories of Katherine Mansfield*, 11–60. London: Constable, 1945b.

———. "The Singing Lesson." In *Collected Stories of Katherine Mansfield*, 343–50. London: Constable, 1945c.

———. "The Fly." In *Collected Stories of Katherine Mansfield*, 422–28. London: Constable, 1945d.

Maugham, W. Somerset. "The Colonel's Lady." In *The Complete Short Stories of W. Somerset Maugham*, 587–604. Garden City, NY: Doubleday, 1953.

Maupassant, Guy de. "La Chambre 11." In *Contes et Nouvelles Maupassant*, Vol. 2, 596–601. Paris: R. Laffont, 1988.

———. "The Necklace." In *The Necklace and Other Stories*, compiled and newly translated by Joachim Neugroschel, 3–12. New York: Modern Library, 2003.

166 Works Cited

May, Charles E. "Introduction." In *The New Short Story Theories,* edited by Charles E. May, xv–xxvi. Athens: Ohio University Press, 1994.

McCartney, George. "The Only Impressionist." *National Review,* Sept. 30, 1988: 54–55.

Michel-Michot, Paulette. "Katherine Mansfield's 'The Fly': An Attempt to Capture the Boss." *Studies in Short Fiction* 11, no. 1 (1974): 85–92.

Miller, J. Hillis. *The Ethics of Reading: Kant, de Man, Eliot, Trollope, James, and Benjamin.* New York: Columbia University Press, 1987.

Moi, Toril. *Sexual/Textual Politics.* 2nd ed. London: Routledge, 2001.

Moldenhauer, Joseph J. "Murder as a Fine Art: Basic Connections between Poe's Aesthetics, Psychology, and Moral Vision." *PMLA* 83, no. 2 (1968): 284–97.

Morrow, Patrick D. *Katherine Mansfield's Fiction.* Bowling Green, OH: Bowling Green State University Popular Press, 1993.

Mortimer, Armine Kotin. "Second Stories." In *Short Story Theory at a Crossroads,* edited by Susan Lohafer and Jo Ellyn Clarey, 276–98. Baton Rouge: Louisiana State University Press, 1989.

Muecke, D. C. (1982). *Irony and the Ironic.* New York: Methuen.

Mullen, Harryette. "Optic White: Blackness and the Production of Whiteness." *Diacritics* 24, nos. 2–3 (1994): 71–89.

Murry, J. Middleton, ed. *The Letters of Katherine Mansfield.* New York: Knopf, 1929.

———. *Journal of Katherine Mansfield.* London: Constable, 1954.

Nagel, James. "Stephen Crane's Stories of War: A Study of Art and Theme." *North Dakota Quarterly* 43, no. 1 (1975): 5–19.

———. *Stephen Crane and Literary Impressionism.* University Park: Pennsylvania State University Press, 1980.

Napolitano, Geneva. "Spinsters and Old Maids as Defined by the Victorian Age." Accessed February 21, 2012, at http://www.umd.umich.edu/casl/hum/eng/classes/434/geweb/Spinster.htm

Nathan, Rhoda B. *Katherine Mansfield.* New York: Continuum, 1988.

———. " 'With Deliberate Care': The Mansfield Short Story." In *Critical Essays on Katherine Mansfield,* edited by Rhoda B. Nathan, 93–100. New York: Hall, 1993.

Nesbitt, Anna Sheets. "The Fly." In *Short Story Criticism,* Vol. 34, edited by Anna Sheets Nesbitt, 239–40. Detroit: Gale, 2000.

New, W. H. "Reading 'The Escape.' " In *Katherine Mansfield—In from the Margin,* edited by Roger Robinson, 90–111. Baton Rouge: Louisiana State University Press, 1994.

———. *Reading Mansfield and Metaphors of Form.* Montreal: McGill-Queen's University Press, 1999.

Nünning, Ansgar. "Reconceptualizing Unreliable Narration: Synthesizing Cognitive and Rhetorical Approaches." In *A Companion to Narrative Theory,* edited by James Phelan and Peter J. Rabinowitz, 89–107. Oxford: Blackwell, 2005.

Nussbaum, Martha. *Love's Knowledge: Essays on Philosophy and Literature.* New York: Oxford University Press, 1990.

Oleson, Clinton W. " 'The Fly' Rescued." *College English* 22, no. 8 (1961): 585–86.

O'Sullivan, Vincent. "The Magnetic Chain: Notes and Approaches to K. K." In *The Critical Responses to Katherine Mansfield,* edited by Jan Pilditch, 129–55. Westport: Greenwood Press, 1996.

———. "Signing Off: Katherine Mansfield's Last Year." In *Celebrating Katherine Mansfield: A Centenary Volume of Essays,* edited by Gerri Kimber and Janet Wilson, 13–27. New York: Palgrave Macmillan, 2011.

O'Sullivan, Vincent, and Margaret Scott, eds. *The Collected Letters of Katherine Mansfield,* 4 vols. Oxford, UK: Clarendon Press, 1993.

Works Cited 167

Parkin-Gounelas, Ruth. *Fictions of the Female Self*. Hampshire, UK: Macmillan, 1991.

Pearsall, Judy, ed. *The New Oxford Dictionary of English*. Oxford: Oxford University Press, 1998.

Peel, Ellen. "Semiotic Subversion in 'Désirée's Baby'." *American Literature* 62, no. 2 (1990): 223–37.

Petry, Alice Hall. "Introduction." In *Critical Essays on Kate Chopin*, edited by Alice Hall Petry, 1–33. New York: Prentice Hall, 1996.

Phelan, James. *Worlds From Words: A Theory of Language in Fiction*. Chicago: University of Chicago Press, 1981.

———. *Reading People, Reading Plots: Character, Progression, and the Interpretation of Narrative*. Chicago: University of Chicago Press, 1989.

———. *Narrative as Rhetoric: Technique, Audiences, Ethics, Ideology*. Columbus: Ohio State University Press, 1996.

———. *Living to Tell about It: A Rhetoric and Ethics of Character Narration*. Ithaca, NY: Cornell University Press, 2005.

———. *Experiencing Fiction: Judgments, Progressions, and the Rhetorical Theory of Narrative*. Columbus: Ohio State University Press, 2007.

———. "The Implied Author, Deficient Narration, and Nonfiction Narrative: Or, What's Off-Kilter in The Year of Magical Thinking and The Diving Bell and the Butterfly." *Style* 45, no. 1 (2011): 119–37.

Phelan, James, and David H. Richter. "Introduction: The Literary Theoretical Contribution of Ralph W. Rader." In *Fact, Fiction, and Form: Selected Essays*, edited by James Phelan and David H. Richter, 1–28. Columbus: Ohio State University Press, 2011.

Phillips, Elizabeth. *Edgar Allan Poe: An American Imagination*. Port Washington, NY: Kennikat, 1979.

Poe, Edgar Allan. *Letters of Edgar Allan Poe*, edited by John Ward Ostrom. Cambridge, MA: Harvard University Press, 1948.

———. Review of *Twice-Told Tales*, by Nathaniel Hawthorne. In *Essays and Reviews*, edited by G. R. Thompson, 568–88. New York: Literary Classics of the United States, 1984a.

———. "The Philosophy of Composition." In *Essays and Reviews*, edited by G. R. Thompson, 13–25. New York: Literary Classics of the United States, 1984b.

———. "The Poetic Principle." In *Essays and Reviews*, edited by G. R. Thompson, 71–94. New York: Literary Classics of the United States, 1984c.

———. "The Tell-Tale Heart." In *Edgar Allan Poe: Poetry and Tales*, edited by Patrick F. Quinn, 555–59. New York: Literary Classics of the United States, 1984d.

———. "The Black Cat." In *Edgar Allan Poe: Poetry and Tales*, edited by Patrick F. Quinn. 597–606. New York: Literary Classics of the United States, 1984e.

———. "The Fall of the House of Usher." In *Poetry and Tales*, edited by Patrick F. Quinn, 317–36. New York: Literary Classics of the United States, 1984f.

———. "The System of Doctor Tarr and Professor Fether." In *Edgar Allan Poe: Poetry and Tales*, edited by Patrick F. Quinn, 699–716. New York: Literary Classics of the United States, 1984g.

———. "The Cask of Amontillado." In *Edgar Allan Poe: Poetry and Tales*, edited by Patrick F. Quinn, 848–54. New York: Literary Classics of the United States, 1984h.

———. "Hop-Frog." In *Edgar Allan Poe: Poetry and Tales*, edited by Patrick F. Quinn, 899–908. New York: Literary Classics of the United States, 1984i.

Polonsky, Rachel. "Poe's Aesthetic Theory." In *The Cambridge Companion to Edgar Allan Poe*, edited by Kevin J. Hayes, 42–56. Cambridge: Cambridge University Press, 2002.

Pratt, Susan Leslie. *Reading the Feminine in the Major Stories of Katherine Mansfield (New Zealand)*. Dissertation, University of Illinois at Urbana-Champaign, 1992.

168 Works Cited

Quinn, Arthur Hobson. *Edgar Allan Poe, A Critical Biography*. New York: Cooper Square Publishers, 1969.

Rabinowitz, Peter J. "Truth in Fiction: A Reexamination of Audiences." *Critical Inquiry* 4, no. 1 (1977): 121–41.

———. *Before Reading: Narrative Conventions and the Politics of Interpretation*. Ithaca, NY: Cornell University Press, 1987.

———. "'Betraying the Sender': The Rhetoric and Ethics of Fragile Texts." *Narrative* 2, no. 3 (1994): 201–13.

Rader, Ralph W. "Exodus and Return: Joyce's *Ulysses* and the Fiction of the Actual." *University of Toronto Quarterly* 48, no. 2 (1978/79): 149–71.

———. "The Logic of *Ulysses*, or Why Molly Had to Live in Gibraltar." *Critical Inquiry* 10, no. 4 (1984): 567–78.

———. "Tom Jones: The Form in History." In *Ideology and Form in Eighteenth-Century Literature*, edited by David H. Richter, 47–74. Lubbock: Texas Tech University Press, 1999.

Rajan, Gita. "A Feminist Rereading of Poe's 'The Tell-Tale Heart.' " *Papers on Language and Literature* 24, no. 3 (1988): 283–300.

Rankin, Daniel S. *Kate Chopin and Her Creole Stories*. Philadelphia: University of Pennsylvania Press, 1932.

Ray, Isaac. *A Treatise on The Medical Jurisprudence of Insanity* (1838), edited by Winfred Overholser. Cambridge, MA: Belknap Press of Harvard University Press, 1962.

Reilly, John E. "The Lesser Death-Watch and 'The Tell-Tale Heart.' " *American Transcendental Quarterly* 2, Second Quarter (1969): 3–9.

Reilly, Joseph J. "Stories by Kate Chopin." In *Critical Essays on Kate Chopin*, edited by Alice Hall Petry, 71–74. New York: Prentice Hall, 1996.

Richardson, Brian, ed. *Narrative Dynamics: Essays on Time, Plot, Closure, and Frames*. Columbus: Ohio State University Press, 2002.

Rimmon-Kenan, Shlomith. *Narrative Fiction: Contemporary Poetics*. 2nd ed. London: Methuen, 2002.

Robinson, E. Arthur. "Poe's The Tell-Tale Heart." *Nineteenth-Century Fiction* 19, no. 4 (1965): 369–78.

Rohrberger, Mary. *Hawthorne and the Modern Short Story: A Study in Genre*. The Hague, Netherlands: Mouton, 1966.

Runkle, Kim Denise. *Persona and Patriarchy in the Fiction of Katherine Mansfield*. Dissertation, California State University, 2002.

Rush, Benjamin. *Medical Inquiries and Observations upon Diseases of the Mind*. 4th ed. Philadelphia: John Grigg, 1830.

———. *Two Essays on the Mind*. New York: Brunner/Mazel, 1972.

Sandley, Sarah. "The Middle of the Note: Katherine Mansfield's 'Glimpses.' " In *Katherine Mansfield—In from the Margin*, edited by Roger Robinson, 70–89. Baton Rouge: Louisiana State University Press, 1994.

Saussure, Ferdinand de. *Course in General Linguistics*, translated by Wade Baskin. London: Peter Owen, 1960.

Schaefer, Michael W. *A Reader's Guide to the Short Stories of Stephen Crane*. New York: G. K. Hall, 1996.

Seyersted, Per. *Kate Chopin: A Critical Biography*. Baton Rouge: Louisiana State University Press, 1969.

Shakespeare, William. *King Lear*, edited by Burton Raffel. New Haven, CT: Yale University Press, 2007a.

———. *Troilus and Cressida*, edited by Barbara A. Mowat and Paul Werstine. New York: Washington Square Press, 2007b.

Shaw, Harry E. "Why Won't Our Terms Stay Put? The Narrative Communication Diagram Scrutinized and Historicized." In *A Companion to Narrative Theory*,

Works Cited 169

edited by James Phelan and Peter J. Rabinowitz, 299–311. Oxford, UK: Blackwell, 2005.

Shaw, Mary. "Stephen Crane's 'An Episode of War': A Demythologized Dramatization of Heroism.' " *Studies in Contemporary Satire* 18 (1991/92): 26–34.

Shaw, Mary Ann. "Crane's Concept of Heroism: Satire in the War Stories of Stephen Crane." Dissertation, Texas A&M University, 1985.

Shelden, Pamela J. " 'True Originality': Poe's Manipulation of the Gothic Tradition." *American Transcendental Quarterly* 29, no. 1 (1976): 75–80.

Shen, Dan. "Defence and Challenge: Reflections on the Relation Between Story and Discourse." *Narrative* 10, no. 3 (2002): 422–43.

———. "Story-Discourse Distinction." In *Routledge Encyclopedia of Narrative Theory*, edited by David Herman, Manfred Jahn, and Marie-Laure Ryan. London & New York: Routledge, 2005a: 566–67.

———. "What Narratology and Stylistics Can Do for Each Other." In *A Companion to Narrative Theory*, edited by James Phelan and Peter Rabinowitz, 136–49. Oxford, UK: Blackwell, 2005b.

———. "Why Contextual and Formal Narratologies Need Each Other." *JNT: Journal of Narrative Theory* 35, no. 2 (2005c): 141–71.

———. "Non-Ironic Turning Ironic Contextually: Multiple Context-Determined Irony in 'The Story of an Hour.'" *JLS: Journal of Literary Semantics* 38, no. 2 (2009): 115–30.

———. "What is the Implied Author?" *Style* 45, no. 1 (2011): 80–98.

———. "Implied Author, Authorial Audience, and Context: Form and History in neo-Aristotelian Rhetorical Theory." *Narrative* 21, no. 2 (2013): 140–58.

———. "Unreliability." In *The Living Handbook of Narratology*, edited by Peter Hühn, John Pier, Wolf Schmid, and Jörg Schönert. Hamburg: Hamburg University. Accessed 28 March, 2012, at http://wikis.sub.uni-hamburg.de/lhn/index.php/Unreliability

Silverman, Kenneth. *Edgar A. Poe: Mournful and Never-Ending Remembrance.* New York: Harper Collins, 1991.

Simpson, Paul. *Stylistics.* London: Routledge, 2004.

Skaggs, Peggy. *Kate Chopin.* Boston: Twayne, 1985.

Solomon, Eric. *Stephen Crane: From Parody to Realism.* Cambridge, MA: Harvard University Press, 1966.

Stallman, Robert Wooster. "Mansfield's 'The Fly.' " *The Explicator* 3, no. 6 (1945), item 49.

———. "Stephen Crane: A Revaluation." *Critiques and Essays on Modern Fiction,* edited by John W. Aldridge, 244–69. New York: Ronald, 1952.

———. "Stephen Crane." *HarperCollins Reader's Encyclopedia of American Literature,* edited by George Perkins, Barbara Perkins, and Phillip Leininger. New York: HarperCollins, 2002: 216–18.

———, ed. *Stephen Crane: An Omnibus.* New York: Knopf, 1976.

Sternberg, Meir. *Expositional Modes and Temporal Ordering in Fiction.* Baltimore: Johns Hopkins University Press, 1978.

———. "Telling in Time (I): Chronology and Narrative Theory" *Poetics Today* 11, no. 4 (1990): 901–48.

———. "Telling in Time (II): Chronology, Teleology, Narrativity." *Poetics Today* 13, no. 3 (1992): 463–541.

———. "Telling in Time (III): Chronology, estrangement, and stories of literary history." *Poetics Today* 27, no. 1 (2006): 125–35.

Stowe, Harriet Beecher. *The Key to Uncle Tom's Cabin.* Boston: John P. Jewett, 1854.

———. *Uncle Tom's Cabin.* New York: Norton, 1994.

Swann, Charles. "Stephen Crane and a Problem of Interpretation." *Literature and History* 7, no. 1 (1981): 91–123.

170 Works Cited

Taylor, Helen. *Gender, Race, and Region in the Writings of Grace King, Ruth McEnery Stuart, and Kate Chopin.* Baton Rouge: Louisiana State University Press, 1989.

Thomas, J. D. "Symbol and Parallelism in 'The Fly.' " *College English* 22, no. 4 (1961): 256, 261–62.

Todorov, Tzvetan. *The Fantastic: A Structural Approach to a Literary Genre,* translated by Richard Howard. Ithaca, NY: Cornell University Press, 1975.

Toolan, Michael J. *Language in Literature: An Introduction to Stylistics.* London: Arnold, 1998.

———. *Narrative: A Critical Linguistic Introduction.* 2nd ed. London: Routledge, 2001.

———. *Narrative Progression in the Short Story: A Corpus Stylistic Approach.* Philadelphia: John Benjamins, 2009.

Toth, Emily. "Kate Chopin and Literary Convention: 'Désirée's Baby.' " *Southern Studies* 20, no. 2 (1981): 201–8.

Tucker, B. D. "Evil Eye: A Motive for Murder in 'The Tell-Tale Heart.' " In *Readings on the Short Stories of Edgar Allan Poe,* edited by Hayley Mitchell Haugen, 114–17. San Diego: Greenhaven Press, 2001.

Ward, Alfred C. *Aspects of the Modern Short Story: English and American.* London: University of London Press, 1924.

Wertheim, Stanley. *A Stephen Crane Encyclopedia.* Westport, CT: Greenwood Press, 1997.

Whitley, John S. "Introduction." In *Tales of Mystery and Imagination* by Edgar Allan Poe, vii–xxiii. Hertfordshire, UK: Wordsworth Editions Limited, 2000.

Williamson, Joel. *New People: Miscegenation and Mulattoes in the United States.* New York: Free Press, 1980.

Wilson, Kathleen, and Marie Lazzari, eds. *Short Stories for Students,* Vol. 4. Detroit: Gale, 1998.

Witherington, Paul. "The Accomplice in 'The Tell-Tale Heart.' " *Studies in Short Fiction* 22, no. 4 (1985): 471–75.

Wolff, Cynthia Griffin. "Kate Chopin and the Fiction of Limits: 'Désirée's Baby.' " *The Southern Literary Journal* 10, no. 2 (1978): 123–33.

Wolford, Chester L. *Stephen Crane: A Study of the Short Fiction.* Boston: Twayne, 1989.

Woods, Joanna. "Katherine Mansfield, 1888–1923." In *Kōtare 2007, Special Issue— Essays in New Zealand Literary Biography Series One: "Women Prose Writers to World War I."* Wellington: Victoria University of Wellington, 2008. Accessed March 7, 2012, http://www.nzetc.org/tm/scholarly/tei-Whi071Kota-t1-g1-t8.html

Young-Eisendrath, Polly. *Gender and Desire: Uncursing Pandora.* College Station: Texas A&M University Press, 1997.

Zimmerman, Brett. " 'Moral Insanity' or Paranoid Schizophrenia: Poe's 'The Tell-Tale Heart.' " *Mosaic* 25, no. 2 (1992): 39–48.

———. "Frantic Forensic Oratory, Poe's 'The Tell-Tale Heart.' " *Style* 35, no. 1 (2001): 34–49.

Index

actual reader 17–18, 22
aesthetics 1, 3–4, 29–31. *See also*
  ethical-aesthetic
aesthetic judgment 22–23, 34, 50,
  57. *See also* ethical judgment;
  interpretive judgment; reader's
  response; authorial reading
Aristotle 3, 11, 13, 20, 145
Arner, Robert D. 70–71, 75–76,
  156n6
authorial audience 15–18, 19, 25
authorial reading 15–16, 23, 25,
  152n12

Bakhtinian critics 18
Bais, H. S. S. 59
Baker, Joseph E. 13
Bardot, Jean 84
Barnard, Anja 128, 139–40
Bateson, F. W. and B. Shahevitch 125,
  159n1
Bauer, Margaret D. 91–92
"Belle Zoraïde, La" (Kate Chopin)
  85–88, 158n21
Benfey, Christopher 67
"Bênitous' Slave, The" (Kate Chopin)
  88–90
Berkman, Sylvia 95, 111, 126, 135
"Beyond the Bayou" (Kate Chopin)
  89–90
"Black Cat, The" (Edgar Allan Poe)
  153n7
Bledsoe, Thomas 127, 140, 142
Bonaparte, Marie 34, 44, 47
Booth, Wayne C. 13, 18, 20, 152n10;
  on context 17; on ethics 3–4,
  22, 151n3; on implied author
  16–19, 20, 88; on narrative
  or structural irony 8, 41; on

shared response 17; on style
  13, 15–16; on authorial norms
  15–16, 83; on unreliability 41
Brooks, Cleanth and Robert Penn
  Warren 2, 7–8, 11
Brooks, Peter 2–3
Buranelli, Vincent 31
Butler, Judith 101, 108
Bynum, Paige Matthey 45, 47

Chatman, Seymour 3, 14–15
Chicago School 13, 16–21. *See also*
  rhetorical criticism
Chopin, Kate 19–20, 25–26, 84–85,
  92
Cleman, John 31, 45, 47
cognitive narratology 18
"Colonel's Lady, The" (Somerset
  Maugham) 10
complicated response 4, 23–25, 83.
  See also reader's response
Coroneos, Con 127
covert progression: and character's
  covert motives 147; and
  different kinds of reading
  21–22; and implicit interaction
  among textual details 147–48;
  and textual details peripheral
  or irrelevant to the plot 3,
  21, 59–60, 62, 69, 131, 141,
  147; and reader's complicated
  response 21–25; brief sketches
  of 4–7; consequences of
  overlooking 26; definition
  of 1, 3–4; difference from
  underthought 1; difference
  from second story 9; difference
  from Rohrberger's "short
  story" 10; different forms of 2,

172 *Index*

26; eight theses for uncovering
146–48; ethically agreeable
23–24; ethically problematic
23; subverting overt plot 3,
22–24, 26, 50, 80, 110, 149;
supplementing overt plot 1,
3, 22, 24, 26, 49, 145, 149;
versus other types of covert
meaning 1, 8–12. *See also* dual
dynamics; irony
Crane, R. S. 3, 13, 17–18
Crane, Stephen 21, 25–26, 50, 54,
58–59, 66–68
cultural studies 18

"Daughters of the Late Colonel, The"
(Katherine Mansfield) 108
"De Mortuis" (John Collier) 7
"Désirée's Baby" (Kate Chopin) 5, 20,
23, 70; aesthetic quality of 23,
83; covert racist progression
in 71–83; extratextual
information concerning 84–85;
how to uncover the covert
progression in 92; intertextual
comparison 84–90; overt plot
of 5, 71–80, 83, 85; previous
criticisms of 70–71, 73, 75–76,
81–83, 90–92, 156n8, 157n13;
relation between text and
context of 90–91
different implied authors 20, 88–90,
92, 146. *See also* implied
author
Doll's House, A (Henrik Ibsen) 21,
103–5, 107
"Dresden Lady in Dixie, A" (Kate
Chopin) 88–89
dual dynamics 12, 16, 25–26,
92, 146. *See also* covert
progression

Elfenbein, Anna Shannon 70, 157n9
"Episode of War, An" (Stephen Crane)
4–5; date of publication of
67–68; intertextual comparison
54–57, 59, 60, 64–67,
68–69; main emasculating
undercurrent in 50, 52–60;
plot development of 4–5, 50,
52, 63, 66; previous criticisms
of 50, 53–54, 58–60, 62,
64, 66–69; relation between
Crane's war experiences

and 66–69; rendering battle
meaningless in 63–66;
subsidiary undercurrent in
60–63
ethical-aesthetic 3, 12, 24–25, 49, 131
ethical import 1, 24, 26, 29, 32,
48–49, 60, 69, 149
ethical judgment 22–23, 34, 42, 50,
57, 74, 116, 130, 134, 147.
See also aesthetic judgment;
interpretive judgment; reader's
response
ethically oriented 3, 29, 44–49, 112
ethics 1, 3–4, 22–26, 29–31, 48–50,
151 n.1. *See also* ethical-
aesthetic

"Fall of the House of Usher, The"
(Edgar Allan Poe) 153n7
feminist theory 99, 108–9, 158n2,
159n5
Fitz, Brewster E. 73
flesh-and-blood author 84, 90, 92,
148. *See also* real author
flesh-and-blood reader *see* actual
reader
"Fly, The" (Mansfield, Katherine)
10–11, 24; extratextual
information concerning
125–26, 139; ironic covert
progression in 7, 129–39; plot
development of 6, 125–28,
130–31, 134–38; previous
criticisms of 125–28, 135,
139–43; relation between
covert progression and plot in
139–43
focalization/point of view 6, 14, 73,
96, 100, 119–21, 123, 135–36
Fogle, Richard H. 9
"For Marse Chouchoute" (Kate
Chopin) 89
free indirect discourse 6, 33, 96–99,
104–7, 113, 115–16, 123, 135,
137; interaction between direct
discourse and 101; slipping
into 115
Freeman, William 40–41

Gibson, Donald B. 58, 61, 155n6
Great Expectations (Charles Dickens)
40
Greenfield, Stanley B. 142–43
Gullason, Thomas A. 67

Index 173

Hanson, Clare 10–11, 127–28
historical author *see* real author
historical context 16–21, 148–49
Hoffman, Daniel 37, 47, 59
Holton, Milne 61, 66
Hopkins, Gerard Manley 1

implied author 4, 8, 12, 15–19, 21, 41, 149. *See also* different implied authors
implied reader *see* authorial audience
instabilities 2–3, 11, 59, 147
interplay between unreliable and reliable narration 29, 48–49. *See also* unreliability
interpretive judgment 22–23, 34, 40, 50, 57. *See also* aesthetic judgment; ethical judgment; reader's response
intertextual comparison 12, 16, 20–21, 25, 149
intertextual contrast 21
intertextual similarity 21
irony: in covert progression 5–6, 7–8, 10, 11, 16, 21; narrative or "structural" 8; situational 7; two levels of 8; verbal 7

Jones, Kathleen 127, 135

Kaplan, Sydney Janet 109, 127
King Lear (Shakespeare) 7, 125–26, 139–40
"Kicking Twelfth, The" (Stephen Crane) 68–69
Knapp, Bettina 58, 66
Kobler, J. F. 95

Lawrence, D. H. 123
Lundie, Catherine 70, 83, 87, 156n2

Maeder, Thomas 45
Mais, S. P. B. 111
Mansfield, Katherine 19, 26, 101–2, 146, 159n5; on religion 158n3; on the fly 125–26; on the real self 109; on vanity 139; on women 121; purpose of writing 19, 108, 122, 124; reasons for concentrating on analyzing 26
May, Charles E. 11
Michel-Michot, Paulette 127
Moldenhauer, Joseph J. 31

Morrow, Patrick D. 98–99, 121, 127
Mortimer, Armine Kotin 9, 11
Mullen, Harryette 85
Murry, John Middleton 126, 141
"Mystery of Heroism, A" (Stephen Crane) 54–56, 59, 66, 68

Nagel, James 50, 58, 61, 64
narrative distance 8, 34, 96–97; changing 95–103; obliterating 104–6
narratology 145–46; complementarity between stylistics and 13–14, 151n5
Nathan, Rhoda B. 95, 97–98
"Necklace, The" (Guy de Maupassant) 7
neo-Aristotelians *see* Chicago School
Nesbitt, Anna Sheets 42–43
New Criticism 7–8, 9–10, 13
New, W. H. 110
norms of the text/implied author 12, 15–16, 18–20, 90

Oleson, Clinton W. 127
"Open Boat, The" (Stephen Crane) 55–57
O'Sullivan, Vincent 111, 126
overthought 1

Peel, Ellen 70, 82, 151n4, 155n1, 156n7
Petry, Alice Hall 87
Phelan, James 13, 15, 18, 152n9, 152n12; on distinction among interpretive, ethical, and aesthetic judgments 22; on instabilities and tensions in progression 2; on style 2, 15, 151n7; on unreliability 8, 34
Phillips, Elizabeth 37, 47
Prichard, James Cowles 45
plot 1–3, 7, 9–11, 145, 147; brief sketches of 4–6; of resolution 3, 11; of revelation 3, 11
"Prelude" (Katherine Mansfield) 101–2, 108–9
Poe, Edgar Allan 10,19, 25–26, 153n2, 154n10; distinction between prose fiction and poetry 29–30, 153n1; on prose fiction 29–30; on structural unity 30–31; stressing Hawthorne's ethical concern 30
primacy of the text 20

174 *Index*

Rabinowitz, Peter J. 17–20, 23, 151n7
Rader, Ralph W. 18–19, 152n9
Rankin, Daniel S. 84
reader's response 1–3, 12, 21–25
Reading for the Plot (Peter Brooks) 2–3
real author 16–20, 139, 152n10. *See also* flesh-and-blood author
Red Badge of Courage, The (Stephen Crane) 60, 66–67
"Revelations" (Mansfield, Katherine) 12, 21, 23–24; covert progression and changing narrative distance in 6, 98–110; extratextual information concerning 101–2, 108–9, 158n3; intertextual comparison 21, 101–5, 107–9; overt plot of 5–6, 96–98, 107–8; previous criticisms of 95, 98–99, 109–110; protagonist's real self in 100–1, 105, 108–9, 159n5
Rhetoric of Fiction, The (Wayne C. Booth) 8, 13, 15, 17–18
rhetorical criticism: 1–2, 12–13, 21; and context 16–20; and intertextual comparison 20–21; and style 13–16, 146
Rimmon-Kenan, Shlomith 40
Robinson, E. Arthur. 34, 37, 47
Rohrberger, Mary 9–11, 126
"Room 11" (Guy de Maupassant) 9
Runkle, Kim Denise 101, 108
Rush, Benjamin 45
Russian Formalists 145

Sandley, Sarah 110
Saussure's theory of the sign 152n13
second story 9
Seyersted, Per 84–85, 90, 92
shared reading 17, 22, 25, 152n12
Shaw, Harry 18
Shaw, Mary 50–51, 53–54, 59–60, 66, 68–69, 155n7
short fiction/story 1–2, 9–11, 25–26
"short story" (Mary Rohrberger) versus simple narrative 10
"Singing Lesson, The" (Mansfield, Katherine): covert progression in 6, 112–18; devices of camouflage and clues to the covert progression in 121–23; historical context of 19, 115, 122, 124; interactive point of

view in 112–13, 119–21; kind woman versus wicked woman in 118–19; overt plot of 6, 111–19; previous criticisms of 111, 116, 121, 123–24
Skaggs, Peggy 70, 85
Solomon, Eric 66
Stallman, Robert Wooster 50, 66, 126–27, 140, 159n3
Sternberg, Meir 2–3
story and discourse 2, 14, 52, 62, 148
Stowe, Harriet Beecher 20, 84
style 2, 12, 14–16, 21, 25, 146
stylistics 2, 14, 145–6; relation with narratology 14–15, 151n5
stylistic analysis 1–2, 12, 21, 92, 95, 99, 145–6
stylistic patterning 2, 12, 29, 32–34, 36, 146
"System of Doctor Tarr and Professor Fether, The" (Edgar Allan Poe) 45–46, 48–49

Taylor, Helen 84, 90–92
"Tell-Tale Heart, The" (Edgar Allan Poe) 4, 10–11, 19, 24, 147–49; complex interplay between unreliable and reliable narration in 29, 34–35, 39–42, 48–49; covert progression and overall dramatic irony in 32–44, 48–49; historical context of 44–48, 148–49; intertextual comparison 37, 40, 45–46, 48–49, 153n7, 154n10; plot development of 4, 32–34, 41–44; previous criticisms of 34, 37–38, 40–44, 46–47; reasons of overlooking the covert progression in 40–43; un/reliable sanity defense in 44–48
tensions 2
Thomas, J. D. 127
Toolan, Michael 2, 14
Toth, Emily 75–76, 81, 156n8, 158n16
transitivity 51, 53, 155
Troilus and Cressida (William Shakespeare) 7
Tucker, B. D. 37, 38
Twice-Told Tales (Nathaniel Hawthorne) 29

Index   175

Uncle Tom's Cabin (Harriet Beecher Stowe) 84
undercurrent *see* covert progression
Understanding Fiction (Cleanth Brooks and Robert Penn Warren) 2, 7, 11
underthought 1
unreliable narrator *see* unreliablility
unreliability 8, 29, 34, 39, 41–42; multiple 48–49
"Upturned Face, The" 68

"Wakefield" (Nathaniel Hawthorne) 30
"War is Kind" (Stephen Crane) 64–65

Ward, Alfred C. 38, 42, 46
Wertheim, Stanley 59, 62
Whitley, John S. 31
Witherington, Paul 41, 44
Wolff, Cynthia Griffin 71, 156n8, 157n13
Wolford, Chester, L. 50, 58, 60
Woods, Joanna 95, 125

"Young Goodman Brown" (Nathaniel Hawthorne) 8
Young-Eisendrath, Polly 102

Zimmerman, Brett 40, 44

CPSIA information can be obtained
at www.ICGtesting.com
Printed in the USA
JSHW011439221219
3113JS00001B/10

9 780415 635486